CW00506059

SACRIFICE: MAGIC BEHIND THE MIC

ISAAC WEISHAUPT
AKA
THE ILLUMINATIWATCHER

Written, edited, and cover artwork by Isaac Weishaupt a.k.a. Illuminati Watcher, publication date September 2014; Revision publication date January 2016

© Copyright January 2016 by Isaac Weishaupt

ISBN-13:
978-1502431448
ISBN-10:
1502431440

For more information on any of the topics presented in this book please visit www.illuminatiwatcher.com

Contents

The Sordid State of Affairs in Hip Hop: A Disclaimer

My educational and professional background is in Systems Engineering and I use that to approach subjects "from the whole" and put pieces together. I have independently studied the Illuminati and occult symbolism for over 20 years and have formulated a deeper insight by managing a website that covers these things on a daily basis (IlluminatiWatcher.com). I'd like to point out that I'm **not** an industry insider, nor do I have 'professional' experience in music, the occult, history, pop culture, philosophy, rocket science, brain surgery, etc. I'm just a guy trying to make sense out of all these things that I have a deep, lifelong interest in.

Please research all of these suggestions for yourself before believing it or repeating it to others. Educate yourself and come to your own conclusions of what you find viable and what you don't and *always* question authority. The problem at hand is that we're dealing with conspiracy theories that have small grains of truth that can get extrapolated out to the point of sensationalism. The occult realm is hidden from common view, hence the origin of the word in Latin "occultus" meaning "hidden" or "secret." Blending occult theories with conspiracy

5

theories provides an easy way of things getting out of hand quickly.

I also have no personal knowledge of any of these musicians, or anyone in the entertainment industry. I say that so you know I don't have an agenda one way or another with them, and I also have no firsthand knowledge of what these people truly believe or do; although I've got an exhaustive list of sources at the end to back up all of the material in this book. I'm merely pointing out theories and correlating facts together in an attempt to explore an overarching theory.

Another disclaimer is the use of the word "Illuminati" where I am merely suggesting that *if* a group of secret elitists are attempting to manipulate the masses covertly for whatever gains, then I'll simply refer to them as the Illuminati. The rabbit hole goes deep and wide if you want to explore whether or not an Illuminati exists, or if it is even the original 1776 Bavarian Illuminati that supposedly disbanded. I will not explore these things here. That takes far too much text, and I'd like to stick to hip hop and the music industry.

Hip hop in its present state is not the art form it was intended to be. Like anything else; it went through a cycle of smaller evolutionary changes, but also momentous revolutionary game changers. Things must change and evolve in order to stay relevant and prosper, but did hip hop change for the better? Or has it been diluted by evil forces to pollute the minds of the listeners with explicit lyrics that propagate themes of low vibrational thinking and lack of empathy for one another?

Chapter 1- The Origins of Hip Hop

Let's start by covering the origin of the culture known as hip hop. I refer to it as a culture because it is *not* a music genre. Rap is a music genre, hip hop is a culture. The foundation of this culture took place in 1971 at 1520 Sedgwick Avenue in the South Bronx borough of New York City; today known as the birthplace of hip hop.

The culture of the time was post-60s gloominess. The South Bronx was plagued with high crime, drug use, and gang activity. The popular counterculture music of the time was disco music but black people couldn't identify with the flashy 'white' upbeat style of the disco dance music. In response to seeing this void, DJ Kool Herc built a sound system for his community's social gatherings and he would tend to the musical maestro duties.

Kool Herc would watch the crowd and noticed that they would groove to the instrumental break beat and he started experimenting with it. He took the disco DJ's two record turntable setup and figured out a way to manipulate the break beat portion so that it was much longer than what was originally on the record. He would go back and forth between two different records, prolonging the instrumental break beat section. This experiment he referred to as the "Merry Go Round" and the concept of mixing records was born.

From this the hip hop culture branches out into the four main elements; DJ-ing, breakdancing (aka B-Boying or Breaking), rapping, and graffiti art. The DJ was the gatekeeper to the beat and therefore set the mood of the party. The DJ would determine if an MC was worthy enough to grab the microphone and make announcements or rap. The early MC only served the purpose of hyping the crowd up, but the DJ was the star of the show.

Another Bronx DJ by the name of Afrika Bambaataa took on this new art form and helped expand its reach. He was a gang leader of the notoriously violent Black Spades gang until he decided he had enough of that deadly lifestyle. He would place a positive spin in his community and created what would eventually be dubbed the Zulu Nation. This movement literally transformed the neighborhoods from gang life and fear, to a culture embracing music and the gathering of likeminded people.

"There are certain things that they say you can't do, there are all these secret people behind the scenes who make things available for you to do. That's why you have so much crime and violence."
- Afrika Bambaataa

The block parties of the Bronx would eventually find their way to being recorded on a tape medium and exported out to the other boroughs of New York City, and eventually the entire tri-state area. In 1979 a woman named Silvia Robinson heard a tape and wanted to record an album based on this rapper/DJ concept for a music label she would call Sugar Hill Records. This song was recorded and called *Rapper's Delight*;

the first mainstream rap song to be released on vinyl. It was powerful on many levels, but mostly for its controversy within the hip hop community. The hip hop purists disapproved the way it used a beat over a taped loop instead of having an actual DJ spin the records. This would have devastating effects on the art form and eventually force DJs into an endangered species once the money making machine chewed it up and spit it back out on the masses.

The funding for Sugar Hill Records came from a man named Morris Levy; a record executive for Roulette Records who would later be convicted of conspiring to extort with alleged ties with the Genovese Mafia crime family. The hip hop industry's proclivity for crime would rear its ugly head throughout its entire lifespan.

A couple of years later in 1981, the commercially viable group Blondie released a song called *Rapture* that featured lead singer Debbie Harry rapping over a beat about Fab Five Freddy whom she met in the New York art scene. The graffiti on trains would be seen all over the city to the point that they were considered artistic and coveted by the counter culture group of punks and new wavers (who both had distaste for the disco movement). The punk groups and the hip hop crowd would share common interests and Blondie was merely detailing part of that relationship in this revolutionary hit song. *Rapture* reached #1 on the US charts in 1980 and everyone had now been introduced to the art of rapping.

After Blondie's rapping, the momentum started the ball rolling and acts like Afrika Bambaataa and Run DMC would release their own efforts to the mainstream. It wasn't until MTV embraced the rap genre that it truly took off. In the mid to late 1980s one could see Run DMC or Beastie Boys videos, or even Fab Five Freddy on the MTV show *Yo! MTV Raps*; devoted entirely to the category. Once rap had a foothold, it began to get more comfortable in the role and a group named Public Enemy released songs and videos that featured lyrical messages of empowerment and black pride. This agenda was unheard of at the time, and the visual cues of militant black men (the S1W security team) in the videos caused a reaction of fear and misunderstanding in the white communities.

This fear would be exacerbated when Public Enemy and Boogie Down Productions (BDP) held a concert in which one of the fans died in an altercation. Rapper KRS-One of BDP initiated a movement called "Stop the Violence" that attempted to restore hip hop to its original vision of a peaceful gathering of communities. This attempt was short lived because a sub-genre of rap called Gangsta Rap was lurking right around the corner...

West coast acts such as NWA and Ice-T hit the scene around the same time in the late 1980s. Their commercial achievement was so unpredictably colossal that record companies scrambled to find any kind of rapper they could tweak into a pop-rap success. And in walked MC Hammer and Vanilla Ice.

These bubblegum type rappers enabled the record industry to further suffocate the original messages behind hip hop music and keep filling the pockets of executives who had no clue what they were getting into. The controversy behind west coast gangsta rappers would come to a head when a group of rappers from Miami, Florida released an album called *As Nasty As They Wanna Be*.

In 1989 The 2 Live Crew rap group released the album that featured controversial tracks like *Me So Horny* that glorified sex and misogyny and it prompted white parents nationwide to go up in arms. The album was banned in Miami to the point that police arrested anyone who merely sold it. The white youth was being polarized further into actually enjoying it, and the parents continued to lean harder on banning it. The group defended themselves successfully in 1990 under the right to freedom of speech and the album was free to be sold again, and that resulted in everybody buying the album to hear what all of the fuss was about.

The 2 Live Crew rap group holds the dubious distinction of having the first album with a non-removable Parental Advisory Explicit Lyrics sticker with their appropriately titled *Banned in the USA* album.

Various patterns took place over the early to mid-1990s that demonstrated the profitability of violent rap music. This in turn supported the machine that kept churning out more extreme behaviors and lyrics. Incidents such as the song *Cop Killer* from Ice-T were political responses to events like the beating of Rodney King, but the coverage and condemning of them only fueled public interest more and more. Gangsta rap was so successful that everyone wanted to push the envelope further with more violent lyrics talking about murder, drugs, and violence against women.

In 1992, NWA's Dr. Dre released a solo album entitled *The Chronic* which was full of lyrics about drug use; particularly marijuana (obviously). On that album he featured another new west coast rapper named Snoop Doggy Dogg. His popularity on songs like *Nuthin' But A G Thang* prompted him to immediately release his own album on Death Row Records; a label devoted to gangsta rap. Unlike Dr. Dre, Snoop Dogg was *actually* a gangsta with multiple convictions against him, adding to the street cred and allure of the rap genre.

In a case of predictive programming, Snoop Dogg actually had a case of murder against him (he previously had a song called *Murder Was the Case*). His actual gangsta reputation stepped the bar up for expectations of a rapper's street cred, while swaying the American masses to consider that gangsta rap might actually be *causing* the inner city problems.

At the same time, there was the somewhat manufactured deadly feud between east coast and west coast rappers, Tupac Shakur and the Notorious BIG. The two were essentially friends for the most part, and Tupac was actually an east coast guy from Baltimore. He had a lot of deep and insightful outlooks on life, even though he was living up to the gangsta image to his own detriment. In 1994 Tupac was in New York on his way to visiting BIG at the studio when he got shot several times. He lived through the ordeal, only to be found guilty for a rape charge and was ordered to serve time in prison while he was still recuperating from the attack.

The "low vibrational revenue" formula worked again for the music industry in 1995, as his next album entitled *Me Against the World* immediately went to debut at #1 on the charts, making him the first artist to have a number one album while being incarcerated.

After his release from prison he linked up with Suge Knight's Death Row Records and in 1996 released *All Eyez On Me*, arguably one of the greatest rap albums of all time. His success was short lived when he was shot to death in Las Vegas on September 13th, 1996. Although the case is officially unsolved, many speculate that it was a spillover from gang warfare or perhaps an East Coast vs. West Coast rivalry.

The violent coastal feud continued and in March of 1997 BIG was shot to death in Los Angeles. Two weeks later his double disc, *Life After Death,* went to number one on the charts, bringing more support for the equation of violence, music, and money. Both rappers were shot and killed in public with no convictions in either case. Some implied that zealous fans might have played a role, driven to murder in order to appease their rap "gods."

The emptiness left behind of Tupac and BIG was filled with acts like Puff Daddy and his flashy pop vibe that glorified money and possessions (e.g. platinum chains, exotic cars, MTV *Cribs*, etc.). Other rappers filling the void included Jay-Z, Wu-Tang Clan, and DMX.

In 1999 Jay-Z pled guilty to stabbing a record executive who leaked his multi-platinum album, *Vol. 3… Life and Times of S. Carter*. The next album he released called *The Dynasty* debuted at #1. In fact, in his 2010 book *Decoded* he notes the irony from the incident in which he applied the "low vibrational revenue" formula and walked away the winner:

"The hilarious thing, if any of this can be considered funny, is that the Rocawear bubble coat I was wearing when they paraded me in front of the cameras started flying off the shelves the last three weeks before Christmas."
– Jay-Z

The early 2000s brought in an unexpected lyrical genius with a white rapper named Eminem. The last white rapper to make it big was Vanilla Ice, approximately 10 years earlier. It was during the early 2000s that there appeared to be a notable shift from making rap music not only mainstream, but actual top 40 pop music. The 90s saw a large mainstreaming of the genre, but the 00s provided a new cooperative between pop artists and rappers. Rappers like Ja Rule would find success with R&B singers such as Ashanti or Jennifer Lopez. The Pussycat Dolls teamed with Busta Rhymes and Snoop Dogg, Justin Timberlake with T.I., 50 Cent and Jay-Z. The rapper Nelly even teamed up with country star Tim McGraw for *Over and Over*.

14

The 2010s deviated from the original concept of hip hop even *further* and merged rappers with pop artists that are popular with a younger crowd of teenagers. Justin Bieber was singing with rappers like Ludacris, Big Sean, or Nicki Minaj, while Ariana Grande was with rappers like Mac Miller or Big Sean. Katy Perry was singing alongside Snoop Dogg and Kanye West, while Miley Cyrus (aka Hannah Montana) had support from rappers like French Montana, Big Sean, or Future.

So where does that leave us today; how far has hip hop strayed from its origins? Is this a natural evolution or has there been a destructive force pushing it down the path it's on? Let's reexamine the history of hip hop from the perspective of a conspiracy theorist...

Chapter 2- Illuminati Manipulation of Hip Hop

As we already know, hip hop was an elemental art form. It was comprised primarily of four elements: DJ-ing, breakdancing, rapping, and graffiti art. The personality known as Black Dot breaks down the fundamentals of hip hop and explains that the original, sacred art of music incorporated the four elements: the sacred word (the spoken word), drum beats, dance, and a Master of Ceremonies. This is analogous to the four elements of earth, water, air, fire; implying a more cerebral and religious experience. Over time this eroded and the "natural" evolution was to break them up in a divide and conquer strategy. I posit that the Illuminati could've been the ones to implement this strategy in order to keep the hip hop culture down. Just like the Illuminati are able to twist and pervert anything and everything in this world to their advantage, they've managed to do the same to hip hop's art.

The idea that there is a secret society of people who control the masses behind the scenes is not a new one. People have been paranoid about this for hundreds of years, including George Washington himself who thought that the Bavarian

Illuminati wanted to cause conflict between the early US government and the people. He wrote in various letters that are now in the Library of Congress:

> *It was not my intention to doubt that, the Doctrines of the Illuminati, and principles of Jacobinism had not spread in the United States. On the contrary, no one is more truly satisfied of this fact than I am.*

The Bavarian Illuminati disbanded in 1785, but conspiracy theories claim that it merely went underground due to the unwanted exposure. After all, George Washington was even aware of this group so it wasn't so "secret" anyways. One train of logic is that it went underground and split into various other groups, some even joining the Freemasons and reaching the highest status for initiates and then creating a sub-Freemasonic secret society. One such splinter was allegedly the Boule Sigma Pi Phi fraternal society.

The Boule was established in Philadelphia in 1904 and was the first society to be founded by African Americans. The Boule was organized by a group of black professionals and setup to have democratic governance that included a Council of Chiefs to watch over the individuals, referred to as Archons. The society allows all races and colors in, which includes Jack Greenberg, a Jewish attorney and Director-Counsel of the NAACP Legal Defense Fund from the 60s to the 80s. The cut is extremely selective though; only around 5,000 members are active. One of the founders of the Boule was Henry Minton who said his fraternity would include the "*best of Skull and Bones of Yale and of Phi Beta Kappa.*" The Skull and Bones are a secret society long alleged by conspiracy theorists to connect elites through a secret society full of occult rituals and even satanic rites.

Several high profile members of Boule include the co-founder of the NAACP W.E.B. Du Bois, baseball player Hank Aaron, UN Ambassador Ralph Bunche, Atlanta Mayor Andrew Young, Council of Foreign Relations and Bilderberg Group member Vernon Jordan, Virginia Governor Douglas Wilder and American Express President Kenneth Chenault. Another member was US Secretary of Commerce Ron Brown who mysteriously died in an aircraft crash while on a trade mission in Croatia. Some conspiracy theories exist surrounding this crash, highlighting that the Boeing 737 was rebuilt as a military aircraft so it wouldn't have a flight data recorder or cockpit voice recorder. Brown was at the time under investigation for corruption allegations regarding a trip he made to Vietnam under the Clinton Administration, and so goes the theory that he was taken out for snooping around where he didn't belong.

Some oddities about the Boule that make it noteworthy are the symbols they incorporate in their distinction of members and logo. They have the Egyptian Sphinx as the logo for the fraternity, even though they are a Greek society. The Egyptian Sphinx is reminiscent of the ancient Egyptians and their culture. The ancient Egyptians were known for having esoteric mystery schools and the inexplicably built Pyramids of Giza. I've already gone into detail with these things and the Golden Age concepts in my book *A Grand Unified Conspiracy Theory: The Illuminati, Ancient Aliens, and Pop Culture* so please reference that for more. The Boule also uses a black ball to cast votes; a concept that was repeated in the MTV reality contest show *From G's to Gents* that took 'gangstas' and 'thugs' and tried to reform them into gentlemen.

Members of Boule reference each other as Archons, which is symbolic of the democratic society of ancient Greece. The term "Archon" is used to signify a ruler, or a king. In the field of conspiracy theory an Archon is a shape shifting deity

19

or demon that manipulates humanity for their benefit. This concept stems from the belief of interdimensional beings that can pervert mankind's attributes in order to harvest their energy (mostly negative energies) as a form of sustenance. We'll revisit this idea later on.

Sticking with the more sensationalized side of the spectrum, the Boule has been described by theorists such as Henry Makow as a black Skull & Bones secret society. On his website he asserts that the Boule consists of only the wealthy elites and they serve the even wealthier white elite. This elite is the global franchise known as the Illuminati. The Boule was established by the Illuminati in order to patrol the black communities and prevent any uprisings. Conspiracy theorist Steve Cokely claims that Dr. Martin Luther King, Jesse Jackson, President Barack Obama, and Bill Cosby are all members of the Boule. I've read that some of these men were actually members of different Greek societies that had ties with the Boule, but that doesn't necessarily make it so. He claims they are posing as civil rights activists, but ultimately supporting the Illuminati agenda. The allegation is that they perform homosexual rituals that are recorded for the sake of blackmail and do the bidding of the super-elites in order to gain access to even higher positions of power.

Some of the things that actually support this theory are the perpetuation of negative messages throughout the black community and rap music. Gangsta rap that glorifies black on black violence, calling each other the 'N' word, referring to the women as bitches, or just reinforcing the message that poor, urban, black youths are doomed to stay in the ghetto are all pervasive. This concept of selling out will continue throughout our reading as we explore ideas of musicians selling their soul in order to appease the executives of the industry. Perhaps they believe the only escape from their 'doomed' fate is to sign the contract that puts them under someone else's control.

Professor Griff, former member of revolutionary rap group Public Enemy, has released several books and lectures in an attempt to expose the conspiracies and issues surrounding the hip hop culture and black community. He seems to suggest that the origin of rap music has a basis with the human spirit's resistance to the slave trade. Typically, the struggle against the higher powers forced the black community to join together to have harmonious, positive messages in order to lift their emotional state of mind. To support this idea, there was an experiment conducted when Dr. Masaru Emoto used water crystals to demonstrate the effect of positive versus negative messages. He exposed some water crystals to labels that had positive messages on them, while the others had negative messages. Examination of the water after being subjected to the messages showed very different patterns. The positive messages produced beautiful echoing patterns, while the negative messages produced dispersed and unpleasant patterns.

The Illuminati viewed these positive messages found in gospel hymns to be troubling because it helped keep the slaves spirits' high. They needed to persuade some members of the black community to help keep their own people's spirits down. The Boule and Illuminati would've been the ones to recruit what was referred to as the "house negro" who did the bidding of the elites in order to attain a slightly better living condition, meanwhile selling out their counterparts.

Rap provides the ideal vehicle for implanting negative messages. The media and entertainment industry portrays the inner city urban environments as a gritty, dangerous place to be. The crime rates support this somewhat, but the point is that nobody is suspicious of lyrics about violence and thuggin' when they're placed in rap music. It's an accepted fact that the art imitates life, but it doesn't take it a step further to see if life is imitating art at all. It seems that hip hop is a trial for experimentation in programming young minds because it works hand in hand with the film industry in glorifying violence. The film industry produces gangster flicks like *Scarface* and *Goodfellas* that show appealing viewpoints of criminal lifestyles. Even when Al Pacino's Tony Montana dies at the end of *Scarface*, one can't help but admire his legacy for going out like a gangster as he unloads his machine gun while inhaling mounds of coke from his personalized monogrammed chair. You can see the influence of film on rap music because there are so many rappers who name themselves after real-life gangsters, drug dealers, and mafia members (e.g. Rick Ross, Capone, Noreaga Nas Escobar, Daz Dillinger, Kurupt Young Gotti, Beanie Siegel, 50 Cent, Scarface, French Montana, Yo Gotti, and Machine Gun Kelly).

The fact is that rap had origins of a rebellious form of music, not all that different from punk music; only to succumb to the music industry and churn out the nonsense that keeps the audience fighting among themselves for the alpha dog position. This begs the question of "What happened?"

Public Enemy and Ice-Cube used to rap about rebelling against the system that was being used to keep an entire race down, and now the rappers talk mostly about who is the king of the money hill. This message distracts the already overwhelmed disadvantaged people and prevents them from focusing on who is really keeping them down. It rarely challenges authority and merely redirects anger and strife towards one another through rap beefs, battles, or gang warfare.

The conscious music of Public Enemy was tied into the Black Panthers and other black power movements. The FBI allegedly viewed this as a resurgence of the uprising of the black man against the system. The FBI responded to the original threat of the Black Panthers by creating a counter-intelligence program called COINTELPRO that was used to neutralize certain activists. They used psychological operations, false flag stories in the media, and even alleged assassinations in order to protect national security and "keep the peace." They aimed at taking down communists, socialists or anyone with a civil rights agenda, particularly Dr. Martin Luther King Jr. In fact, there was a trial held in 1998 where the King family filed a wrongful death suit against Loyd Jowers, who claimed that he was involved with a conspiracy involving the Mafia and government figures in order to assassinate Martin Luther King in Memphis. Contrary to the 'official story,' the jury found that James Earl Ray *wasn't* the shooter, and there was in fact a plan intact to set him up as the fall guy. Counter-theorists claim that Jowers story was full of holes and he only confessed to being involved in order to make money off of it. The US Department of Justice performed an investigation of the claims and found no solid evidence to support the theory that there was a conspiracy to assassinate King, yet there are FBI files on King that you can read on the FBI's Vault website, proving that he was being monitored. Before King was assassinated at the Lorraine Motel, police officers and FBI agents were watching him under surveillance from across the street. Add all of that information in with the fact that the FBI tried to discredit King by portraying him as an adulterer and Communist, one must wonder if a conspiracy is in fact what took this voice of civil rights and justice out for good.

The COINTELPRO project managed to deter many subversive groups like the Ku Klux Klan, the Socialist Workers Party, and the Black Panthers. The program didn't end until

1971 when it was exposed and turned over to media outlets. Similar to the MKULTRA mind control program of the CIA, we are left to believe that it simply no longer exists under a different name, even though it was shut down only *after* its exposure. No matter what ever became of this program, its effects were long lasting.

Surveillance and Governance: Crime Control and Beyond compiles several reads on different aspects of government surveillance programs. One of which is *"WHAT IF SHE'S FROM THE FBI?" THE EFFECTS OF COVERT FORMS OF SOCIAL CONTROL ON SOCIAL MOVEMENTS* by David Cunningham and John Noakes, which details the agenda of the COINTELPRO program with some examples. The agenda had multiple goals and they include:

1. Create a negative public image (e.g. digging up dirt on civil rights activists and political leaders with "subversive" ties)
2. Break down internal organization (e.g. cause infighting)
3. Create dissension between groups (e.g. the FBI wrote letters to related black activist groups alleging that the other was misusing resources allocated to them by the other group; more infighting)
4. Restrict access to organizational resources (e.g. cut off funding to keep organizations going)
5. Restrict organizational capacity to protest (e.g. psychological operations to keep activist groups from maintaining organization)
6. Hinder the ability of targeted individuals to participate in group activities (e.g. the FBI released the criminal record of John Franklin to the New York

Daily News in order to create negative publicity for this Manhattan Borough Presidential candidate in 1961)

The authors proceed to explore the emotional impact of surveillance on the social movement and argue that it has a powerful influence over behavior, beliefs, and feelings. It invokes feelings of fear and paranoia, which, in this case, may have stoked the inevitable belief in a conspiracy against the black community (and even the non-black populations since *all* of the subversive groups were targeted by COINTELPRO). Perhaps the rock/rap group Rage Against the Machine summed it up best in their song about COINTELPRO, *Wake Up*:

Yea, the several federal men
Who pulled schemes on the dream
And put it to an end
Ya better beware
Of retribution with mind war
20/20 visions and murals with metaphors
Networks at work, keepin' people calm
Ya know they murdered X
And tried to blame it on Islam
He turned the power to the have-nots
And then came the shot
- Rage Against the Machine, *Wake Up*

There are several theorists that claim the COINTELPRO project persisted under different names and different purposes to the present day. The online personality known as Mr. Gates was on a podcast called The Higherside Chats where he points out the irony and inconsistency of the FBI being able to shut down the well-organized Black Panthers, yet are unable to eliminate low level street gangs like the Crips and Bloods. In fact, the two street gangs seemed to have been twisted *into* a violent culture even though their acronyms allegedly stand for more benevolent meanings. For example, one pair of definitions for the gang names includes CRIP- Common Revolution In Progress and BLOOD- Brotherly Love Overrides Oppression & Destruction. The wordplay and double speak is a calling card of the Illuminati and Archon race. They twist and confuse things to send one message while actually delivering another.

One of the deadliest riots in US history was the 1992 Los Angeles riots that sparked as the result of the trial that found LAPD officers not guilty on charges of excessive force against Rodney King, even though there was video evidence. This event was covered in detail by all major media outlets, and 53 people died from April 29th to May 4th of 1992. Many hip hop artists spoke out against the LAPD, but I'd like to mention some occult aspects of this event that suggest a potential ritual of the Illuminati.

Sadly, this tragedy occurred (or perhaps was "orchestrated") over the pagan holiday of Beltane. This holiday used to be observed with sacrifices to the deity Ba'al through bonfires (which derive from Bailfires or Ba'alfires). Some theorists claim that Adolf Hitler and his wife Eva Braun had their wedding and suicide rituals over the course of Beltane (April 29th-30th) in order to commit a sacrifice to Ba'al, one of the alleged Illuminati sacrifice deities that is celebrated annually at Bohemian Grove by the elites of entertainment, politics, and various industries.

This same year of 1992 was monumental in the Los Angeles area for more than the riots though. Just one day before the riots on April 28th, the Crips and Bloods signed a truce to stop the gang violence. Fast forward to December of

1992 and Dr. Dre released a revolutionary album, *The Chronic* which influenced rap music forever. This album introduced the masses to Snoop Doggy Dogg and various Death Row Records artists who littered MTV with lyrics of violence, gang activity, and drug use. This spurred gangsta rap to a new level and effectively changed the entire landscape of music due to its popularity amongst the white audience (over eight million copies sold worldwide). Do these things relate to one another? Are they orchestrated and prepared as an overarching plan to perpetuate negativity in the black community? With the acknowledgement of the FBI's COINTELPRO project one can only guess.

Music isn't the only avenue of manipulation; the other coveted tool of the Illuminati is the television. There is much research into this field, with an entire branch called "Cultivation Theory." This is the theory that television has the power to influence people over a long period of time. The findings of various studies on this subject indicate that people tend to think television is closer to reality than it truly is. The oversaturation of violence and sex leads people to believe the world is a far scarier and judgmental place than it truly is. Over time the more people who buy into this concept of the world being more negative, help support it and make it a reality. All of this supports the reptilian brain and ultimately Archonic agendas. The purveyors of negativity help support the elites who benefit from this pessimism and the television works hand in hand with music to make it happen.

It also provides enculturation, in that it demonstrates what roles and responsibilities people *should* have. Eckhart Tolle explains why this is a manipulation in his book *A New Earth* because the concept of fulfilling a role is egoic and pulls a person further from finding their true self and happiness. The purpose for this 'role making' is to make society more manageable, predictable, and controllable. An example would be the concept of the sitcom father. Today's father figures on television are usually comedic characters who are stupid, subservient, and useless in a household. According to many pick up artists and sexual experts like David Shade, women today suffer because men are unable to express their true fiery masculinity in the bedroom due to spillover from the "stupid father" role they actually take on due to the programming of the television. I argue that this comes from this enculturation, which arguably stemmed from the feminist movement. George Gerbner was an expert on studying the effects of television violence and released a University of Pennsylvania article titled *Who is telling all the stories?* In it he breaks down how and why a story is presented. It says:

*They typically present a valued objective or suggest a need or desire, and offer a product, service, candidate, institution or action purported to help attain or gratify it. The lessons of fictitious Little Red Riding Hoods and their realistic sequels prominent in everyday news and entertainment not only teach lessons of vulnerability, mistrust and dependence **but also help sell burglar alarms, more jails and executions promised to enhance security (which they rarely do), and other ways to adjust to a structure of power**.*

In another George Gerbner article from 2000 titled *Cultivation Analysis: an Overview:*

As another example, consider how likely television characters are to encounter violence compared to the rest of us. Well over half of all major characters on television are involved each week in some kind of violent action. While FBI statistics have clear limitations, they indicate that in anyone year less than one per cent of people in the U.S. are victims of criminal violence.

The 'facts' of the television world are evidently learned quite well, whether or not viewers profess a belief in what they see on television or claim to be able to distinguish between factual and fictional presentations. (In fact, most of what we know, or think we know, is a mixture of all the stories we have absorbed. 'Factual,' which may be highly selective, and 'fictional,' which may be highly realistic, are more questions of style than function within a total framework of knowledge.) **The repetitive 'lessons' we learn from television, beginning with infancy, are likely to become the basis for a broader world view, making television a significant source of general values, ideologies and perspectives as well as specific assumptions, beliefs, and images***.*

Perhaps that is why we hear stories of the exorbitant costs of advertising during the Super Bowl (close to $4M for a 30 second ad). The companies that pay for these ads know there is a return on investment otherwise they wouldn't pay that much (subconscious influence). A Consumer Federation of America survey from 1990 detailed the findings that:

Americans are not smart shoppers and their ignorance costs them billions, threatens their health and safety and undermines the economy...

The people who run businesses are savvy marketers and they are well aware of what they can and can't do with the masses. Wages have remained stagnant from 1990 to 2010, and why is that? It's because they can be. Another survey by

Consumer Federation of America from 2012 reflects this disturbing statistic:

*Today, middle class households earn **less** than they did a decade ago, and **little more than they earned two decades ago**. The income of the typical American family, in 2010 dollars, was $49,445 in 2010 but $53,164 in 2000 and $48,423 in 1990.*

More disturbingly, the conclusion of that study provides the 'justification' for why the Illuminati (according to the theory they control all forms of big business, government and economy) believe they can pay the masses so little:

Most middle class Americans are not financially desperate. In 2010, after being battered by economic recession, they typically had:
Sufficient funds in transactions accounts (checking and saving), $3,900, to cover most unexpected expenses.
Total financial assets of $29,000.
Manageable debts, with a debt to asset ratio of 27 percent, and only 9 percent with debt that is at least 60 days overdue.

If there is an Illuminati shadow organization controlling the planet, they surely would've seen these results and decided that they are able to keep wages low so that they can have more. The disparity gap expands further and further every year. The television works hand in hand with the music industry to propagate the same messages that seem so counter intuitive to people who have the cards stacked against them. Statements such as "stop snitching" make it a social norm to not speak to the police, even when it may take a criminal or drug dealer off of the streets. Another common theme is "keeping it real" where you're not able to think outside of the box or venture from the herd without chastisement. Comedian Dave Chappelle famously did a running skit on his Comedy Central about "when keeping it real goes wrong" that highlighted the downfalls of this concept. One theory on why these ideas are kept alive is because of the notion I mentioned back in the section about the Boule society. It's a humiliation and degradation thing. Theorist and mind control expert, Neil Sanders, points out the cruel irony in the fact that rappers are brought up to believe that the bigger the chain around their neck is, the higher their status. These gold chains used to be called Dookie Ropes. When in reality you can see the symbolism of chains and wrapping them around the neck, and how that can be degrading to an African-American, yet it still persists.

Dave Chappelle and comedian Katt Williams both publicly discussed their distaste for black men being forced to wear women's clothing in the name of "comedy." Note that Chappelle and Williams were portrayed as having "gone crazy" after they came out against the system and the perpetuation of emasculating black men. Chappelle went to Africa after a disagreement with Comedy Central on the direction of his wildly popular television show and the media portrayed it as a loss of sanity. He went on Oprah and explained that he was merely taking a break and he proceeded to describe the setup to make him wear a dress. We've seen Hollywood pull this off on a regular basis because it sells to the masses (black *and* white audiences). The list of black men who play a man in drag is exhausting: Tyler Perry dresses as a woman named Madea in his film series about her/him, Martin Lawrence as Sheneneh on his sitcom *Martin* and also as Big Momma in the movie series, Eddie Murphy in *The Nutty Professor* and *Norbit*, Arsenio Hall in *Coming to America*, Miguel Nunez Jr. in the film as the main character *Juwanna Man*, Chris Tucker in *Fifth Element*, Kenan Thompson and Tracy Morgan as characters on *SNL*, Wesley Snipes in *To Wong Foo, Thanks for Everything Julie Newmar*, the Wayans brothers as two white women in *White Girls* and even Jamie Foxx had his start on *In Living Color* playing Wanda. Note that Martin Lawrence had a slight mental mishap in 1996 when he stood in the middle of oncoming traffic and cursed at cars with a pistol in his pocket, screaming "Fight the establishment!" Was this a reaction to the system that seeks to portray strong black men in a nonsensical manner? Dave Chappelle made the argument on *Oprah* that these guys are not weak people, especially Martin Lawrence, yet they've been forced into these roles for one reason or another.

Let's think about why there would be a continuation of the emasculation of black men (or men in general)? One explanation is the psychology behind it. Confusing the roles of a man and/or woman is potentially one of the tools of the Illuminati. If the Illuminati truly seek to break down the family unit (theorists claim this is a divide and conquer strategy), they must do it in a covert way. The families of African-American slaves were far from stable due to the psychological damage inflicted by the slave owners. They were literally unable to legally marry one another in any of the American colonies because they were classified as property. The slaves were even owned by different slave masters so that the family could only see each other on certain nights, and even that wasn't the worst case scenario because the slave owners could sell a family member to another owner that wouldn't allow the visitation at all. At some point during the slave trading days in America the owners decided it might actually benefit them to *force* slaves to marry and create families because they'd be less likely to run away. Since marriage was illegal for slaves, the owners allegedly co-opted the ceremony called "jumping the broom" that would symbolically represent an actual wedding ceremony; a custom that was performed in Africa years before to represent the joining of families.

The effects of broken families and distorted roles have continued through to present day with high numbers of children being raised with absent fathers. New York Senator Daniel Moynihan reported in 1965 that problems from three hundred years of mistreatment play out in today's modern African American families. He claimed that broken slave families started a cycle because it didn't provide black men the ability to learn roles of providing and protecting and this plays out in high unemployment rates and absenteeism. In the 1965 US Department of Labor report *The Negro Family: The Case For National Action*, Chapter III The Roots of the Problem, the problem is summed up fairly bluntly:

With the emancipation of the slaves, the Negro American family began to form in the United States on a widespread scale. But it did so in an atmosphere markedly different from that which has produced the white American family.

The Negro was given liberty, but not equality. Life remained hazardous and marginal. Of the greatest importance, the Negro male, particularly in the South, became an object of intense hostility, an attitude unquestionably based in some measure of fear.

When Jim Crow made its appearance towards the end of the 19th century, it may be speculated that it was the Negro male who was most humiliated thereby; the male was more likely to use public facilities, which rapidly became segregated once the process began, and just as important, segregation, and the submissiveness it exacts, is surely more destructive to the male than to the female personality. Keeping the Negro "in his place" can be translated as keeping the Negro male in his place: the female was not a threat to anyone.

Unquestionably, these events worked against the emergence of a strong father figure. The very essence of the male animal, from the bantam rooster to the four star general, is to strut. Indeed, in 19th century America, a particular type of exaggerated male boastfulness became almost a national style. Not for the Negro male. The "sassy nigger[sic]" was lynched.

Most disturbingly, the conclusion and recommendations in the final chapter of the report are as such:

What then is that problem? We feel the answer is clear enough. Three centuries of injustice have brought about deep-seated structural distortions in the life of the Negro American. At this point, the present tangle of pathology is capable of perpetuating itself without assistance from the white world. The cycle can be broken only if these distortions are set right.

In a word, a national effort towards the problems of Negro Americans must be directed towards the question of family structure. The object should be to strengthen the Negro family so as to enable it to raise and support its members as do other families. After that, how this group of Americans chooses to run its affairs, take advantage of its opportunities, or fail to do so, is none of the nation's business.

This begs the question of how much effort has actually been given to strengthen black families? Just five years after the release of that report the US Congress passed the Comprehensive Drug Abuse Prevention and Control Act of 1970 which classified controlled substances and kicked off the War on Drugs in 1971. Some of the logic for this was to fix the problem of broken families in the black community. Since then, the broken family problem has been exacerbated due to a disproportionate number of black people being incarcerated on drug related offenses, even though statistically white people commit more drug crimes than black people. The Human Rights Watch report released in 2000 detailed that black people were arrested on drug charges at five times the rate of whites due to over allocation of law enforcement resources in low income urban areas.

A controversial topic in the 1980s was crack cocaine and its highly addictive nature. During the War on Drugs, legislation passed through Congress that had a 100 to 1 ratio of lengths of sentencing for crimes involving crack versus cocaine (this was eventually reformed to have an 18:1 ratio in the 2010 Fair Sentencing Act). Possession of crack alone was enough to inflict a five year mandatory minimum sentence. This was disputed as a discrimination against minorities who were more likely to use crack, where as white people were more likely to use cocaine. This law states that someone with 1 gram of crack would suffer the same penalty as someone with *100* grams of cocaine powder. Journalist Gary Webb wrote a book called *Dark Alliance: The CIA, the Contras, and the Crack Cocaine Explosion* where he details allegations that the CIA supported drug smuggling of cocaine to support Nicaraguan rebels who opposed the Sandinista government. Gary Webb was subsequently found dead with two gunshot wounds to the head in 2004 and labeled a suicide. That's right, a suicide with *two* bullets in the head. I'm not sure how someone manages to shoot themselves in the head twice but apparently he did.

Allegedly drug dealer Freeway Ricky Ross was supplied cocaine through a liaison with the CIA and Contra rebels to convert to crack. He would eventually get imprisoned to a life sentence for procuring over 100 kilograms of cocaine but appealed it and served 13 years, being released in 2009. The recurring theme of rappers emulating real-life gangsters played out when William Roberts II debuted in 2006 as a rapper named Rick Ross. Freeway Ricky Ross sued the rapper Rick Ross in 2010 for using his name under a copyright infringement, but the suit was thrown out a few weeks later. Ironically Rick Ross was actually a corrections officer in the late 90s, leading us into the connections between the War on Drugs, the music industry, and the industrial prison complex.

Another important scandal in hip hop's drug history was the Black Mafia Family and their convictions on being part of a criminal enterprise. The organization started out in Detroit by Demetrius (aka Big Meech) and Terry Flenory in the 1980s. They set up drug distribution points in the US that pushed cocaine from the Mexican drug cartel. Before they got arrested in 2005, they set up the BMF Entertainment label with the hopes of using their connections to get involved with music. They allegedly had been intermingling with rappers for years, and helped artists like Young Jeezy while also being involved with murders, like when Big Meech got accused (and then never indicted) of killing Puff Daddy's former bodyguard, Wolf Jones. It's also alleged that BMF tried to kill rapper Gucci Mane, only to have Gucci fire back in self-defense. Gucci was also exonerated in terms of self-defense. Bobby Brown's nephews were stabbed at a restaurant with the alleged assailant being the brother of a BMF rapper, Bleu DaVinci. The alleged assailant, "Baby Blue" Dixson was murdered before charges could be brought against him. In 2006 a case of conspiracy to distribute cocaine and money laundering was brought up against BMF and several of their associates, including Jacob the Jeweler. Jacob would take a plea and served two and a half years in federal prison, while many others face up to life in prison.

The population of prisons in America has ballooned to astronomical figures. The Center for Research on Globalization released an article that cited alarming facts like how the United States contains 25% of the world's prison population; meanwhile the entire US population is only 5% of the world's population. In 1972 there were fewer than 300,000 inmates, and in 2000 that number leaped to 2,000,000. One reason why there are so many prisoners is due to the War on Drugs. Over 50% of the inmates in federal prison are incarcerated for drug related offenses. What's even more rotten is that when you look at that 50% chunk, one quarter of them are imprisoned for marijuana; a drug that is currently legal in Colorado and Washington for recreational purposes.

In *The New Yorker's* article by Adam Gopnik *The Caging of America: Why do we lock up so many people?,* he highlights two different origins on why we need a penal system. One argument is rooted in the Civil War era Northern territory with the idea of reforming prisoners into functional members of society, and the other is claiming a far more unsettling idea:

> *The other argument—the Southern argument—is that this story puts too bright a face on the truth. The reality of American prisons, this argument runs, has nothing to do with the knots of procedural justice or the perversions of Enlightenment-era ideals. Prisons today operate less in the rehabilitative mode of the Northern reformers "than in a retributive mode that has long been practiced and promoted in the South," Perkinson, an American-studies professor, writes. "American prisons trace their lineage not only back to Pennsylvania penitentiaries but to Texas slave plantations." White supremacy is the real principle, this thesis holds, and*

racial domination the real end. In response to the apparent
triumphs of the sixties, mass imprisonment became a way of
reimposing Jim Crow. Blacks are now incarcerated seven
times as often as whites. "The system of mass incarceration
works to trap African Americans in a virtual (and literal)
cage," the legal scholar Michelle Alexander writes. Young
black men pass quickly from a period of police harassment into
a period of "formal control" (i.e., actual imprisonment) and
then are doomed for life to a system of "invisible control."
Prevented from voting, legally discriminated against for the
rest of their lives, most will cycle back through the prison
system. The system, in this view, is not really broken; it is
doing what it was designed to do. Alexander's grim
conclusion: "If mass incarceration is considered as a system of
social control—specifically, racial control—then the system is
a fantastic success."

The system of "convict lease" was prevalent in the
American South from the 1800s-1900s and it basically leased
out prisoners to work for private industry because the states
couldn't afford prisons. As one would expect it led to the abuse
of prisoners and human rights violations, and eventually the
states became responsible to build actual prisons. The costs
became too much to cover and eventually the incarceration
model favored privatizing prisons and letting them run it as for-
profit businesses in the 1980s. The state continued to run some
prisons, but other cash strapped states found a public-private
partnership that contracted the prison workers out to
corporations. This saved the state governments money because
it introduced competition while allowing a business to turn a
profit and provide employment for the local communities.
These newer prison systems gave way to a more
"humane" prison-work model known as Federal Prison

Industries. The name of this corporation is UNICOR and it was originally created in 1934 as a way for the federal prison system to produce goods and services for other branches of government (including the Department of Defense). The argument for this penal work system is that it rehabilitates prisoners and gives them a vocational training they can apply to jobs when they get out of prison. One viewpoint on this is that it is a positive thing and prepares the prisoner for employment when they get out. Another viewpoint is that it is cheap slavery because it only pays on average about a buck an hour for prisoners to do menial labor that won't turn into gainful employment on the outside.

Over time, the trend is leaning towards more privatization of prisons, while there are also financial interests in keeping the vacancy rates of prisons high. A corporation (like Corrections Corp of America or GEO Group) can make more money by keeping a prison populated, and you can guess that private prison lobbyists (over 200 lobbyists according to Justice Policy Institute's *Gaming the System* from 2011) will be pushing for legislation that calls for longer prison sentencing. A Huffington Post article about the privatization of prisons reveals that the Corrections Corp of America proposed to "save the taxpayers money on prisons" if they could agree to maintain a 90% occupancy rate for at least 20 years. They are telling you they have a vested interest in keeping their prisons populated; and why wouldn't they? They are a business out to make profit. That doesn't make it acceptable, instead it just points out the glaring fact that we shouldn't be supporting prisons that would be "interested" in keeping a population incarcerated.

The Justice Policy 2011 report on privatized prisons cited that the Corrections Corp of America cofounder Tom Beasley was also chairman of the Tennessee Republican Party when he and his cohorts decided to flip the prison model on its head and make it a for-profit business. That same report also provides an example of corruption in a system like this, when in Luzerne County, Pennsylvania two private youth prisons illegally gave money to local judges to the tune of 2.6 million dollars in the "Kids for Cash" scandal. The payments influenced the judges to sentence thousands of children to serve time in the privatized prison for petty crimes such as retail theft and trespassing.

If you look at the trends, facts, and graphs of America's prison systems you can see that more people are being locked up even though violent crimes are on the decline. Connecting the privatization of prisons with the cheap slave labor of UNICOR, one could argue that rap music does nothing but *help* these corporations make profit by filling their occupancy rates. This would in fact be a very covert form of slavery, an idea that rapper Kanye West mentioned in his song *New Slaves*:

Meanwhile the DEA
Teamed up with the CCA
They tryna lock niggas up
They tryna make new slaves
See that's that private owned prison
Get your piece today
They Probably all in the Hamptons
Braggin' 'bout their maid
- Kanye West, *New Slaves*

There is a letter online that is supposedly written by an anonymous person who claims to have been a "decision maker" in the music industry back in the 80s and 90s. This letter claims that he/she was at a meeting in Los Angeles in

1991 that was full of executives, music insiders, and a "mysterious" group of unnamed individuals. The purpose of the meeting was to discuss the direction of rap music. The speaker informed the attendees that private prisons were going to go public and the attendees would be able to cash in on this since their representative music companies were also investors in the private prisons. The speaker went on to describe the privatized prison model of more prisoners equaling more profit. They were then instructed to help push rap music into the gangsta genre to promote violence, drugs, etc. in order to turn profits for the prison industry, and to get a little taste for themselves as well.

Even though this tale should pique the interest of any good conspiracy theorist; I'm on the side of the fence of 'not' believing this story. The first argument against it being true is that the author of the letter obviously fears for his/her life. Why not send it to a legitimate news source? We're asked to believe that they would send it to a low-ranking hip hop website (not to knock on HipHopRead.com, but it's not as popular as The Source or XXL). The grammar in the letter is poorly written as well, which leads me to doubt the author's true status of being a "decision maker" high up on the chain of the music industry. It says the person is from Europe but still, most Europeans speak English rather well, and like I already mentioned this person claims to be a professional executive. Another claim made in the letter that I could refute is the following excerpt:

It was also made clear to us that since these prisons are privately owned, as they become publicly traded, we'd be able to buy shares.

The problem with that statement is that the nation's largest private prison corporation; the Corrections Corporation of America (CCA) went public in October 1986 under the NASDAQ symbol CCAZ, but this meeting supposedly happened in 1991. The second largest privatized prison company; however, is GEO (formerly Wackenhut) and they did in fact go public in 1994 on the NASDAQ (CCA and GEO combined account for over 75% of the privatized prisons in America), so take that for what it's worth; maybe it is true…

A more rational argument could be the kick-starting of privatized prisons with the 1973 Rockefeller Drug Laws in New York. These laws were named after then-Governor Nelson Rockefeller. Theorist Fritz Springmeier asserts that there are 13 bloodlines of the Illuminati and the Rockefellers are one of them. Gov. Nelson Rockefeller was grandson to Standard Oil founder John D. Rockefeller, a prominent philanthropist whose legacy continues with the Rockefeller family donating vast sums of financing to various religious causes and the education industry (and even funding the Rockefeller Sanitary Commission that eradicated hookworm disease in the US). The theorists claim that the Rockefeller family has an Illuminati agenda and these drug laws would support an overarching conspiracy of the Illuminati's pursuit of global control, drugs, prisons and rap music.

Hip Hop legend Afrika Bambaataa met with theorist David Icke and said that he confirmed that rap music is a far cry from where it was when he first started DJ-ing. They discussed how the messages of today's rap are designed to destroy empathy for one another, which is definitely not what the original intent was. The twisting and perverting of the message is a trait of the supposed shape shifters referred to as Archons, shape shifters, or Djinn; depending on who you ask. All of these different things are variations of embodiment of evil. Without going too deep, the Archon are a race of evil

42

spirits that have been talked about for hundreds of years since the mystery schools and Gnostic belief systems were circulating. Several conspiracy theorists like David Icke and Jay Weidner point out Archon type activity being conducted by the Illuminati, in which they take one thing and invert it to another. The Archon has no ability to be creative, but rather rely on human creations and then they twist it to the point of it no longer meaning the same thing. Some ironic examples that David Icke uses include correctional facilities where prisoners *don't* get corrected, schools where children *don't* get a real education, and hospitals where people get *sicker* (have you ever looked at the death rate of hospital-acquired nosocomial infections?... approximately 100,000 deaths per year in the U.S. alone). One of the theories is that the Archon shape shifters inhabit the bodies of the Illuminati, driving them to do these evil things. Eckhart Tolle said that '*being creative is a reflection of God's beauty and desire*,' and this goes against what the Archons stand for. This is also the reason why the Archons need to use the musicians for their purposes since they're unable to be creative themselves.

Tupac Shakur had a message that was distorted with his THUG LIFE tattoo. He claimed that THUG LIFE stood for "The Hate U Give Little Infants Fucks Everyone" which is actually fairly well spoken if you take a step back and think about it. We live in a society that has people who lean heavily on a Pro-Life stance and condemn abortions; meanwhile the same people don't want to provide welfare services to the women who are in the position of considering an abortion. I'm not here to take a stance on abortion or welfare, but I do feel that Tupac's THUG LIFE statement is trying to shed light on the social issues surrounding these things. Unfortunately the masses will never know that, and merely think THUG LIFE is what it sounds like, thanks to the evil Archon spirits of the

Illuminati who have taken one thing and twisted the message around to mean another; a form of "double speak" that you've possibly heard of in Orwell's dystopian novel, *1984*.

Just one month prior to his death Tupac recorded an album called *The Don Killuminati: The 7 Day Theory* that took him seven days to write and record. This dark album was based on a concept he formulated in prison and he was establishing his alias as 'Makaveli' to supplant his 2pac stage name. Many believed there was a conspiracy behind this album and Tupac's death (as we'll discuss much later). People were postulating that he faked his death because Makaveli was a play on Niccolo Machiavelli, a philosopher that Tupac studied who had his most famous work *The Prince* release several years after his own death. The term "Machiavellian" is an adjective used to describe someone who is being deceitful, and many believed this supported the conspiracy theory. If you add in the fact that the case is unsolved, even though it happened in front of a Las Vegas crowd on a busy night, you have to wonder where the truth lies.

The "low vibrational revenue" formula worked yet again, as this album went to number one making him the second artist in history to have a posthumous number one album…

Chapter 3- Words Are Weapons; Or Magic?...

The "low vibrational revenue" formula requires the use of negative messages of fear, hatred, anger, violence, etc. These messages are implanted into the music and the listener takes them in on the subconscious level and stores them permanently. The messages will later bubble up to the surface and come through the listener's behavior and cause them to act in a certain manner. This is where the magic happens.

"Music is like magic there's a certain feeling you get when you're real and you spit and people are feeling your shit."
– Eminem, *Till I Collapse*

Understanding the effects of negative messages requires understanding how the mind works. The brain is efficient in that it finds patterns of things you've been exposed to and presents that to your mind as something identifiable. For example, if you've seen an apple before then you'll immediately recognize it when you come across another one based on the memory retrieval system and say "that's an apple." If you envision an apple with a bite out of it, you might think of Apple's logo; a symbol that could represent the Garden of Eden and the origination of sin. Basically, the brain retrieves a pattern that you have previously stored and presents it to you, similar to how a hard drive retrieves information and displays it on a screen. The same concept applies to music and negative messages. If you hear rap songs about how 'all women are scandalous prostitutes,' then you'll be scanning for anything that supports this notion, even though it's not the truth. Or worse yet, you'll believe that it is the 100% truth and it will ruin your relationships with 100% of all women. Another example is the film *Groundhog's Day* with Bill Murray. He repeats the same thing over and over because he has a negative belief system and outlook on life, and the only way he can break the pattern is to change his belief system, and the universe lets him proceed to the next day. The messages of gangsta rap often times perpetuate misogyny, violence, and distrust. While they are sadly part of the daily struggles for some people; they aren't true for all people. Overzealous fans of the gangsta rap genre might take on these belief systems and apply them to their lives, when their reality isn't supportive of it. An example is the film that stars Danny Hoch called *Whiteboyz* where suburban white kids listen to gangsta rap to the point that they think they are legitimately ready for a gangsta lifestyle until they make a trip to Chicago and find out otherwise.

You can see that the introduction of gangsta rap and violence is probably something that is not *good* for the black community, regardless of the effect you may *think* music has on people. An excuse I hear often is that music doesn't control people but I beg to differ. Songs get "ear wormed" into your head with the ability for lyrics to be recalled several years later.

Who doesn't know at least a few lines from Sir Mix-A-Lot's *Baby Got Back*? Can you recall anything else to such detail from 1992?...

Words have power, ipso facto; music has *a lot* of power. Music combines words and melody, providing a perfect method for displacing a message upon our human brains.

I believe you can speak things into existence.
–Jay-Z, *Decoded*

My words are weapons
I use 'em to crush my opponents
My words are weapons
I never show no emotion
My words are weapons
I use 'em to kill whoever's steppin to me
My words are like weaponry on a record
-Eminem, *My Words are Weapons*

The Illuminati are surely aware of this and have taken advantage of it. Take a look at commercials on the allegedly-Illuminati owned television networks. They almost always have a melodic tune in the background; even though nobody is singing. The Illuminati knows they need to hijack the message, strip the truth from it, and implant whatever devious thing they desire. They repeat the tainted message with themes they find profitable. An example would be 1999's Jay-Z ft. DMX song *Money, Cash, Hoes*. They repeat the line several times (about 48 times), implanting the message deeper and deeper of, well, money, cash, and hoes. Anyone familiar with hip hop knows this is a common theme in modern rap music.

A similar example is the 1998 song by The Lox ft. DMX and Lil' Kim called *Money, Power & Respect*. They repeat the lyrics *Money, Power and Respect* about 40 times. The message is quite clear:

It's the key to life.
Money, power, and respect.
Whatchu' need in life.
Money, power, and respect.
When you eatin' right.
Money, power, and respect.
Help you sleep at night.
You'll see the light.
It's the key to life.
Money, power, and respect.
Whatchu' need in life.
Money, power, and respect.
When you eatin' right.
Money, power, and respect.
Money, power, and respect.
Money, power, and respect.
-The Lox, *Money, Power, & Respect*

These repetitions are what the ancient Hindus referred to as mantras. A mantra is a repeated sound that has a psychological and spiritual effect. They implant moods and thoughts, and that is precisely what the Illuminati want with lyrics such as these. They emphasize material concepts and dog-eat-dog, alpha male attitudes. These are meant to divide the people who listen to it, unlike, say, hippie music that sought to unify the people (and we saw what happened with that movement when Manson was placed into the culture to unleash fear and anxiety of the hippies). Only one person can be the alpha male with all of the jewelry and cars, and the perception is that it is going to be the listener. People listen to these songs and get uplifted by them but not in the positive sense. They envision *themselves* as the ones who will have all of the money, power, and respect. They want badly to make this a reality in their lives, and the only path they see to make that happen is to follow the rappers and either sell drugs or perhaps start rapping themselves (and repeating the mantra to the others). That's not to take anything away from people pursuing their dreams of becoming a rapper; more power to them, but the cold reality is that it's much easier to fall into the trappings of the drug game than to be a rich and famous rapper. Similar to the alpha males of the wild, there is always a battle for the top and rats get stuck fighting it out to pretend who that will be, meanwhile the *real* winner is the Illuminati who sit atop the throne orchestrating movements.

One idea held by many theorists (myself included) is that the Illuminati and music industry force the musicians to fit a certain mold and present certain images. Why do you think you see newcomers to the rap scene boast about how much they possess and their endless swagger? How can they talk about having so much when they haven't even blown up on the charts yet? Even Vanilla Ice said he was a few payments behind on his Mustang 5.0 when he was touring with Public Enemy and Ice-T prior to the release of his breakthrough album *To the Extreme*. The Illuminati set these artists up to fit certain molds and images, and then experiment to see what works. If the artist doesn't work out, they're left for dead and of no use to the corporation. In a revealing interview he had with BackWashZine.com, Vanilla Ice explains how the game chewed him up and spit him out:

"I mean it almost killed me, I mean I tried to commit suicide in '94, heavily on drugs, having to escape reality, life sucked. A lot of people thought I was living this famous life, huge ego, but it really wasn't the case. I wouldn't wish my life

on anybody. I've never to this day enjoyed any of my success. I would've turned around and gave it all back if I would've seen the consequences of it all. It's amazing because in 1990 I had two record deals on the table. Before those two records came about I was on Ichibon Records and I played for an all-black audience. I was opening for Ice-T, Stetsasonic, Public Enemy, EPMD, and in '90 I had the two deals, one for Def Jam for $30,000. Hank Shockley was going to produce my album, Public Enemy was going to appear on my record. And I had another deal with SBK to cross my hip hop record to the pop market for $1.5 million. So I took the money. I was 19 years old, three car payments behind on my 5.0, living in an apartment with 3 other guys, couldn't even pay my share of the rent. It was like winning the lottery over night. I didn't see the consequences. The consequences being turned into a novelty act. Something I was very uncomfortable with. Something I didn't want to be. Didn't know it was going to happen. And it was too late once it hit to turn anything around. So I had to ride it out and roll with the punches. And that's what led to tons of criticism. Now you have these groups like 'N Sync, Backstreet Boys, they're designed to be a novelty act. When I started out I was not designed to be that way. When you listen to my record, you could tell it was a hip hop record. It was not a pop record. The image is what crossed it over and made the music acceptable. Maybe because I'm white or whatever. But it happened. The music was always real. The record company completely treated me as a puppet with the image, but the music I had control of, except a few songs like I Love You and those extra songs they had to fill in for that album. But other than that, Ice Ice Baby, Play That Funky Music, Fantasy, and all that shit, that was real. But the image just got so f*ckin' played out. I mean, just beyond what I could see when I signed. So I went through the drugs, '94 tried to kill myself and in '94 I *had millions of dollars in the bank, but here I am on the floor and my friends are dumping buckets of cold water on me and I'm puking blood, I really wanted out. I would've gave everything back to go back to that one moment when I signed and gone with Def Jam because I really believe that would've given me more credibility. I wouldn't have been some pop-f*ckin'- novelty teenie-bopper act. You gotta understand, I'm sitting here lying in front of the camera, "You should stay in school" because I'm a role model I'm a f*ckin' dropout! How can I sit there and tell kids to stay in school? "And you should always do the right thing!" And I f*ckin' sold drugs, I'm a piece of shit, I was in jail. What the f*ck do you want me to be? So I never felt like any kind of role model. So here I am acting. Everything to this point has been an act. It's all fabricated. It's all been staged, from the clothes to everything. They're pulling the strings and I'm going along with it. And I was getting paid tremendously. And I guess that's the one positive thing that came out of all of this, I'm not one of these artists who blew all their money, I saved a lot of it. So here I am in '94 with millions of dollars in the bank trying to die."*

–Vanilla Ice, BackWashZine.com

Given the importance of wordplay in the rap genre, it shouldn't be that much of a stretch of the imagination to think that musicians are using *actual* magic to create their art. Art in and of itself is magic because you're creating something out of nothing. The term Abracadabra has Aramaic roots and literally means "*as I speak; I create.*" It's a magical belief system that projects an illusion and makes the viewer believe it, which makes it a reality. It's no different than the concept of the media or entertainment industry repeating a false theme (e.g. an illusion) to the viewers until it becomes an accepted "reality." You see pharmaceutical companies pushing advertising of new ailments until you *believe* it affects you. They are making something out of nothing: abracadabra.

The ancient Egyptians accredited Thoth as the patron of scribes and the written word (is it ironic that there is a word "THOT" used in the hip hop culture...). He was believed to be the God who invented music, and Osiris used this music to control the world. The first western culture musicians were the Greek Muses (from the Greek word 'mousike' we get 'music', or Muse-ic). They were the goddesses who inspired the written word and the arts. These daughters of Zeus are continually being evoked by musicians in order to create their art: the music. The musicians are literally asking to be possessed by these goddesses in order to obtain inspiration and guidance for their tales or lyrics. They conjure the spirits in their minds, whether it is through mental practices or physical rituals. Sometimes they get so used to it that they begin to self-identify with their muse and attach themselves to them.

"My muse is very fickle. She only comes to me sometimes, which is annoying."
–Lana Del Rey, *Nylon* magazine, November 2013

You could extrapolate the creativeness of music with magic to include one of the other goals of the Illuminati; money. This means of trading for goods and services is only worth what we believe it to be worth in our minds. The paper is inherently worthless, but the magic that we 'will' onto it makes it a valuable product. If you study survival guidebooks you'll quickly find that one of the necessities to have in your bug out bag is coins made of precious metals like gold or silver; not paper cash. That is because there is a potential for the magic spell to be "lifted" someday (e.g. an economic crash).

So how exactly does this magic work? I'll piece together some various things I believe *could* work. First you must believe in the concept of free will. You and I are free to carve out a potential future, and there is no such thing as fate or a deterministic plan where we have *no* control over our lives. I've heard many credible experts on New Age theories and even practitioners of magic provide the guidance that there is no such thing as "the future," yet people spend most of their time there. This proves that even believers of non-traditional systems concur with this idea of free will. This concept is highlighted in the popular New Age book *The Secret*. You must establish a will to work towards a certain future goal. You place this in your mind and repeat the mantra until the universe presents a path of synchronicity in front of you. You are essentially creating something out of nothing.

> *"There is no future, the future is now."*
> –Non Phixion, *There is No Future*

One goal of the Illuminati is to steer your free will (effectively not making it so "free" anymore) to fit their agenda. This is one key tenet of magic and occultist Aleister Crowley defined it as such:

> *Magic(k) is the Science and Art of causing Change to occur in conformity with Will.*
> – Aleister Crowley, *Magick*

The practitioners of true magic believe that they can make the universe harmonize itself to *their* will. They believe they can use symbolic methods to make change in the universe through the paranormal, as Stephen Flowers, PhD describes in his book, *Lords of the Left-Hand Path*. One way they do this is through predictive programming. The concept of predictive programming is to present a certain idea to the masses in order to make it come to fruition by magical means. Some claim that the Native Americans couldn't see the Europeans' ships coming across the ocean because they had no preconception of such a thing. When we see a repetitive concept in entertainment media we can draw a conclusion that the Illuminati are presenting an idea so that we will all take part of the upcoming ritual.

An example of predictive programming would be the pop singer Ke$ha's song *Die Young* that came out in September 2012. In the music video she is depicted as part of a satanic cult performing sex type magick rituals and talking about living life like you were going to die young. Three months later the Sandy Hook mass shootings occurred and the song was pulled from the radio because of the deaths of all the young children (note that the song was #1 on the US Billboard charts). After the Sandy Hook event Ke$ha apologized for the lyrical content of the song and revealed that she was *forced* to sing it. Later she deleted the tweet and claimed she didn't mean to use the term "forced" but what she said didn't make things any clearer for conspiracy theorists, considering the occult nature of the music video:

" 'Forced' is not the right word. I did have some concerns about the phrase 'Die Young' in the chorus when we were writing the lyrics ... because so many of my fans are young," she wrote. "That's one reason why I wrote so many versions of this song. But the point of the song is the importance of living every day to the fullest and staying young at heart, and these are things I truly believe."
– Ke$ha, MTV.com

An example from the film industry is the hip hop community-beloved gangster film *Scarface*. In this film Al Pacino plays a dope dealing murderer who has it all; money, power, and respect (see the Lox lyrics above). He even dies in a glamorous fashion, huffing piles of cocaine and shooting his assault rifle from his mansion's office. Films like this are used to implant themes of gangster fantasy because there are not many points of the film that make his lifestyle undesirable.

The artist Prince was at a concert in the Netherlands in 1998 and he told the crowd that he had to go because "*Osama Bin Laden was going to drop the bomb on America.*" He's also talked about his experience with chemtrails and belief in conspiracy theories on the Tavis Smiley talk show.

Jay-Z could have the most predictive programming out of all of the artists in the industry. His album *The Blueprint* was released on September 11th, 2001 (also note that it was Kanye West's breakout into the industry for its production). As it would turn out it was indeed the blueprint of the Illuminati... We also saw predictive programming with the 9/11 date on Neo's driver's license in *The Matrix*, it also happened on an episode of *The Simpsons* on the front cover of a magazine, and in the film *Terminator 2* there was a 9'11" clearance prominently shown in one chase scene. Some would claim these are all coincidences, and maybe they were, but there were also other oddities of celebrities who seemed to have foresight of disaster. For example, Seth MacFarlane (*Family Guy*), Mark Wahlberg (rapper Marky Mark), Leighanne Littrell (actress and wife of Backstreet Boys' Brian Littrell) and Julie Stoffer (member of MTV's *Real World* from 2000) were *all* ticketed to board the ill-fated American Airlines Flight 11 but didn't get on board for one reason or another.

Getting back to Jay-Z, his album *The Blueprint* (recipient of the coveted 5-mic Source award) prompted two follow-up albums under the same name. *The Blueprint 2: The Gift & The Curse* dropped on November 12th, 2002 (the day that news broke that Osama Bin Laden was behind the 9/11 attacks, and again on Nov. 12th, 2013 when the One World Trade Center was announced as the tallest building in the US). *The Blueprint 2* had a photo of Jay-Z on the cover with what looks like his hand making the gesture of 666. In the lyrics to the song called *Blueprint 2* he references the donations he made from ticket sales to the 9/11 tragedy:

Can't y'all, see that he's fake, the rap version of TD jakes
Prophesizing on your CDs and tapes
Won't break you a crumb of the little bit that he makes
And this is with whom you want to place your faith?
I put dollars on mine, ask Columbine
When the Twin Towers dropped, I was the first in line
Donating proceeds off every ticket sold
When I was out on the road, that's how you judge Hov, no?
- Jay-Z, *Blueprint 2*

After *Blueprint 2* Jay-Z started to transition lyrically to more esoteric and occult subjects. For instance, the next album he released was *The Black Album* with songs like *Lucifer*. This song was produced by Kanye West and some claim you can hear the words "murder, murder Jesus" if played backwards. The lyrics to the song talk about murder out of necessity of street life intermixed with the Luciferianism aspects you would expect from the title:

Lucifer, dawn of the morning!
I'm gonna chase you out of Earth

Lucifer, Lucifer, dawn of the morning...
(I'm from the murder capital, where we murder for capital)
Lucifer, Lucifer, dawn of the morning!

Man I gotta get my soul right
I gotta get these Devils out my life
These cowards gonna make a nigga ride
They won't be happy 'til somebody dies
- Jay-Z *Lucifer*

On that same album was a song called *Justify My Thug* that sampled Madonna's *Justify My Love*; a song that is rumored to have satanic messages when played backwards as well. His album *Kingdom Come* featured a song called *Hollywood* that featured Beyoncé (two years before they were married) and it depicted the dangers of Hollywood and perhaps a subtle cue of demon possession:

And everybody warning you about it (Try to told you)
And once you taste you can't live without it (It's addictive)
Not cause you choose to not live without it (Sure you want this baby)
It's now a part of you (It's a part of you)
It's now a part of you
And everybody warning you about it (I see you blinded)
And once you taste you can't leave
- Jay-Z ft. Beyonce, *Hollywood*

The next album in the Blueprint series was *The Blueprint 3* which was released digitally in the US on September 11th, 2009. This album stepped up the esoteric aspects with songs like *Run This Town* featuring Rihanna and Kanye West and *On to the Next One*. The video for *Run This*

Town depicts a dystopian future that theorists such as Doggstar believe is the direction the Illuminati and Freemasons are seeking to take the country. Jay-Z was seen sporting a hooded shirt that says "Do What Thou Wilt", a phrase commonly used as a greeting by Thelemites (followers of Aleister Crowley's religious order). Doggstar says that the video shows Jay-Z as Osiris (because he goes by Hova or Jay-Hova) the father, Rihanna as Isis, and Kanye as the son, Horus; an alteration to the Egyptian trinity with occult significance. He also points out that the lyrics to the song where Jay-Z says "*We are, Yeah I said it we are*" were taken from the script of a satanic group called The Order of Nine Angles, one of the most dangerous sects of Satan worshippers. The founder of this group, Anton Long, allegedly wrote a letter that was posted in a forum for Order of Nine Angles' followers that said the following:

Whose gonna run this town, tonight? The short answer: **we are,** *however long it takes to undermine by whatever means the societies of the mundanes and replace their rule of law, and their Police forces, with our law of personal honour and our tribal enforcers.*

The song *On to the Next One* also has hidden references in it that suggest Illuminati symbolism as well. Jay-Z timed the video to release precisely at midnight of 2010, making it the very first video of the year which suggests it may be part of a ritual (timing is of the utmost importance to the occult). The lyrics point to his ability to set trends, yet the visuals of the video suggest otherwise. In the video there are images spliced throughout of rams and horned animals; a common symbol for pagan or occult belief systems. This horned deity is expressed in various videos as the bull God Moloch, Pan, or the most obvious horned creature: Satan. The personality known as Mr.

Gates explained his take on the video's theme in his *Jupiturn: Illuminati Special* show/podcast and says it's based on an astrological context, implying that Jay-Z is seeking to push society into the Age of Aquarius, an era of which the New Age is defined. The astrologists believe that this New Age will bring forth a more civilized era of humanity, and the hippie movement of the 60s was thought to be the first step into this next phase.

Mr. Gates supports this by pointing out the disparity between the lyrics and the actual imagery from the video; they seem to have nothing to do with one another (as mentioned earlier). The symbolism shows us sets of wires that appear just like the water waves in the depiction of Aquarius. There are also images and lyrics of yachts, raindrops, and boats, and a jersey with the number "00" across it. He asserts that this could be indicative of starting over into the new Age of Aquarius. Jay-Z is pushing us, or as the lyrics reveal, "coaching us"; telling us it's "On to the next one;" meaning the next Age. One of the lyrics Jay-Z drops says *"No, I'm not a Jonas, I use my cajones"* which is a clever insult against the old Age of Pisces, or the time of Christianity. The Jonas Brothers were known for being a squeaky clean boy band that got their start with a Nick Jonas' song on Christian radio. Jay-Z is juxtaposing himself with them and basically saying this is the old way of the ignorant; join me in the next phase of humanity. The Bible is full of allegories of fish, and Jesus brought us into the Age of Pisces, so moving "On to the next one" would indicate moving from Christianity and into this New Age religion. Another mockery of Christianity is an image that depicts a cross with bullets around it, again showing us death symbolism with Jesus Christ. His lyrics also say *"Big pimpin' in the house now"* and "(I) *tore the house down"*, which Mr Gates points out as references to the destruction of the previous Age, or "House" as astrology calls it. Astrology divides the horoscope into twelve houses based on time and location (some theorists claim this is where Christianity gets its twelve disciples from). In Jay-Z's song he is telling us he is tearing down the old "House" and introducing us to the next House.

One last point Mr. Gates brings up in *Jupiturn* regarding Jay-Z is the MTV production called *Jay-Z in Africa: Water for Life*. In said documentary, Jay-Z is bringing awareness to the global water crisis that is predominantly affecting people in Africa at the moment (which is one of the doomsday scenarios theorists claim will eventually take *all* of us out). The argument for symbolism is that it is all a charade put on by the Illuminati, who are making this water special in an attempt to push more Age of Aquarius symbolism. They are using it as a mass ritual to get attention and energy to focus on water; an aspect of the water carrier of the Aquarius. In fact, one of the chapters of the video is called "Eyes Wide Open"; a reference to the All Seeing Eye (or perhaps the occult symbolism filled film of the similar name). The video was also showing us that the United Nations set everything up for Jay-Z to work on this project; drawing speculation since the UN is one of the hot topics for conspiracy theorists who believe in a One World Government agenda.

One of the seemingly laughable conspiracy theories about Jay-Z is the symbolism behind the naming of his child with Beyoncé. They named their daughter Blue Ivy Carter and theorists all over the world have chimed in on why this is. There are claims that Blue is an acronym for Born Living Under Evil and Ivy means Illuminati's Very Youngest. If you spell them backwards it's Eulb Yvi which supposedly means Lucifer's Daughter in Latin, but the root of that was a joke from Katt Williams and conspiracy theorists ran with it. The real meaning for the odd name of Blue Ivy could have come from a Beyoncé Tumblr post that said "*The world is blue at its edges and in its depths*" which came from a book called *Field Guide to Getting Lost* which she says had great meaning to her.

Another idea is that Ivy is a play on the Roman numeral IV which is 4. The number 4 is symbolic for both Jay-Z and Beyoncé since he was born on Dec. 4th, she was born on Sept. 4th, they were married on April 4th and they had "IV" tattooed on their ring fingers. Jay-Z also has a fascination with the color of blue, given that he had the album series named *The Blueprint*, a song called *Blue Magic* (talking about drugs), another song called *Jay-Z Blue* (about his daughter) and even trademarked a color called Jay-Z Blue that was intended to get painted onto a line of Jeep Commanders. Weeks after Blue Ivy was born they tried to trademark the name "Blue Ivy" but were denied by the US Patent & Trademark Office.

Another conspiracy theory is that Beyoncé was never really pregnant but Blue Ivy was born to a surrogate mother instead. The "evidence" to support this includes footage of Beyoncé bending over and the baby bump folding over. To me it seems like these are the more absurd theories that give conspiracy theorists a bad name, but either way I'm not here to pre-judge these things because the world is too weird to deny ideas on the fringes. Jay-Z did in fact have a record called *The Dynasty: Roc La Familia* where he prominently has the triangle of manifestation on the cover and I can't help but wonder if he was tapped by the powers that be to start a new family of royal blood; a rap dynasty if you will. This would explain his settling down with the wife and kids after all of these years rapping about gaming on women and *not* settling down. Perhaps the obsession with blue ties into the need to be a member of the "blue bloods"- another term used for the elite bloodlines that run the world, making Blue Ivy the first of a new generation of power brokers in la familia Illuminati.

To tie things back into the more legitimate esoteric aspects, I posit that the color blue holds significance for Jay-Z because the blue chakra point (known as the energy wheel Vishuddha) is located in the throat and is known for the ability to verbalize. I don't know many other people that can verbalize like Jay-Z who has the ability to 'express truth through the spoken word'; a trait of the blue chakra.

One indictment of the Illuminati infiltration of the entertainment industry is the clever ruse of redefining magic. They've managed to depict magic as parlor tricks performed by men dressed in black and white pulling rabbits out of a hat. This is a psychological operation (PsyOp) meant to distract the masses from the beliefs held by practitioners. In reality it's more of a self-discipline used to create one's own world; a concept veiled in New Age thought and in books like *The Secret*. There are different forms of magic such as Wiccan, Hermetic, Black, White, etc. and it all depends on what the practitioner believes in using to attain their end goal. Some of the more modern forms of magic have roots in the Hermetic Order of the Golden Dawn, a close offshoot of Thelema, founded by Aleister Crowley. R&B singer Ciara wore a coat that boasted the name of the Golden Dawn in her video for *Keep On Lookin'* and Jay-Z wore the Thelema expression *Do What Thou Wilt* on the aforementioned video shoot for *Run This Town*. Does this mean they practice magic? Not necessarily, but it does beg the question. The two magic sects are a more ritualistic style of magic so it falls in line with the reason why they insist on showing us these symbols.

Carl Jung and Sigmund Freud theorized about a 'collective unconscious' or 'archaic remnants' that the symbolism speaks to. When we see a symbol in a music video it is able to penetrate the message by opening up certain frequencies or chakras with the beat, effectively making the listener part of the ritual. When we see Jay-Z holding up the triangle of manifestation on his album cover, it's working on the collective unconscious level.

Rick Rubin is a name synonymous with hip hop because he found Def Jam Records with Russell Simmons, which provided us with acts like LL Cool J, Public Enemy, Beastie Boys, and Run DMC. He was highlighted in a *New York Times* article when he revealed his fascination with magic:

"From the time I was 9 years old, I loved magic," Rubin recalled as he walked around the cavernous loftlike space. "I was an only child, and I think that had a big impact on me. I always had grown-up friends even though I was a little kid. I would take the train from Lido Beach into Manhattan, and I'd hang out in magic shops. When I was 14, I had magician friends who were 60. I learned a lot from them — I still think about magic all the time. I always think about how things work, the mechanics of a situation — that's the nature of being a magician."
– Rick Rubin, *New York Times*

Theorists Jamie Hanshaw and Freeman Fly wrote about aspects of magic in their book series *Weird Stuff (Operation Culture Creation)*. In their first book they detail various laws of magic. One of which is The Law of Knowledge which asserts that understanding comes with control and power. The more the magician knows the more control he/she has over that subject. Survivalist and *Dual Survivor* star Cody Lundin has a mantra that says *"The more you know, the less you need"* and this same principle is echoed here. In a survival situation, the more a person knows the more control they have over their continued existence. The Law of Knowledge applies in all of these situations when the practitioner controls the symbols and understands what they truly mean, while the audience remains unsuspecting.

Taking that concept a step further goes into The Law of Self Knowledge. This law reflects aspects of Descartes-like philosophy and requires the practitioner to explore who they truly are. Once you know yourself and have fully tested your limitations as a human you are no longer an insecure person, afraid to try new things. Many great minds were aware of the importance of this concept, as is evident at the Temple of Apollo at Delphi in ancient Greece where the oracle inspired the carving of "Know Thyself" to be written in the rocks.

"Know thy self and thou shalt know the universe and God."
– KRS One, *Know Thy Self*

Going a bit further, there is a Law of Words that states knowing the true name of something will give you control over it. The reason for this is because the magicians believe the name holds the true essence of its being. The ancient mystery schools believed words and names held certain amounts of energy. Key words would give the power to shape reality simply by using the vibrational energy of the vocal chords and saying them. In the fifth century BC, philosopher Plato analyzed the properties of names and words in *Cratylus*. He explored the question of what criteria were necessary for naming an object. One of the beliefs the come out of this exercise is that names come from *divine* origin; not arbitrarily derived with community consensus. In fact, we see the *King James Holy Bible* describe just this in Proverbs 18:21:

Death and life are in the power of the tongue: and they that love it shall eat the fruit thereof.

It also appears in John 1:1:

In the beginning was the Word, and the Word was with God, and the Word was God.

On a simpler level, one could think of the way we teach children manners. We ask, *"What is the magic word?"* and the response must be *"Please."* The *magic* is required to make the *will* a reality. These incantations are used with the power of words that can be expressed one letter at a time through spelling. We literally *spell* the powerful words.

Stephen Flowers, Ph.D., writes about Greco-Egyptian magical rituals in his book *Lords of the Left-Hand Path* and in it he details part of a theory that claims Jesus Christ was a magician. There are rituals for obtaining a spirit in order to become a son of God, and in these rituals, the magician is to look for certain signs (including a descending falcon) and then say:

I have been attached to your holy form. ***I have been given power by your holy name****. I have acquired your emanation of the Gods. Lord, God of Gods, master, daimon.*

Going further, Flowers draws parallels between magic rituals and the baptism of Jesus. In the story, Jesus received the Holy Spirit and is able to perform unbelievable (magical) feats by merely saying the word, which the author eludes to being a magical spell or mantra. Although I don't personally believe it, that doesn't make it so. Even more importantly, the believers of these concepts accept these as facts and dedicate their own lives to practicing the magic.

Taking this concept over into rap music, we can easily see that the rapid fire, melodic format of the genre makes the rapper a much more effective sorcerer than most. The rappers do what most practitioners of magic do, in that they use everything as a metaphor. Magicians use a stick as wand, which represents the Will which can be inferred as a microphone. The cup represents understanding (e.g. Lil Jon and Snoop Dogg's 'crunk' cups), and the songs set the mood for the ritual (e.g. gangsta rap sets mood for criminal activities). Rap lyrics are teeming with lyrics that are metaphors:

"Keep one eye open like CBS, you see me stressed, right?"
– Jay-Z, *Can I Live?*

"Devil's Plan is to have you drip in the Clorox, Beast deceiving us ways devious possessing, My peeps to walk streets with stolen heat like Prometheus"
– Jus Allah, Jedi Mind Tricks, *I Against I*

Another trick up these magicians' sleeves is the incorporation of symbolism in the music videos, lyrics, and imagery. The most notorious symbol is the "Roc" diamond that Jay-Z made famous. Most people think this is a triangle because the shape appears to be that way, but originally it was the shape of a diamond. It derived from Roc-A-Fella records; the record label he started with Damon Dash under the Universal Music Group umbrella. Jay-Z's first album, *Reasonable Doubt* was released under this label after being rejected by several other labels (and featured a song called

D'Evils as the 6th track). He truly made something out of nothing in the magical sense. But that doesn't take away from the fact that it appears to look like a triangle and Jay-Z is seen doing it with the All Seeing Eye symbolism as well. At his concerts you can see thousands of devoted fans throwing up the diamond in reverence to this modern day "God." The same hand gesture shape is also used by actual Illuminati elites as a "power triangle" known as the Merkel-Raute (or the Merkel Diamond), and you'll see them do this while giving speeches and on the campaign trail. It's no coincidence that Jay-Z's Roc-A-Fella label was named after an alleged main bloodline of the Illuminati known as the Rockefeller family.

In Texe Marrs' book *Codex Magica* he highlights symbolism held by the Illuminati and displays an image of David Rockefeller Sr, then President of Chase-Manhattan Bank and founder of the Trilateral Commission. The image was from *Town & Country* magazine and it shows him in a masonic pose with diamonds on his necktie. The diamonds are claimed to be a symbol for the Hermetic mystery school maxim of *"As above, so below."* It can be shown as two triangles butted together and you'll come across this in various studies of occult, magic, and Kabbalah related organizations. The basic premise is that anything that happens in this realm of the microcosm will *also* occur in the macrocosm. This supports the idea that the magician can bend the universe to *their* Will. If they make something happen in their mind it will reflect in reality of the universe.

In fact, Jay-Z's influence has caused a chain reaction of rappers and celebrities to throw the Roc diamond up. This list includes (but is not limited to): Denzel Washington, Warren Buffet, Kanye West, Rihanna, Tom Cruise, Kobe Bryant, Drake, Lebron James, Jason Kidd, Al Sharpton, Ellen DeGeneres, NY Police Commissioner Ray Kelly, New

England Patriots and business mogul Robert Kraft, and even Jay-Z's wife, Beyoncé did it at the 2013 Super Bowl performance, prompting many theorists to speculate on her involvement in the Illuminati.

The rapper/R&B singer Drake throws up the Roc diamond but he is primarily known for having depictions of owls on his albums and jewelry. The owl is usually confused as the symbol for the deity of Moloch, but that is not the case. Moloch is depicted as a bull, while Minerva is shown through the owl. The owl shows up near ancient goddesses like the Greek Athena and Roman Minerva. The symbol represents wisdom because the owl can see through the darkness. His metaphor represents the illumination of education and seeing through pervasive ignorance and deception. Not only do we see the owl on Drake's "October's Very Own" label (it gets truncated to "OVO" which is cleverly disguising the owl's eyes and beak), but also at the infamous Bohemian Grove where world leaders get together and perform a ritual called The Cremation of Care where they do a mock sacrifice to a giant owl God.

Another rapper named A$AP Rocky released a video in January 2012 called *Wassup* that depicts him forming a sequence of pentagrams inside of an Enochian magic circle while the All Seeing Eye of Horus is displayed in the background inside the apex of a pyramid. This video released before he even had a debut album (that was called *Long.Live.ASAP* that released in January 2013). The purpose of the Enochian circle is to evoke spirits and form a sacred space that protects the magician from the evil they are summoning, so what we are witnessing is a spiritual evocation of an evil entity.

The practice of evocation or invocation of spirits is to magically lure the energies of the spirit world into the material world. Evoking draws from *external* spirits and sources, while invoking is harnessing power *within you*. Aleister Crowley was believed to have summoned his higher form of self through invocation of his holy guardian angel Aiwass (whom he believed to be Lucifer). This proved to Crowley that one can be God like if they invoke their higher form of consciousness. The Left-Path followers claim that Crowley was referencing Satan from a different viewpoint than what we currently think of it as. Using the principles of opposites, or yin and yang, he believed that Satan would merely be the God of anything others dislike. He believed that Satan was needed to unite the world because he provided opposition and you need opposites to clearly define the boundaries.

The list of symbolism found in music videos is also fairly exhausting, and it includes Rick Ross' artwork for *Black Barmitzvah* that has the Rothschild family crest and Seal of Solomon, which is used to control demons. Solomon supposedly used this magical symbol to control demon spirits and force them to build his Temple of Solomon. In Rihanna's video for *Umbrella* there is a symbol made from splashing water that clearly outlines the shape of the Baphomet. This symbol of the horned goat is another symbol for the inverted Pentagram with the horns being the bottom legs of the star. In dozens of videos we see the depiction of the All Seeing Eye of Horus inside of a triangle, outside of a triangle, or in combination with the 666 hand gesture. The same goes for the Mano Cornuto sign of the Devil horns. This symbol is commonplace for representing rock 'n' roll but its true meaning is far more sinister and resides in the satanic doctrine which traces back through the Canaanites' worship of the bull God Ba'al. The fact that most people laugh at those of us who point out the evil aspects of the Devil horns, is just a testament for how commonplace the Illuminati have made these symbols in our daily lives. We're led to believe that they are harmless jokes, when in reality people like Church of Satan founder Anton LaVey admitted they are used to place hexes on others.

So why do these artists throw these symbols up? Some believe in it, while others don't know what they are doing and are told by their handlers to do it. Willard Smith (better known as "Will" and you'll see a terrible pun on it here in about one sentence...) went on the Tavis Smiley show and proceeded to talk about how he wanted to represent magic. He said that 2+2 is going to equal what he *wants* it to be (that's a subtle way of saying he will bend the universe to his "Will"). One of his favorite books is *The Alchemist* and he says he believes he can learn patterns and create whatever he wants to. In the novel the boy named Santiago follows his prophetic dreams to go to Egypt and along the way he learns to pursue his "Personal Legend" which is "what you have always wanted to accomplish." Again, this is the occult version of the Will, and also notice the synchronicity of two of Will Smith's other films like *The Pursuit of Happyness* and *I Am Legend* coinciding with the 'Personal Legend' from this novel. High profile celebrities like Oprah Winfrey and Pharrell Williams have also gone on record to proclaim their devotion to *The Alchemist*.

Allegedly Will Smith is into Scientology and tried to convert his son, Jaden, but as the Hollywood Street King reports on his website, his son rejects the teachings. Instead, it claims that Jaden is into "black magic and triangles." Again, the source of this information isn't listed on the HSK website, but he apparently has several insider connections because he maintains one of the most popular black culture gossip websites.

The rapper 2 Chainz has gone on record in an interview with DJ Vlad to say that they had no idea they were conducting such things:

71

"In my opinion, I feel like directors or people that do imagery, who went to school the past last 10 years, these are some things that they learn. Which is symbols, different icons, different things – whether they be negative or positive, just to get us talking. So if I shoot a video, Vlad, and I look behind you, I have these statues behind you. You don't know these two statues behind you. I'm the director. I'm shooting this sh*t. You don't know that's f*ckin' behind you–you don't know what the f*ck I'm doing. ... Boom, you leave. Boom, people go online and say, 'Vlad is in Illuminati.' And guess what happens? The views go up. The views don't help Vlad. The views help me, the f*ckin' director."

– 2 Chainz interview with DJ Vlad, 2013

The concepts laid out here will be elaborated on further in this book, so keep the basic fundamentals in the back of your mind as we proceed. The mind works by identification through retrieving stored information, and this information is often times first presented to the audience through predictive programming in films and music. The ability for the rappers to express concepts lyrically allows them to become the sorcerer, using magic rituals to shape the universe according to their Will. The listener participates in the ritual and devotes their energy towards that same Will. Whether you believe this idea or not is beside the point. The fact of the matter (or more appropriately the fact of this theory/speculation) is that the musicians and/or the executives handling the musicians (e.g. the Illuminati) believe in this process and apply it into their products.

Chapter 4- Alter Egos, Possession, and Mind Control

We've explored the power of rituals and also the magical laws of names and words. This shows us the importance in selecting a good name. This could explain why rappers change their names from their "governments" into aliases and alter egos. Many will claim the stage names are a tradition handed down through the hip hop culture since its inception, but one has to wonder where this concept originated. Practically *every* rapper or R&B artist has at least one alias stage name; many have more than one (with Prince the reigning champ with over seven aliases):

Shawn Carter = Jay-Z = Hova = Jigga = Iceberg Slim
Marshall Mathers = Eminem = Slim Shady
Cordozar Calvin Broadus = Snoop Doggy Dogg = Snoop Dogg = Snoopzilla = Snoop Lion
Dwayne Carter Jr. = Lil Wayne = Young Weezy = Young Tuneche = Weezy F. Baby
Curtis Jackson = 50 Cent
Sean Combs = Puff Daddy = P. Diddy = Diddy

William Roberts = Rick Ross
Cameron Thomaz = Wiz Khalifa
Tauheed Epps = Tity Boi = 2 Chainz
Onika Maraj = Nicki Minaj = Roman Zolanski = The Harujuku Barbie
Rakim Mayers = A$AP Rocky
Ben Haggerty = Macklemore
Jhene Aiko = J. Hennessy
Tracy Marrow = Ice T
Janet Jackson = Damita Jo
Prince Rogers Nelson = Prince = Jamie Starr = Alexander Nevermind = Joey Coco = Paisley Park = The Purple One = The artist formerly known as Prince
Beyoncé Knowles = Beyoncé = Sasha Fierce = Yonce = Beezus
Will Smith = The Fresh Prince
O'Shea Jackson = Ice Cube
Robert Diggs = The Rza = Bobby Digital
Taalib Johnson = Musiq Soulchild = Purple
Justin Bieber = Shawty Mane
Mariah Carey = Mimi = Bianca

Dropping a government name for an alias could be an extension of the form of rebellion from the time of the early African slaves. The American slave owners would try to destroy their sense of identity with Africa and part of this required a change in name. The belief was that the slave would fit into the program more easily if they identified themselves with the American version of themselves. Over the course of a couple of generations the youth would have no identity or concept of their true home or origin. This is why the story depicted in *Roots* shows Kunta Kinte refusing to say his name is Toby; he doesn't want to give up his identity. He knew there was a larger programming taking place and didn't want to give in.

Followers of the left-hand path (a term typically reserved for those who dabble in the occult) often times come up with new names as well. They refer to their government names as "mundane" names. Their magical names are used to protect their real-life identity and provide a constant reminder of their higher calling. Even Aleister Crowley changed his name from his original Edward Alexander Crowley to fit the formula of a dactyl followed by a spondee (it's the rhythm of the first name's three syllables). The founder of the Brotherhood of Saturn magical order (a group inspired by Crowley with roots tracing to the OTO) was Eugen Grosche and he changed his name to Gregor Gregorius to satisfy his occult beliefs.

You see the controversial groups like the Latter Day Saint Mormons practice the concept of alias names when they perform their private endowment ceremonies. The founder of the LDS faith, Joseph Smith, heavily borrowed symbolism from the secret society of Freemasonry, and this is evident in many aspects of the LDS faith. In a ritualized recreation of the fall of Adam and Eve, they are provided new, secret names. They believe these and other powerful tokens will be required to approach God in the afterlife and they are to keep them secret. Pagans and Wiccans also have a magical name they receive when they get initiated into their Craft, and this is also kept secret until the appropriate setting in which it can be used (*recall that I said dates and times were important in the occult). Ironically, noted British occultist and founder of Hermetic Order of the Golden Dawn, Samuel Mathers added the name MacGregor to his middle name in order to claim a Highland Scottish heritage. This draws similarity to the rapper Marshall Mathers who goes by Eminem as a play on M & M (his initials) so we have yet another M & M, but this one was *definitely* in the occult.

Many of the rappers have criminal names because they want to portray the violent, mobster image (e.g. Rick Ross, 50 Cent, Nas Escobar, Daz Dillinger, Young Gotti, Capone 'N' Noriega, etc.). The name selected is of importance because it generally is indicative of the reality around that person. Professor Griff talks about how it lines up your chakras and frequencies of being. This is why a rapper with the name C-Murder ends up going to jail for murder. The issue at hand is the magic behind the name selection. There are magic practices like contagious magic or sympathetic magic that basically adhere to the principle of 'fake it until you make it,' and eventually it will become a reality. You take attributes of what you're trying to emulate and do them until the universe opens that path up for you. This principle is exhibited in students or workers dressing in business attire. The professional look and feel of the attire gets translated onto the person and they feel they need to function at that professional level, and often times do. The same logic goes for wearing uniforms to private high schools or Catholic schools.

In the context of sympathetic magic (aka contagion magic), one can create an energetic reaction against a person based on a smaller energetic field from that person. An example most people know of is the voodoo doll, where the magician can take a lock of hair from the person they seek to interfere with and attach it to the doll. They can use the doll and hair to disturb the victim from a distance using magical spells and imitation. You've also seen this concept in the *Lord of the Rings* tale with 'one ring that can control them all.' The one ring forged by the Dark Ruler Sauron had the ability to control all of the other rings through sympathetic magic.

Musical artists like Ke$ha (or "Kesha" as she has renamed herself; yet another reference for the musical name game) requests that her fans send their teeth to her so she can make jewelry, or arguably cast spells, as I postulate. Madonna is also known for taking a sterilization team with her on the road for concert tours so they can clean up all traces of DNA so that others can't use this type of sympathetic-imitation magic against her. She claims that the reason for it is so nobody can keep a genetic souvenir of her, which sounds more ridiculous than just saying it's to block magic spells.

The sympathetic magic is also played out through product lines from the artists. A clear example of this would be Michael Jordan's Nike shoe line. The hip hop community generally goes nuts when the latest Air Jordans get released, leading into robberies, assaults, and even murders in order to obtain these pieces of pop culture history. People buy the product in order to perform a subtle form of sympathetic magic and be more like the person. Remember the phrase "Be like Mike" from Gatorade commercials? Well, the shoes are akin to this, where the people who pay for them seek to play at the level of Michael Jordan. This concept continues on with perfume lines from every musician possible (e.g. Puff Daddy, Beyoncé, Bieber, Kim Kardashian, Nicki Minaj, etc.). Lady Gaga released a fragrance called *Fame* that was based on the molecular structure of blood and semen; two very important bodily fluids used in magic rituals. She even said that it was based on her blood molecules to have "*a sense of me on your skin.*"

Another oddity is the religious aspect for some of these aliases that imply they are actually gods. They take the typical rap bravado to the next level and assume the identity of a savior or even more sacrilegiously assume the name of God:

Jay-Z = Hova
Kanye West = Yeezus
Beyoncé = Beezus

We see this because one of the main tenets of the supposed Illuminati is the pursuit of becoming God. The Illuminati group beliefs are a blend of Freemasonry, Luciferianism, occultism, Satanism, etc. which are all in the pursuit of enlightenment. The idea presented is that one can perfect themselves to the point of becoming God-like. This spiritual journey can be done without the help of a guiding hand (e.g. religious groups). This is why some theorists claim the New Age movement is the Illuminati in disguise, even going as far as to claim David Icke is a secret disinformation agent since his presentation has New Age concepts in it. Any movement that seeks to divide one another with an illusion of independent freedom will usually follow with a conquering of the group, and this is precisely what the Illuminati want to do. It's the classic divide and conquer strategy.

The Latter Day Saints are allegedly affiliated with the Illuminati (at the high levels, unknown to the lower level 'civilians'). In fact, they have something about becoming God on their website:

Through the Atonement of Jesus Christ, all people may progress toward perfection and ultimately realize their divine destiny. Just as a child can develop the attributes of his or her parents over time, the divine nature that humans inherit can be developed to become like their Heavenly Father's.

The desire to nurture the divinity in His children is one of God's attributes that most inspires, motivates, and humbles members of the Church. God's loving parentage and guidance can help each willing, obedient child of God receive of His fulness (sic) *and of His glory. This knowledge transforms the way Latter-day Saints see their fellow human beings.* ***The teaching that men and women have the potential to be exalted to a state of Godliness clearly expands beyond what is understood by most contemporary Christian churches*** *and expresses for the Latter-day Saints a yearning rooted in the Bible to live as God lives, to love as He loves, and to prepare for all that our loving Father in Heaven wishes for His children.*

Aleister Crowley's Thelema religious beliefs included self-realization of the "true will." This concept believed that you could find your reason for being in the universe without the aid of God or any other divine authority. The popular mainstream book, *The Purposeful Life,* was written by Pastor Rick Warren, who is allegedly involved with the Illuminati plot. Truth be told I've never read the book, but the title begs the question of juxtaposition of a "purposeful life" with finding your "Will" (as in "do what thou wilt"). The support for this theory comes from conspiracy theorist Texe Marrs who points out that Rick Warren is a member of the alleged Illuminati-front, the Council on Foreign Relations (it's true, he's on the CFR.org website as a member, as of June 12, 2014). He even goes as far as to say that Robert Murdoch's Fox network and the media teamed up to push the book's sales (over 30 million to date). Rick Warren also quotes from Eugene Peterson's New Age version of the Bible called *The Message* which in fact has distorted the Lord's Prayer as such:

Our Father in heaven, Reveal who you are. Set the world right; Do what's best- as above, so below.

Of course you will notice this isn't exactly what you would read in the Holy Bible for the Lord's Prayer; but rather a message from the Hermetic mystery schools and occult beliefs of the Illuminati. "*As above, so below*" is a message familiar to occultists and magicians used to reveal the importance of the microcosm and the macrocosm. The universe lies in the person, and the person lies in the universe. The fact that these musicians work their way up from nothing to something (a concept highlighted in Drake's *Started From the Bottom*) only reinforces these ideas, and on top of that the fame elevates them to a God like status, further stroking their ego. The 60s music movement allowed the musician to become a powerful influence in the way people dress, think, and act, and it gave rise to the idea of 'rock and rap gods' of present day. Satanism is about being your own God, and having a God complex, and that is very much what we're experiencing today.

Songs like Eminem's *Rap God*, Kanye West's *I Am A God* (from the album *Yeezus*) and *New God Flow*, Rick Ross's *God Forgives, I Don't*, and Jay-Z's *Izzo H.O.V.A.* are all examples of juxtaposition of religious gods and rappers. In the music video for Nas ft. Puff Daddy *Hate Me Now*, Hype Williams shot a scene where Nas and Puff Daddy were depicted on crosses as if they were Jesus Christ. Granted the rap culture is built on who can be more over the top with their swagger, but things have been changing in the last several years with a turn towards actual deification. Kanye West did an interview with MTV where he said he believes he'd be in the Bible if he was around back then.

Besides the self-elevation to God status, programming, magical, and occult practices, another theory to support the reason we see alter egos is that of mind control experimentation. The conspiracy theory behind mind control goes back to the C.I.A. MKULTRA experiments that subjected people to dissociation of the mind through trauma. This trauma based mind control has since been relabeled as Dissociative Identity Disorder. The idea is that you can expose someone to various levels of trauma and the mind will respond by breaking it up into chambers so that it can hide the pain from the rest of the mind. These small chambers are self-contained and referred to as "alters." The idea is that you can channel various alters through triggers and place the person under a state of hypnosis (like in the film *Manchurian Candidate*). While one of the alter egos is triggered, the subconscious mind controls the body, and in our example, it provides the delivery of lyrics from the rappers. Even though you generally only hear about MKULTRA from conspiracy theorists, it does have a basis in reality and the C.I.A. deliberately destroyed most of the records in the early 1970s in an attempted coverup.

On August 3rd, 1977, the US Senate published a report on Project MKULTRA and it was titled *PROJECT MKULTRA, THE CIA'S PROGRAM OF RESEARCH IN BEHAVIORAL MODIFICATION*. The aim of the report was to review the CIA program and detail its abuses in an effort to prevent it from happening again in the future. MKULTRA was a secret CIA program that started in 1953 and ran until its termination in 1963 (it was actually rebranded MKSEARCH until 1972), with most of the documentation being destroyed in 1973. It is speculated that then CIA Director Richard Helms ordered the destruction in response to fears of another Watergate type scandal. It ran unnoticed by the upper-brass because the operatives found clever ways to fund the projects like finding private donors of whom the government would match donations, or using subprojects to fund other subprojects. The proper chain of command for approval was overlooked as well. Eventually in 1963 the program would somewhat come to light and get shut down. However, a full investigation wouldn't happen for at least another decade, with a full Senate investigation in 1977.

In 1973 the documents were destroyed due to a regulation cited as CSI-40-10 that defines the destruction as a form of "retirement" in order for there to be *conscious judgment in the application of the rules modified by knowledge of individual component needs.* The destruction of the documents left the Senate Committee very little to go off of in determining the extent of the activities of this program. They could tell that then-Director of CIA Allen Dulles authorized the program on a higher level of abstraction (he authorized MKULTRA; but not necessarily the smaller subprojects like administering LSD). It started with the fear that China and the Soviet Union were researching brainwashing techniques. There was a rumor that the Soviets bought up the world's supply of LSD and that stoked Cold War fears. The early 1950s had similar mind control projects called Project BLUEBIRD and Project ARTICHOKE that eventually spawned MKULTRA.

Some of the controversial aspects of MKULTRA include the use of chemical and biological agents in order to research human behavior and also determine if behavior could be controlled. The drugs used were initially with willing participants, but later were administered to unknowing and non-volunteering subjects. The idea was to see if the enemy could brainwash our people or use it as a truth serum; or if it could be used clandestinely against the enemy in the same manner.

This three-phase umbrella operation would start with seeking the appropriate materials needed for the experiments, then performing laboratory testing on willing volunteers, and then finally confirming findings via application in "normal life settings" (which sounds an awful lot like unknowing participants/victims). MKULTRA used universities, hospitals, prisons and private research groups to find and administer various drugs. This includes an addiction rehabilitation prison in Lexington, Kentucky:

The test subjects were volunteer prisoners who, after taking a brief physical examination and signing a general consent form, were administered hallucinogenic drugs. As a reward for participation in the program, the addicts were provided with the drug of their addiction.

The document claims that the program was run so covertly that the universities and citizens weren't aware of their participation in it. Without acknowledgement by those running the tests, there is no way to determine which universities and citizens played a part unless they come forth. This is a strategy used by the alleged Illuminati to keep the research going. David Icke talks about this in his lectures, using an example of a bank teller not knowing what happens with the check after he/she cashes a check. The superior above the bank teller doesn't know what their superior does, and so on and so forth. It's a system of compartmentalization that keeps everyone worried about their own little sector, meanwhile those at the top (the Illuminati) know the big picture and keep everything moving in their direction.

Admiral Stansfield Turner, then Director of the CIA, provided a statement on the history of MKULTRA, explaining that they discovered seven boxes of documents that detailed the program. It ran from 1953-1964 and had several subprograms (at least 149); all used to research human behavior modification, hypnosis, "magicians' art", ESP, eletro-shock, harassment techniques, sabotage (including crops and animals; a subprogram called MKNAOMI out of Fort Detrich,

Maryland) and drugs. When describing a tactic of police in India in the document about interrogation drugs:

"It is far pleasanter to sit comfortably in the shade rubbing red pepper in a poor devil's eyes than to go about in the sun hunting up evidence."
– Sir James Stephens, 1883

MKULTRA subproject 3 involved the administration of LSD to subjects, including Dr. Frank Olson who committed suicide while under the influence. He was a civilian employee of the Army who died after participating in an LSD experiment. He was given 70 micrograms of LSD and suffered paranoia and schizophrenia and was being treated in New York City when he fell from a tenth story window in the Statler Hotel.

To tie MKULTRA into the magical concepts, the document goes into a subproject that sought to apply covert communication (perhaps symbolism) to influence others. The project that investigated "magician's art" was seeking ways of administering materials to someone without them knowing (a deceptive practice or distracting someone's attention). It also looked for a way to covertly communicate without others knowing what the information being passed was. In the document, Senator Huddleston asks Admiral Turner if there were any projects with a motive of debilitating someone to the point that they could kill another and Admiral Turner replied with:

"Yes; I think there is. I have not seen in this series of documentation evidence of desire to kill, but I think the project turned its character from a defensive to an offensive one as it

went along, and there certainly was an intention here to develop drugs that could be of use."
    – Admiral Turner

One of the controversial theories of mind control is the alleged Project MONARCH program that Cathy O'Brien campaigns against. She alleges that she was a victim of this MKULTRA sub-program in her *Trance Formation of America* book. She says that she was exposed to these dissociative identity disorder processes and can recall them through hypnosis. She goes further to claim that she was passed around as a sex slave through various Illuminati groups and high ranking individuals, including Country Western musicians. Oddly enough, Nicole Kidman (ex-wife to Scientologist Tom Cruise and his co-star in the occult symbolism riddled film *Eyes Wide Shut*) married Country Western singer Keith Urban in 2006. He's been placed on the cover of *GQ* magazine with one hand covering his eye and the other placed inside of his jacket, which are two Illuminati symbols; one for the All Seeing Eye and the other for the Freemason hidden hand. Nicole Kidman was in the film *Stepford Wives* that portrays a group of mind controlled programmed women. In real life she is also deathly afraid of butterflies; a symbol referenced in Project MONARCH (for the Monarch butterfly).

Some theorists believe that not only do the rappers suffer from mind control, but they are actually under possession of evil spirits. The Crowley influenced magical group Ordo Templi Orientis (OTO) uses symbols and rituals to transmit entities *into* the practitioner. Depending on how far down the rabbit hole you follow Crowley, he seemed to have a belief that these externally evoked spirits were actually being invoked from inside the person's self, like a holy guardian angel, but either way we're dealing with supernatural energies possessing the artist's body. Supposedly this type of practice is used to infect or possess the musician to allow them to harness musical abilities of the entity. Musicians regularly reference these types of things in interviews or song lyrics:

> "*I get possessed by the, ... by the spirits.*"
> – Jay-Z, Interview

> "*I can sing notes and sing strong and do all these things that when I'm just by myself I can't do. And I remember right before I performed I raised my hands up and it was kind of the first time I felt something else come into me.*"
> –Beyoncé, BET Presents

Nicki Minaj channels up to 15 different alter egos, including a blonde homosexual male named Roman Zolanski, who is named after the director Roman Polanski who was allegedly involved in sexual acts with children. She also evokes the sexually explicit Nicki Lewinsky, named after Monica Lewinsky.

> "*I ask him to leave but he can't, he's here for a reason. People have brought him out. People conjured him up and now he won't leave.*"
> – Nicki Minaj, Interview on alter ego Roman Zolanski

She later came out to provide some small glimpse of hope that she has been freed from the demons, even though the media did quite a number on covering up the story. Nicki Minaj appeared at the 2014 BET Award Show and announced that she almost died, and the crowd proceeded to *laugh* at the story:

"The other day, literally I didn't tell anybody this, I really thought I was about to die. Like, I was saying my prayers to die. And I didn't even want to call the ambulance because I thought, 'Well, if I call the ambulance, it's going to be on TMZ. And I'd rather sit there and die.'"

Later on, she claimed that she almost died from a marijuana contact high. If you believe she could've died from a contact high you might be high yourself because studies show that there have been no deaths from marijuana by itself. The media made practically no mention of this near-death experience, but rather focused on a staged fake-beef between Minaj and Iggy Azalea. Even though Nicki never did anything to promote it, the media proceeded to say that she was "throwing shade" at Azalea when she was performing. During the show Minaj said:

"...when you hear Nicki Minaj spit, Nicki Minaj wrote it..."

The media took that to mean that Iggy had a ghostwriter and Nicki was calling her out for it. In reality, I believe she might've been trying to say she's shaking off the demon spirits that had previously possessed her (e.g. Roman Zolanski).

R&B singer Jhene Aiko is another player in the music industry who seems to sport Illuminati symbolism and possession traits. She has various album titles that could be referencing selling one's soul (*Souled Out, Sailing Soul(s), Sail Out*), and she might be talking about this because she's potentially signed the pact; the selling of one's own soul to the Devil or the music industry. She's been depicted with the All Seeing Eye imagery and even wearing the horns of Moloch in her videos. Following suit to the other musicians, she talked about her alter ego, J. Hennessy:

"I literally feel throughout the day I go through 12 different personalities in my head."
- Jhene Aiko, Rap-Up.com interview

The reason why magic practitioners perform spirit evocations (and internal invocations) is to pull energy or information from another realm. The artist can pull knowledge, lyrics, or energy through the ritual. Any energetic being can be evoked, and that is why even fictional characters like H.P. Lovecraft's Cthulhu are used in evocation. So long as you have a defined set of characteristics you can perform magic to have an energetic conversation with them in order to gain their insight. Everyone practices this on a very small scale when they name their inanimate objects (e.g. a car, computer, etc.), or even animate objects such as a newborn child (just take a look at baby name meanings; you'll see characteristics that the name invokes). It takes an incredible amount of energy and focus in order for these people to get in touch with this other realm of existence, so it drains them emotionally and physically, perhaps explaining the overwhelming amount of drug abuse found in the industry.

Some more practical examples of sympathetic magic that will appeal to all of you rational types out there includes the real life exploitation of Facebook users in their 2012 study where they skewed either happy or sad news items on users' news feeds in an attempt to gauge their responses. After one week of experimentation they found that emotional contagion could in fact occur through transfer of emotions in avenues like online social media. Professor and evolutionary biologist Richard Dawkins coined the term "meme" in reference to the behavioral equivalent of a gene. The memes are small units of information that carry from one person to another. These conveyances of energy can be schools of thought, like an entire religion, or perhaps a simple idea like the more familiar internet memes. Either way, the memetics are able to be transferred and evolve from one concept to another simply by passing on from one person to the next.

"A poet's mission is to make words do more work than they normally do, to make them work on more than one level."
–Jay-Z, *Decoded*

Even more unbelievable is the theory that the headphones crafted by Dr. Dre and Jimmy Iovine in 2008 are used for a satanic purpose. The support for this idea is that the products are placed in various Illuminati-symbol-loving artist videos such as Miley Cyrus, Nicki Minaj, Robin Thicke, Ariana Grande, etc. The elites of the asset management Carlyle Group invested around 500 million dollars into Beats, and you might recognize that name because Michael Moore highlighted their conspiracy involvement in the film *Fahrenheit 9/11*. They allegedly held a conference on September 11th, 2001 in which members of the Bin Laden family were in attendance because they had assets with Carlyle, only to allegedly help usher them out of the country when the events of 9/11 transpired. In just six short years the Beats headphones got sold to Apple for over three billion dollars, making Dr. Dre the richest human being to come from the hip hop culture ever. Some question why Apple bought the headphones because true audiophiles have claimed they are some of the worst quality headphones on the market (some claim Apple bought them in order to capture the Beats music streaming audience). They've been shown to only cost $14 to make, yet they sell for over $400 at times. The sales and marketing are shrewd enough that people continue to snatch them up, even with the horrible reviews. This makes the parties involved true sorcerers as they've made something out of nothing (a concept I keep highlighting).

You could've seen this coming if you analyzed the name and logo for Beats. They have a lower case 'b' that looks like a 6 and theorists have claimed that makes the 666 if you add up all the 'b's on the product. If you also move the letters in the word you'll go from "Beats" to "Beast." If you go a bit further you'll find out that the company who originally made these headphones is named "Monster" which is analogous to the beast known as Satan (and their logo is an "M" that looks like a pair of horns).

When it comes to finding evidence to support the notion that these artists are possessed by spirits (whether they be good, evil, or the Devil himself), you need to look no further than the lyrics, interviews, statements and actions of the artists themselves.

Beyoncé's 2008 album *I Am... Sasha Fierce* birthed her alter ego (obviously the alias is Sasha Fierce). In a BBC interview she said this character she invokes allows her to be more aggressive and sexy than how she acts in real life. On her website she shows this character in dark makeup sporting Devil horns or even wearing a suit that resembles the satanic Baphomet-goat image. She allows this entity to take control over her; a classic sign of possession:

"I have someone else that takes over when it's time for me to work. When I'm on stage, this alter ego that I've created that kind of protects me and who I really am."
– Beyoncé, BBC Interview 2008

She said that when she performed *Crazy in Love* on the 2003 BET Awards she saw it all in her head before it even happened. She says that Sasha Fierce can do things that she can't do when performing rehearsals by herself. She goes on to reveal that she actually felt this entity go into her:

"I remembered right before I performed, I raised my hands up, and it was kinda the first time I felt something else come into me, and I knew that was going to be my coming out night..."
- Beyoncé, BET Interview

In 2013 she would reveal that she was using a *new* alter ego named Yonce, but only after saying she had to kill Sasha:

"Sasha Fierce is done. I killed her. I don't need Sasha Fierce anymore because I've grown and now I'm able to merge the two."
– Beyoncé, interview with *Allure* magazine in 2010

Somewhat contradictory, she also said that she originally conceived the Sasha Fierce character while making the video for *Crazy in Love*, supporting theorists Jamie Hanshaw and Freeman Fly with their "Project Crazy Bitch" concept found in *Weird Stuff: Operation Culture Creation Part 2*. In this theory the artists truly go crazy from the various doses of mind control experimentation and spirit possession. The claim is that various brands actually use marketing campaigns to push certain ideals into the minds of the young and impressionable. This can be seen in the product lines that emphasize the importance of the princess archetype found in Disney, Barbie, and whatever new "it" doll is on the market. The multitude of princess characters push a sense of entitlement, narcissism, greed, and a lack of empathy for others. The princess will get what she wants, and it is of no concern what effect it has on others. We've seen these attitudes by others in the entertainment world because it's a dog-eat-dog industry. Of course one could argue that the destruction of empathy is an Illuminati agenda because it allows the Archons to feed from that low vibrational energy, while also providing a way to keep the masses culled from one another.

Hanshaw and Freeman suggest that Project Crazy Bitch is being rolled out because it's part of a magical, satanic agenda. Anton LaVey wrote a book called *The Satanic Witch* that says a successful witch makes a pact with Satan (at least symbolically), and uses the powers of lust to have magnetic power over men and other women. LaVey is perpetuating Aleister Crowley's suggestion that letting go of sexual inhibitions releases a vast amount of energy that the sorcerer could use to their advantage. These are all the reasons why we see marketing of such a sexual nature, including such blatant sexualization as in beauty pageants and racy Halloween costumes for young girls.

The theorists point out the overwhelming references to girls going crazy in songs and lyrics from pop princesses, and although they are usually references to falling 'crazy' in love, there are also other examples referencing mental health craziness. Even when they are referencing falling in love, it plays on the princess programming because fairy tales depict a girl who finds all of her self-worth and importance in finding a prince to live happily ever after with.

On the track *Dark Side*, Kelly Clarkson sings about what could be the music industry and the dark side it pulls out of you:

Oh oh oh, there's a place that I know
It's not pretty there and few have ever gone
If I show it to you now
Will it make you run away?

Or will you stay
Even if it hurts
Even if I try to push you out
Will you return?
And remind me who I really am
Please remind me who I really am

Everybody's got a dark side
Do you love me?
Can you love mine?
Nobody's a picture perfect
But we're worth it
You know that we're worth it
Will you love me?
Even with my dark side?

Rihanna had a hit song with Eminem called *Monster*:

And you think I'm crazy, yeah, you think I'm crazy

She also had a song called *Disturbia*:

What's wrong with me? Why do I feel like this? I'm going
crazy now

Rihanna once also tweeted:

I'm crazy, and I don't pretend to be anything else

Perhaps this is from the attempt to cross the Kabbalah Tree of Life's "Abyss"; an occult practice that Aleister Crowley admitted would make one go crazy. A succinct explanation for this crossing of the Abyss would be that the practitioner is seeking to pass through Da'at; a realm where fallen angels exist in an attempt to attain spiritual bliss in Heaven (the sephirot point on the Tree of Life known as Keter) directly from Earth (Malkhut). There will be more on that later, so don't get too wrapped up in it quite yet.

Sia Furler, who goes by 'Sia', is a singer and songwriter who rose to fame for writing lyrics for a plethora of pop artists, including Katy Perry, Britney Spears, Ke$ha, and Rihanna. You've heard her voice on the Flo Rida song *Wild Ones* (although the video had a model named Analicia Chaves lip syncing her lines) and David Guetta's *She Wolf (Falling to Pieces)*. What's interesting about Sia is that she spoke about the process in which she derives her song lyrics on an interview with Howard Stern in 2014. After she says she believes in a higher power, Howard asks if she knows where that comes from or if she has to be in some weird state to come up with them and her producer, Greg (maybe her handler?...), replies with:

"She's always in that state of mind... There's no, like, analytical part of song writing, it's just like, from the brain, out of her mouth."
– Greg Kurstin, Howard Stern Show, June 2014

One of the songs Sia wrote included the Rihanna track *Diamonds*. The lyrics indicate a love that doesn't seem terrestrial, but rather a devotion to a God or deity; perhaps a reference to Lucifer; the light bearer:

Shine bright like a diamond
Shine bright like a diamond

Find light in the beautiful sea
I choose to be happy
You and I, you and I
We're like diamonds in the sky

You're a shooting star I see
A vision of ecstasy
When you hold me, I'm alive
We're like diamonds in the sky

I knew that we'd become one right away
Oh, right away
At first sight I felt the energy of sun rays
I saw the life inside your eyes

She continues with the light and All Seeing Eye theme:

At first sight I felt the energy of sun rays
I saw the life inside your eyes

So shine bright tonight, you and I
We're beautiful like diamonds in the sky
Eye to eye, so alive
We're beautiful like diamonds in the sky

On the Britney Spears track *Brightest Morning Star* she also references an otherworldly love:

96

You're my light when it gets dark
You will always in my heart
You're my brightest morning star
You're my light when it gets dark
You will always in my heart
You're my brightest morning star
You are the light of my beautiful life
I can never let go, you're my brightest morning star
You are the light of my beautiful life

I can never let go, you're my brightest morning star
In your arms I feel alive, I'm not afraid
I will keep you this encloses me,
I look for signs everyday
I lift my hands and pray cuz life's tough somedays

Another song Sia helped write is Beyoncé's *Standing on the Sun*, which follows the same logic:

My body is magnified
In the sun set me alight
My body, and your delights
Burn me up, set me alight

I can't deny, your desire
Feel like I'm on fire
When you touch me
I feel the flame, baking up my feet, ohh

Can you feel the heat on my skin
Can you feel it all over it
You and me, standing on the sun

97

Can you feel my heart burning
Make you feel all my good loving
You and me, standing on the sun

Of course, one could argue I'm looking far deeper than necessary with these lyrics, but if you take into consideration what Sia said on Howard Stern you could guess that it's possible for her to be using Luciferianism inspired words from a spirit in order to derive these lyrics. This is precisely how Aleister Crowley dictated the *Book of the Law* from his holy guardian spirit of Aiwass:

The voice was of deep timbre, musical and expressive, its tones solemn, voluptuous, tender, fierce or aught else as suited the moods of the message. Not bass – perhaps a rich tenor or baritone. The English was free of either native or foreign accent, perfectly pure of local or caste mannerisms, thus startling and even uncanny at first hearing.
- Aleister Crowley, *The Equinox of the Gods*

Britney Spears also had the song (*You Drive Me) Crazy* that foreshadowed her mental breakdown when she actually went crazy (more predictive programming in action). In 2007 she walked into Esther's Salon in Tarzana, CA and told the owner she wanted her head shaved because her extensions were too tight. Esther tried to talk her out of it when Britney grabbed the electric razor and shaved it off herself. Afterwards she went to Body & Soul tattoo in Sherman Oaks and got two tattoos (one was a pair of lips on her wrist, the other was a black, white, and pink cross on her hip). When the tattoo shop asked her why she shaved her head she said "*I don't want anyone touching me. I'm tired of everybody touching me.*"

Freeman Fly says that there is a much deeper esoteric meaning to Britney's moment of craziness if you step back and examine the details of the event. Britney checked herself out of Eric Clapton's Crossroads rehab facility just prior to the head shaving incident. The term "Crossroads" is of great importance here because it appears so often. For example, Britney Spears had a film called *Crossroads* in 2002 and she found herself in Eric Clapton's Crossroads rehab center some years later. There's also a 1936 blues song by Robert Johnson called *Crossroads* (or *Cross Road Blues*) where he talks about selling his soul to the Devil in exchange for his musical abilities, and the Faustian bargain myth was depicted in the 1986 film *Crossroads*. Rap group Bone Thugs 'n' Harmony released a song dedicated to Eazy-E in 1996 called *Tha Crossroads* that stars a grim reaper marking people for death and was featured on the album *E. 1999 Eternal* that had songs like *Mr. Ouija 2* that asks the Ouija board if the rappers will die of murder. Additionally, Freeman asserts that Britney chose the salon called Esther's because Esther is another name for the Illuminati-Babylonian goddess Ishtar. It was also chosen by Madonna as an alter ego for her Kabbalah personality, Esther Madge.

Kanye West is no stranger to acting crazy, but if you put his antics aside you might think that he is in a struggle with good and evil. One of his first hits was *Jesus Walks* where he told us the Devil was trying to drag him down, but then years later he'd talk about the eventual success of Satan. His lyrics for *Black Skinhead* make a short reference that could indicate he's taken a turn for the worse:

"Four in the morning, and I'm zonin', They say I'm possessed, it's an omen"
– Kanye West, *Black Skinhead*

He was interviewed by *The Breakfast Club* radio show with DJ Envy, Angela Yee, and Charlamagne Tha God, and in it he tried to lay out his frustrations with trying to get a fashion label off the ground (his company named after his mother, "Donda"). He said that we're all slaves to symbols, and how society destroys our creative abilities. He reinforces David Icke concepts like how societal norms are put in place so that we police each other and actually keep each other down while elitists continue with their power quest in the background. He even goes as far as to subtlety claim that we're worshipping Saturn; which is occult in nature and is depicted as the Nike swoosh logo:

"We're controlled by a Nike sign; we're controlled by peer pressure."
    – Kanye West, *The Breakfast Club* interview, 2013

All of the talk about destroying creative abilities is also David Icke 101 because he asserts that the Gnostic Archon race (the Illuminati, or reptilian shape shifters) are known for their inability to be creative. They use the artists' creative abilities to push their message and propaganda to our subconscious. In that same interview he goes into Illuminati bloodlines like the Medici Family and Charlamagne Tha God tells him he's *"not on his square"* which is a reference to Freemasonry. Perhaps he was trying to remind Kanye of who he was talking about before he took it too far. He disregards the warning and says that *"Black people don't have the same connections as Jewish people."* He later went on Sway's talk show and reinforced the same concepts, but not before almost getting into an altercation with Sway. The media picked up on it and instead of looking at

100

his message, they pushed the video of the altercation and tried to label Kanye as a crazy person.

Around the same time, Kanye and Kid Cudi were performing a show in Atlanta, Georgia and Kanye tells the crowd that artists are afraid to speak out against the system because they're afraid to lose everything. He then does some spoken word and says the following:

"I sold my soul to the Devil, I know it's a crappy deal, At least it came with a few toys like a Happy Meal."
– Kanye West

Prolific guitarist Santana was interviewed by *Rolling Stone* in 2000 about his album *Supernatural* and he described a spirit he evokes named Metatron, who tells him that he is responsible to connect people with this 'light' (which I read as Lucifer; the light bearer since there is so much rampant Luciferianism and black magic happening in these industries):

*"Metatron is the architect of physical life. Because of him, we can French-kiss, we can hug, we can get a hot dog, wiggle our toe." He sees Metatron in his dreams and meditations. He looks a bit like Santa Claus – "white beard, and kind of this jolly fellow." Metatron, who has been mentioned in mystical disciplines through the ages, also appears as the **eye inside the triangle**.*
Santana credits Metatron with alerting him to the recent changes in his life. In the mid-Nineties, he met some people in a spiritual bookstore near his home, and they invited him to their afternoon meditations in Santa Cruz. The last time he was there, Metatron, delivered some important messages. "You will be inside the radio frequency," Metatron told him, "for the purpose of connecting the molecules with the light."

101

Carlos Santana understood. He would make a new album and be on the radio again. **And he would connect the molecules with the light: He would connect an audience with some of the spiritual information he now had**.

To demonstrate all of the concepts of this chapter in one thorough example, let's take a look at the entity known as the Rain Man. Anyone who's been online and searched for Illuminati in the music industry is familiar with the Rain Man, but I'm going to put some supporting evidence behind the argument. The Rain Man is an entity that is evoked by musicians in order to harness its abilities for rapping or performing.

Eminem had a song titled *Rain Man* on his 2004 album *Encore*. On this song he raps about his soul being possessed by a devil named Rain Man:

"Hi, my name is...
I forgot my name!
My name was not to become what I became with this level of fame
My soul is possessed by this devil my new name is....
Rain Man"
- Eminem, *Rain Man*

At the end of the track he spits out random incoherent numbers, alluding to the idea that he is referencing the character from the film *Rain Man* played by Dustin Hoffman, which is the mainstream explanation for the term of 'Rain Man' being used by these artists. The film is called that because the main character is an autistic man named Raymond, based after a real life savant of a different name (Kim Peek). In the film the character's name is confused with Rain Man because of the similar pronunciation, but it played such a small part in the film's plot it makes one wonder if there wasn't more to it (especially considering the argument I'm presenting). One outlandish theory is that the film is actually talking about a demon named Rain Man possessing Tom Cruise's character who, at one point, decides to take advantage of Dustin Hoffman's character for financial gain and use his abilities in a casino. The demon of greed and all things monetary makes this man take advantage of his disabled brother, but as you can imagine the film ends on a happy note when Tom Cruise purges the evil spirit and regains his relationship with Raymond.

You can see Eminem and Dr. Dre doing a reenactment of the gambling (or possession as I theorize) scene from *Rain Man* in the music video *We Made You* at the Palms in Las Vegas. The fact that they are parodying the film *Rain Man* would make most people drop it but this is the world of conspiracy theorizing so you know that is unacceptable. Instead, we'll point to the fact that the song is literally talking about a devil possessing Eminem.

He also makes the crowd chant his new alter ego in concert footage that can be found online. It appears that he is trying to make the name Rain Man more than just a pop culture reference. In fact, it's not the only track he references him. On *Old Time's Sake* he mentions it:

"Speak of the devil it's attack of the rain man
Chainsaw in hand, blood stain on my apron"

This album on which *Rain Man* was featured is notorious in that he attributes it to being the start of his prescription pill addiction. His next album after a four year break was *Relapse* and the very first track is a skit called *Dr.*

103

West. On this skit you can hear a back and forth between Eminem and a disguised demon who eventually shows itself by his true nature and tells Marshall "*you'll never leave me*" before Marshall turns back into Slim Shady again. This leads into the next track with is a song called *3 a.m.* in which Eminem is depicted murdering folks at the witching hour of 3 A.M.; an inversion of 3 P.M., the hour that Jesus Christ died after His crucifixion. One of the tracks on the extended version of the album (*Relapse: Refill*) is called *My Darling* and he continues to talk about selling ones soul for the rap game:

"And the dark shall emerge from the fiery depths of hell
And swallow the shell of the hollow who dwell
And the shadows of all who are willing to sell
Their souls, for this rap game, and it g-g-goes
My Darling, I don't ever want you to leave me
My Darling, you and me were meant to be together
My Darling, And if I cannot have you, no one can, you're my
My Darling, cause I possess your soul, your mind, your heart
and your body

"I'm not in the mirror, I'm inside you, let me guide you"
Fuck you, die you son of a bitch
"Put the gun down", Bye Bye!
Ok I'm still alive, "So am I too!
You can't kill a spirit, even if you tried to
Haha, you sold your soul to me, need I remind you?
You remember that night you, prayed to God
You'd give anything to get a record deal, well Dre signed you
This is what you wanted your whole life Marshall, right
through
Look at this house, look at these cars, I'm so nice, wooo!
Oh, but you didn't know, fame has a price too

That you're just now seeing the downside to
Lose your best friend from high school, your wife too"

As a side note, *Encore* also featured a song with the aforementioned "crazy" theme with *Crazy in Love* as well.

Eminem isn't the only one who references the Rain Man demon. There are numerous references to raining in the music industry, but *most* of them can be attributed to the weather or even the urban slang for "making it rain" (throwing wads of cash in the air such that it falls down like rain; typically on a stripper's stage). Jamie Foxx's *Rain Man* is about the weather, as is Missy Elliott's *The Rain (Supa Dupa Fly)*, and the numerous "making it rain" references include Fat Joe's *Make It Rain*, Lil Wayne's *Got Money*, Gucci Mane's *Rain Man*, and The Game's *Cali Sunshine*. Rock bands do it as well, but here is where the line starts to blur as to what or who the Rain Man really is. For example, in W.A.S.P.'s *The Burning Man* they are definitely talking about demons:

"Hang man coming better run to save your
Kids, your wives, your lives, your babies
Hang the wire round the necks of liars alright
Rain man on fire from the hells of Hades"

Bob Dylan talked about the Rain Man a couple of times as well, including the song *I Wanna Be Your Lover*:

"Well, the rain man comes with his magic wand
And the judge says, "Mona can't have no bond"
And the walls collide, Mona cries
And the rain man leaves in the wolf man's disguise"

He also talks about it in *Stuck Inside of Mobile with the Memphis Blues Again*:

"Now the rainman gave me two cures
Then he said, "Jump right in"
The one was Texas medicine
The other was just railroad gin
And like a fool I mixed them
And it strangled up my mind
And now, people just get uglier
And I have no sense of time
Oh, Mama, can this really be the end
To be stuck inside of Mobile
With the Memphis blues again."

The Counting Crows had a poppy little hit called *Rain King* that featured lyrics much more disturbing than the melody implied:

"Oh, it seems night endlessly begins and ends
After all the dreaming I come home again

When I think of heaven
Deliver me in a black-winged bird
I think of dying
Lay me down in a field of flame and heather
Render up my body into the burning heart of God
In the belly of a black-winged bird
Don't try to bleed me
I've been here before
And I deserve a little more

I belong in the service of the queen

106

I belong anywhere but in between
She's been dying and I've been drinking
And I am the Rain King"

The rapper MIMS had a song called *Doctor, Doctor* that we can use to segue into the next case of Rain Man possession with Jay-Z:

"I done came in the game in a dash like Damon, predicted the reign man just like "Rain Man"."

The context of the lyrics is that he is seeing a doctor for mental health issues and we see by the end of the song he goes crazy (yet again; Project Crazy Bitch, this time with a man):

"I mean damn doc, I can't take this no more man.
I'm crackin under pressure.
It's a little too much for me man.
My minds goin crazy right now.

I'm crazy man, I'm crazy.
I'm crazy man, I'm crazy.
I'm crazy man, I'm crazy.
Uh, I'm crazy man, I'm crazy.
I'm crazy man, I'm crazy.
We goin to the next one now, MIMS, yeah."

Going back to the first line I posted, he talks about Damon Dash and predicting "the reign;" but who, or what, is he talking about? I propose it's Jay-Z since he had such tight affiliations with Damon Dash and Roc-A-Fella Records.

Jay-Z is known for his ability to spit rhymes without having to write them down or memorize; a skill known in the rap game as freestyling. In an interview explaining this process he said that he used to write words down until he got into his "Rain Man" thing and referenced how Rain Man spits numbers in a rapid fire sequence:

"I start doing uh, you know, these different hidden messages in the music, you know, just as to replace the technical aspect of it and it evolved from there."
- Jay-Z, MTV Interview

In the song *La La La (Excuse Me Miss Again)* he raps alongside Pharrell Williams and says the following:

"No prescription, you could prescribe to subside his affliction
He's not a sane man, more like Rain Man twitchin'
You can't rain dance on his picnic
No Haitian voodoo, no headless chickens can dead his sickness (whoo)
No Ouija board, you can't see me dog, nigga you CB4"

Jay-Z also appeared on the song *Umbrella* with his protégé, Rihanna, and says the following:

"In anticipation for precipitation, stack chips for a rainy day,
Jay, Rain Man is back with little Ms. Sunshine,
Rihanna, where you at?"

Conspiracy theorists online (mostly YouTube) have attempted to debunk the music video for *Umbrella* to show that it is an occult ritual that the Illuminati put out in order to tell others that Rihanna is now transitioning to a new, malevolent image. They point out a pose she makes that appears to be in the form of a Baphomet goat, and hidden symbols in splashing water (claiming that it's Rain Man's semen impregnating Rihanna) that support a theme of a demon taking her over and making her go from good to bad. In fact, the name of the album is *Good Girl Gone Bad* so maybe it's not all that far-fetched. The next album she released was a reissue of *Good Girl Gone Bad: Reloaded* and it featured a song called *Disturbia* that had a video full of dystopia imagery (and the lyrics I referenced earlier about her going crazy). When she released her next album, *Rated R*, we most definitely saw a transition from good girl to bad. The album cover shows her giving us the pose for the All Seeing Eye and the songs take a much darker turn from her previous albums. Music news website Pitchfork reviewed the album and said the following:

> *Fallouts mark Rated R as well, though they are decidedly heavier. Over the course of the album, Rihanna puts a revolver to her temple on "Russian Roulette", recalls "white outlines" on "Cold Case Love", and even threatens to crash head-on into a boyfriend on "Fire Bomb"-- not exactly the most politically correct metaphor in the age of IEDs, but it does get her point across. In a recent interview, Rihanna described the Rated R recording sessions as "theraputic* (sic)*," and the vitriolic, rough, raw end product is about as brutal as you'd expect.*
> *Like its lyrical themes, **Rated R's tones are decidedly darker than anything Rihanna's done.***

The affiliations of this Rain Man entity (if you're willing to accept that it is in fact a demonic entity) seem to mark a spiritual descent based on the output of the artists evoking him. Meanwhile, the artists are selling more records and achieving higher levels of fame and fortune. I've laid out that argument over the previous examples including Eminem's addiction issues, Jay-Z's rise to the top of rap music, and Rihanna's darker, yet pervasive music on the Top 40's charts. Do these behaviors represent what the Rain Man is capable of? The definition of rain, according to Merriam-Webster Dictionary includes the following:

The descent of this water
A fall of rain
A heavy fall ("a rain of arrows")

Dictionary.Reference.com lists similar definitions, including:

A heavy and continuous descent or inflicting of anything

It appears that we can safely say that *if* there is a demon called Rain Man, then they are capable of inflicting an artist while "raining" fame and fortunes down upon them. Rain Man would gladly trade ones soul for the bestowing of his "blessings". We can see this in the symbolism and behavior of these artists. Once the artist takes part of this agreement they are forever tied to this demon spirit, and that is why they often talk about hearing whispers or having demonic thoughts which explains why we see rappers like Eminem making such violent references in his lyrics:

"I'm Dr. Hyde and Mr. Jekyll, disrespectful,
Hearing voices in my head while these whispers echo
"Murder Murder Redrum""
- Eminem, *Low Down Dirty*

"These voices, I hear them, I hear them,
And when they talk I follow, I follow"

-Eminem, *Guilty Conscience*

Eminem did a song with Rihanna called *The Monster* that had her crooning similar messages:

"I'm friends with the monster that's under my bed,
Get along with the voices inside of my head,
You're trying to save me, stop holding your breath,
And you think I'm crazy, yeah, you think I'm crazy,
Well that's nothing"

And that wasn't the only song Rihanna had with these themes either:

"I hear voices in my head
They go oh, oh, oh"
-Rihanna ft. Justin Timberlake, *Hole In My Head*

Even if you could look past *all* of these examples and conjectures, there is one documented case of a demon entity possessing a man named Don Decker. As you probably anticipated, the name of the demon was Rain Man. Don Decker's story has been featured on *Unsolved Mysteries* and *Paranormal Witness* and it illustrated him as a teenager in 1983 who found himself possessed by the spirit of a demon (or perhaps his own grandfather as he suggests) that could make it rain. The rain was able to drop inside of houses and jail cells without explanation. While Don was serving time in jail a priest was sent in to perform an exorcism because of the rain he was causing. Over some time and multiple exorcisms the priest was able to draw the Rain Man spirit from Don.

It appears these artists are choosing alter egos and aliases for nefarious reasons, or even worse being possessed by evil spirits. What isn't up for debate is the fact that mind control experiments happened, and marketing strategies take advantage of similar research in order to sell products or themes. The artists appear to be subtlety trying to tell their story of possession or mind control, and the evidence is piling up to support it. The Faustian Bargains and deals with the Devil could very well be more than just myths, and actually be the key to success in the entertainment industry; particularly rap music.

Chapter 5- Enter the Aeon of Horus

At this point we can start to frame an agenda of where the Illuminati believe they can take us. In order to understand where they want us to go, we must first switch gears and explore some of the origins of the modern day beliefs of magic and where they fit into the music industry. The issues at hand start with the ceremonial magician, Aleister Crowley. He was associated with various magical and occult groups such as the Hermetic Order of the Golden Dawn, the Freemasons, and the Ordo Templi Orientis. He would regularly evoke spirits, including his Holy Guardian Angel Aiwass ("Aiwass" mean "Lucifer" in Gnostic terms). In 1904, Crowley evoked Aiwass and he dictated a document to him called *The Book of the Law* that would be the foundation for Crowley's Thelema religion. This book details various ages of man, including what would be the modern day Aeon of Horus, a time period associated with his catch phrase "*Do what thou wilt.*" Present day followers of Thelema greet each other with "*Do what thou wilt shall be the whole of the law*" and respond with "*Love is the law, love under will.*" These statements support The Law of

Self Knowledge, indicating that the followers will seek their own path in life and find their true will, or purpose for being, through the practice of magic (or "magick" as Crowley asserts).

In this aeon the emphasis is on the self or will, not on anything external such as Gods and priests.
– Aleister Crowley, *Book of the Law*

The 20th century ushered in this Aeon of Horus and many credit Crowley as the man who inspired them to find their "true will"; most notably musicians. The birth of the concept of a rock God can be traced directly to Crowley, given the praise due to him from legends such as The Beatles, David Bowie, the Rolling Stones, and Led Zeppelin. You can see Crowley embedded in the background of The Beatles' *Sgt. Pepper's Lonely Heart Clubs Band* album amongst other famous people whom they found influential. Jimmy Page from Led Zeppelin bought the Boleskine House that Crowley inhabited when he summoned demon spirits during some of his famous rituals, and Page even claimed to have seen a spirit head floating around the house. Iron Maiden and Ozzy Osbourne both have works dedicated directly to Crowley (Ozzy's *Mr. Crowley* song and Maiden's front man Bruce Dickinson's *Chemical Wedding* film), and he is also featured on the back of The Doors' *13* album.

The Aeon of Horus arguably hasn't been *fully* realized yet. Thelema beliefs state that the previous Aeon of Osiris revolved around the worship of a singular, patriarchal God, and the Aeon of Isis revolved around the matriarchal goddess and a time of harmony. The last age is the Aeon of Horus and this will be the worship of the child God. This period is believed to be a time in which individuality and the principles of the child will be evident. It is a time of self-realization and holds characteristics in common with the Age of Aquarius, or simply, the New Age movement. Attributes like devotion to being more "spiritual" instead of being more "religious", and being more aware of the connection of the collective human consciousness dominate all of these supposed Ages. Given the various pop culture phenomenon that I will lay out, you'll see that we are being led down this path of the New Age; or Crowley's Aeon of Horus. It seems that we are witnessing a mass ritual that uses sympathetic magic in order to force this period, given the help of the occult beliefs of the music industry.

The support for the argument of the music industry forcing us into the Aeon of Horus starts with the emphasis on individuality. Our culture is experiencing never before seen levels of narcissism with social media and interconnectivity with one another. Through social media people can highlight themselves in whatever way they like; generally with a favorable outlook on how "exciting" their lives are, or perhaps how good looking they are. Psychologist and author Dr. Jean Twenge points out several studies of data and trends that indicate the millennial generation (people born after 1982) on average have a higher amount of narcissism and selfish behavior. This appears to be directly correlated with the technology and social media the millennials grew up with. Just taking a look around at pop culture and fashion indicates that there is an ever growing trend of people focusing on themselves and less worried about our society as a whole (e.g. crude shirts that put other people down without reason, fascination with death and skulls, lack of empathy for one another, etc.). The University of Michigan study entitled *You're so vain* took a look at how people interact with social media and found the younger people used it as a tool for boasting and carving an image of extraordinary individuality. This supports the idea that we're living in an age of self-actualization and trying to find our place in this world, but at the same time not being able to separate ourselves from desiring to be the celebrities we are so consumed with. Aleister Crowley's *The Book of the Law* 1:3 states:

Every man and every woman is a star.

People put on a persona online that fits the image of a celebrity, and in a sense they believe they *are* a celebrity when they accumulate followers. Many online personalities have actually become celebrities through their YouTube channels or perhaps from starring on a reality show. In this modern time, anyone can become Crowley's "star."

Some of the occult institutions have publically stated that we're already in the Aeon of Horus. The Ecclesia Gnostica Catholica is a Gnostic church and is a branch of Crowley's OTO magical order, and they have a manifesto on their website that states the following:

The world has entered the New Aeon, the Age of the Crowned and Conquering Child. The predominance of the Mother (Aeon of Isis) and of the Father (Aeon of Osiris) are of the past. Many people have not completely fulfilled these formulas, and they are still valid in their limited spheres; but the Masters have decided that the time has come for the administration of the Sacraments of the Aeon of Horus to those capable of comprehension.

I said previously that the music industry is forcing this movement because that is the trend of music; particularly rap. We see rappers like Jay-Z wearing shirts that specifically state

117

occult beliefs like *"Do What Thou Wilt"* and Lil Wayne covering one of his eyes in a symbolic ritual denoting the All Seeing Eye of Horus. Lady Gaga and R. Kelly teamed up to make a song with lyrics of *"do what you want with my body"* which I could loosely decipher as *"do what thou wilt with my body."*

If you aren't yet convinced that the music industry believes in Crowley's Aeon of Horus, take a look at the trend of rappers collaborating with young, white pop stars. Many years ago this would crush your street cred to share the stage with the likes of Justin Bieber or Katy Perry, but today it's a common occurrence. Street credentials used to be of importance if a rapper wanted to keep their fans, but today it appears to be more acceptable to be a poser. Even Rick Ross was ousted as a prior Corrections Officer in the penal system but it didn't affect record sales, even though the hip hop community was generally anti-establishment for some time (and mostly still is). If people found out that Chuck D used to be a police officer, Public Enemy's reputation would've been destroyed in the 90s. It just goes to show there is some serious financing going on behind the scenes to push certain artists and agendas, and it doesn't necessarily matter what the fans think. An article on Mic.com called *The Music Industry Is Literally Brainwashing You to Like Bad Pop Songs- Here's How* explains how it works:

Research suggests that repeated exposure is a much more surefire way of getting the general public to like a song than writing one that suits their taste. Based on an fMRI study in 2011, we now know that the emotional centers of the brain — including the reward centers — are more active when people hear songs they've been played before. In fact, those brain areas are more active even than when people hear unfamiliar songs that are far better fits with their musical taste.

This happens more often than you might think. After a couple dozen unintentional listens, many of us may find ourselves changing our initial opinions about a song — eventually admitting that, really, Katy Perry's "Dark Horse" isn't as awful as it sounds. PBS' Idea Channel's Mike Rugnetta explains, it's akin to a musical "Stockholm syndrome," a term used originally by criminologist Nils Bejerot to describe a phenomenon in which victims of kidnapping may begin to sympathize with their captors over time.

The rappers are being teamed up with young pop stars in an effort to draw the youth into the negative messaging and "low vibrational revenue" formula as well. The Illuminati that control the music industry know that they can create more energy for their purposes by drawing in the youth to their rituals. This is based on an old belief system that blood sacrifices of infants provided more energy desirable to deities like Moloch, and in return they'd bestow blessings on the families. Here's how it works: the music industry pulls a bait and switch on the youth by introducing these adolescent stars on television shows or music videos. They allow it time to build a large fan base of impressionable children, and then switch the persona of the musician to a dark place. One moment the parents think their child is following a squeaky clean child-star, and before they know it their image has changed drastically. Another reason the Illuminati do this is because from a marketing perspective: it works. You can build brand loyalty for an entire lifetime if you start embedding the symbolism and imagery on the fully imprintable mind of a child. Just ask the cigarette industry or McDonald's; they've perfected the craft, as mentioned in books like *Fast Food Nation*:

> *The competition for young customers has led the fast food chains to form marketing alliances not just with toy companies, but with sports leagues and Hollywood studios. McDonald's has staged promotions with the National Basketball Association and the Olympics...*
> *...McDonald's and Fox Kids Network have all formed partnerships that mix advertisements for fast food with children's entertainment...*
> *...All of these cross-promotions have strengthened the ties between Hollywood and the fast food industry. In the past few years, the major studios have started to recruit fast food executives. Susan Frank, a former director of national marketing for McDonald's, later became a marketing executive at the Fox Kids Network. She now runs a new family-oriented cable network jointly owned by Hallmark Entertainment and the Jim Henson Company, creator of the Muppets. Ken Snelgrove, who for many years worked as a marketer for Burger King and McDonald's now works at MGM. Brad Ball, a former senior vice president of marketing at McDonald's is now the head marketing for Warner Brothers...*
> *...Forty years after Bozo's first promotional appearance at a McDonald's, amid all the marketing deals, giveaways, and executive swaps, America's fast food culture has become indistinguishable from the popular culture of its children.*

One might ask why there is so much marketing towards children. It's because it puts money in big business' pockets. Canada's Centre for Digital and Media Literacy analyzed this and found that in 2009 over $17 billion was spent by companies to advertise to children; double what was spent in 1992. In 2000 the Federal Trade Commission conducted a study that found the music industry was targeting children under 17 with songs that had violent content. 55 music recordings with explicit content labels were reviewed and *all* of them were targeted to children under 17 through advertising in media that was aimed at this age group.

Teenage oriented pop star Katy Perry and Triple-6-Mafia (that's the "666 Mafia") rapper Juicy J performed a witchcraft-like ritual at the 2014 Grammy Awards show when they performed the hit single *Dark Horse*. It featured various occult symbols, including the horned deity of child sacrifice, Moloch, and placing Katy Perry on a burning witch's stake. Conspiracy theorists clamored about the ritual, going as far as to claim she was drawing in evil spirits from another dimension. Of course we should've known the ritual was coming because the music video was full of Egyptian symbolism including the All Seeing Eye and pyramids. Within a year the song became so pervasive that viral videos of babies throwing fits until their parents played the *Dark Horse* song hit the internet to much fanfare and little questioning of why it had this effect on them. One could take a look at the video she released for her song *Roar* which came out right before *Dark Horse* and see that she had juvenile imagery of tigers, butterflies and crocodiles in a cartoonish jungle scene. This is obviously appealing to a younger audience, so pushing *Dark Horse* as the next video seems a bit odd (*technically there were two less successful videos released before *Dark Horse* but you get the point).

Another pop artist who is collaborating with rappers is Lady Gaga. She released her first album, *The Fame*, in 2008 but has since started introducing more rappers onto her songs. For example, in 2009 she was on Wale's *Chillin*, in 2011 she had Kendrick Lamar on *Bitch, Don't Kill My Vibe*, in 2013 she paired with R. Kelly on *Do What U Want*, and also had a song on *Artpop* called *Jewels N' Drugs* with T.I., Too Short, and Twista that talked about getting with someone for their drugs. On that same album, *Artpop*, she coordinated with ABC to be on a *Lady Gaga and the Muppets' Holiday Spectacular* where she proceeded to perform songs from the album amidst various poses of Illuminati symbolism (e.g. the All Seeing Eye and goddess worship). This wasn't the first time she worked with the Muppets; in fact she had a Thanksgiving special with them in 2011 and she took Kermit the Frog with her to the 2009 MTV Video Music Awards.

Another rapper that appears to be in the mix on this stuff is Nicki Minaj. The 2012 Grammy Awards featured Nicki Minaj dressed as the Scarlet Whore of Babylon with a red satin Versace cape (a concept that is important in the Aleister Crowley belief system) and a man mocking the Pope. The Whore of Babylon is mentioned in the Bible in the Book of Revelations as an embodiment of evil. Crowley believed that the Scarlet Woman is the physical manifestation of the feminine goddess; similar to "the Beast" being an incarnation of evil. That night she performed her song *Roman's Holiday* in which she channels a spirit named Roman; one of the many spirits that she claims takes over her body. During the controversial performance she conducted a satanic ritual and was depicted receiving an exorcism. In a subsequent interview with Rap-Up.com she said the following about it:

"I had this vision for him to be sort of exorcised—or actually he never gets exorcised—but people around him tell him he's not good enough because he's not normal, he's not blending in with the average Joe. And so his mother is scared and the people around him are afraid because they've never

seen anything like him. He wanted to show that not only is he amazing and he's sure of himself and confident, but he's never gonna change, he's never gonna be exorcised. Even when they throw the holy water on him, he still rises above."
    – Nicki Minaj, Rap-Up interview

That same year she would appear as the voice of Steffie on the children's cartoon *Ice Age: Continental Drift*, and then in 2014 as the voice of Sugilite on the Cartoon Network's *Steven Universe*.

Miley Cyrus started her career on Disney's children's show *Hannah Montana*. Eventually she launched a music career and had a video for her hit song *We Can't Stop* and in it you see a rap producer named Left Brain from the rap group Odd Future Wolf Gang Kill Them All. In the video Left Brain is sporting a hoody with a pentagram on it, which is no surprise to me because he founded Odd Future with rapper Tyler the Creator, who has been depicted with images of Aleister Crowley propaganda. Tyler the Creator helped produce a song called *666* and also directed a racially charged Mountain Dew commercial that featured a goat; a subtle cue to the Baphomet, a logo for the Church of Satan. Left Brain has been depicted with symbolism of the All Seeing Eye of Horus, and it should also be mentioned that the 'left brain' concept is an Illuminati manipulation in and of itself. The ancient Egyptians had a harmonious culture that used *both* sides of the brain, where the right brain was able to think more abstractly and connect with the planes of consciousness. The left brain is used for material concepts and adhering to rules. The Illuminati reinforce and build up our left brains by providing a reward system based off of memorization of facts (e.g. school), which is primarily a left brain function. I explain this process in detail in *A Grand Unified Conspiracy Theory* so please reference that for more.

Miley Cyrus even has a concert tour called *Bangerz* that features Illuminati pyramids and a blow up doll of Big Sean. She mounts blowup phalluses and instructs the fans to kiss other members of the same sex and take drugs. They aired the concert on network television and you can see that most of the crowd consists of 12-16 year old girls. The occult rituals of Aleister Crowley believed that these types of activities would connect to certain energies. He would perform homosexual and drug usage rituals on a regular basis; a practice he learned while with the Hermetic Order of the Golden Dawn. Even more disturbing, in Hanshaw-Freeman's *Weird Stuff 2* book they quote Crowley's *The New and Old Commentaries to Liber AL vel Legis, The Book of the Law*:

Moreover, the Beast 666 adviseth that all children shall be accustomed from infancy to witness every type of sexual act, as also the process of birth, lest falsehood fog, and mystery stupefy their minds, whose error else might thwart and misdirect the growth of their subconscious system of soul-symbolism.

Justin Bieber is another one of the ultra-young that found his way to stardom by going to any and every radio station to perform before Usher Raymond and Scooter Braun eventually signed him. The Illuminati may have helped him get out on the forefront, only to do a bait and switch on the impressionable young fans when they see him acting out, like getting Minerva-owl and All Seeing Eye tattoos, and allegations of vandalism, reckless driving, popping' Xannies, and hanging out with rappers like Lil Wayne.

Ariana Grande started out as an actress on Nickelodeon sitcoms, obviously targeted at children. Now we see her giving the All Seeing Eye of Horus symbolism and letting rappers like

124

Big Sean lounge about churches in a mocking fashion in her video for *Right There*. So what brought that about? We have to take a look from a macro-level at where she comes from. Her mother, Joan Grande, is the President and CEO of Hose-McCann Communications; a piece of the military industrial complex that sells communications solutions to the US and Canadian militaries. Does that necessarily indicate some kind of nefarious involvement? Not really, but like everything else in this book, you can throw all of this evidence on a table and come to your own conclusion. Without going too far off track, the conspiracy theorists generally have distrust for the military contractors, claiming that they are in bed with the politicians and help line their pockets with taxpayer money (effectively claiming that the contractors are benefiting from wars). There is plenty of evidence to support this notion, but that doesn't mean Grande's company is involved with all of that.

Getting back to Ariana's career, we can see that she came up through the Nickelodeon route like Miley Cyrus. In fact, Miley suggested that she was going to influence Ariana to come to the dark side on PerezHilton.com:

"I don't have a bunch of celeb friends, because I feel like some of them are a little scared of the association. I was backstage with Ariana Grande. I'm like, "Walk out with me right now and get this picture, and this will be the best thing that happens to you, because just you associating with me makes you a little less sweet."

She's trying. I see her wearing the shorter things. She comes in, and she goes, "This made me feel like you." And I'm like, "That was like my sixth grade prom dress."
-Miley Cyrus on PerezHilton.com

Ariana could possibly be subjected to mind control, just like I spoke of earlier with the MKULTRA and Project MONARCH topics. The supporting evidence for this is numerous images that show her covering up one of her eyes with a butterfly, or perhaps just posing with them. The Monarch butterfly knows its history through genetic transfer. This means that the offspring know *who* they are without having to manually trace through their genealogy. The Nazis wanted to do a similar process by weeding out what they deemed "inferior" races in part because they thought the ancestry of those bloodlines were inferior; thus the offspring were inferior. It's all crazy stuff, but some of these people subscribe to these types of things. They believe that children of certain abusive bloodlines are more able to dissociate from trauma, so they go after them to brainwash them through MKULTRA. Practices like yoga and meditation help one enter into a trance like state, which is actually dissociating; hence one reason why we see so many Hollywood types pushing these types of things. In one YouTube video Ariana is seen hanging out with her friend and acting very strange. At one point she appears to be trying to pull her own teeth out. Similarly, we saw the actress who played Lois Lane in the original *Superman* films (Margot Kidder) go through an odd breakdown where she suffered from paranoid delusions before being found in the woods pulling her own teeth out.

One more tie-in with this manipulation of Ariana is that confession she made in 2013 that she was switching from Catholicism to Kabbalah after "*the Pope told me everything I loved was wrong.*" Since then she's been seen wearing the Kabbalah red string bracelet that so many other stars wear. She wore it at award show performances and also in her more recent music videos like *Break Free*. And guess who persuaded her to go that route? Madonna, the O.G. of

126

Illuminati symbolism. She has more than her fair share of occult links including wearing her Isis garb during a Super Bowl ritual, posing with the All Seeing Eye, and her outspoken following of New Age belief systems.

The trend of establishing childhood stars and then converting them into drug induced, over sexualized, occult symbolism ridden maniacs is disturbing to say the least. The idea of a hardcore gangsta rapper (who debuted on an album named *The Chronic*) performing over the beats of a top-10 pop song aimed at 5-15 year olds was inconceivable at the block parties of the South Bronx in the 1970's. But that is exactly what we're being exposed to when Snoop Dogg raps with Katy Perry on *California Gurls*:

"Homeboys,(gang) *bangin' out, all that ass, hangin' out."*
— Snoop Dogg, *California Gurls*

In fact, in 2011 Snoop Dogg was tapped to perform at the Nickelodeon Kids' Choice Awards. This was during the time that he was under much heated publicity for releasing a caffeinated alcoholic drink aimed at children. This drink was called Blast and was made by Colt 45 in various flavors like raspberry watermelon and strawberry lemonade. Senior VP at the rehabilitation center Daytop Treatment Services said:

"You look at this product, and you think it's a fruit drink. They (breweries) are creating a demand, and then offering the supply."

Hip-hop activist Minister Paul Scott said:

127

"It's called Colt 45 Blast because they are trying to blast the minds of our young people. Snoop Dogg of all people you should know what alcohol has done to all oppressed communities."

The fact that he was pushing this alcoholic beverage aimed at the youth, while simultaneously performing at a kid's award show is just one more odd "coincidence" that supports this theory of a manipulative agenda in the works. Rampant drug use in the music industry could also go back to Aleister Crowley. He would partake in mind expanding drugs and this was glorified by groups like The Beatles and Led Zeppelin who paid homage to Crowley in various pieces of art. They also allegedly employed back masking (playing the song backwards to hear the true message) in order to push a Satanic agenda. They believe they are using music and symbolism to "awaken" dormant parts of the mind, while simultaneously destroying Christianity and allowing Satan to reign free. They know that children are influenced by music and drugs, and are able to tap into both realms. I know this sounds an awful lot like the "Satanic Panic" movement of the 80s and 90s but there is enough evidence to support it, in my opinion.

Another idea that supports the notion that there is an agenda to push drugs to the youth is looking at the drug trends. Some people are aware of the various links that exist between the MKULTRA mind control experiments and the 60s hippie movement. To briefly explain this; the CIA had mind control experiments and they gave LSD to unknowing test experiments. This eventually sparked a hippie movement with mind expansion drugs, which some theorists point out as a purposeful manipulation by the "Illuminati" to destroy a socialist movement (effectively making people reliant upon the government to make decisions instead of entrusting the people to do so). There are plenty of resources out there that explain how it went down, including mind control expert Neil Sanders' various works on the subject, or perhaps one of the books on the infamous Laurel Canyon area of Los Angeles. The link I'm trying to make here is that there is a solid foundation of evidence to support the idea that some forces used drugs and music together in order to steer an entire generation of people. This process could've easily floated through the generations to the millenials of today. One clear example of this is Eminem.

Marshall Mathers, aka Eminem, came out in 1999 at the tail end of the 90s golden era of rap. He was discovered by Dr. Dre and immediately dominated the charts. He would enjoy a reign over the rap music industry for several years over the course of several albums. I believe that he was instrumental in mainstreaming rap music and grabbing the attention from the pop music fans who would otherwise still have no interest in the genre. Another "contribution" Eminem made to pop culture was the expanded use of prescription pills as a recreational drug. Before Eminem hit the scene, marijuana was the recreational party drug of choice for America's youth (to be fair; so was ecstasy). The artwork on Eminem's first CD was a depiction of a Vicodin pill being broken open. On the song *I'm Shady* he says:

"I think I got a generation brainwashed to pop pills and smoke pot til they brains rot"

Of course we could go on all day with lyrical references to Eminem's prescription pill fetish, but nothing could convey its hold on him more than his actual stint in rehab. After years of rapping about taking pills, it turned out that he really had a problem with it. Unfortunately, the damage was done and the pills were a recurring theme on most of his albums (if not all). The glorification of pill usage in the lyrical content of this bestselling rapper paralleled the actual pill abuses in America over the course of the 2000s-2010s. The US government National Institute on Drug Abuse released a report on a study they conducted from 1991-2010 on prescription pills and the findings were shocking. Some of the factoids that convey the message include:

In 2007, the number of overdose deaths from prescription opioids outnumbered deaths from heroin and cocaine combined.

Abuse of prescription drugs is highest among young adults aged 18 to 25.

Young people are strongly represented in this group (referring to users of prescription drugs for nonmedical reasons). *1 in 12 high school seniors reported past-year nonmedical use of the prescription pill Vicodin in 2010 and 1 in 20 reported abusing OxyContin- making these medications among the most commonly abused drugs by adolescents.*

While marijuana was still being used by a high percentage of adolescents; the fact that an album released by one of the most influential rappers of all time depicted a Vicodin being used is quite ironic with the fact that Vicodin abuses increased during the same time frame.

Another link we can explore is a man named Scott "Scooter" Braun. He is a talent agent who works with Usher to represent artists like Justin Bieber, Ariana Grande, Carly Rae Jepsen, and Psy. He began his career as an 'after-party' organizer for Eminem & Ludacris' Anger Management Tour, which I'm sure, had its share of "party favors" (although I have zero proof to back that up- I'm just conjecturing based on the lyrics of both rappers). The fact that he works with many of these artists who are involved with this overarching agenda to mix rap with pop music makes me suspicious of his involvement in this theory. I've already covered Bieber and Grande, but I haven't discussed Psy yet. This South Korean rapper was America's sweetheart in 2012 for his viral song *Gangnam Style* (the first video in YouTube history to break the one billion views mark in 2012; only to break the record again in 2014 with *two* billions views). What most Americans *don't* know is that he used to boast anti-American lyrics in songs like *Dear American* (a song originally performed by a South Korean rock band called *N.EX.T*):

"Kill those fucking Yankees who have been torturing Iraqi captives and those who ordered them to torture. Kill daughters, mothers, daughters-in-law and fathers, Kill them all slowly and painfully."

Although there is a controversy as to whether or not that is the actual translation of the song; it was still fairly close to the interpretation. There was much more to the lyrics than what was on the surface as well; the group was trying to protest some accidental (and some purposeful) deaths that were allegedly caused by South Korea's involvement with America's occupation in the country. The fact remains that he seemed to support this, yet somehow was able to become so popular in the US that he would appear at the Christmas in Washington charity concert in 2012 with the President and first wife in attendance. Some people put a petition up on the *We the People* website used for petitions such as this; however it was taken down that same day for "violating the Terms of Participation." All of these oddities are why I don't call him Psy; I call him Psy-Op (Psychological Operation).

It all seems fairly innocuous on the surface when you're sitting in the dentist office, listening the top 40 pop radio station, worrying about more relevant worries in your day; but just know that there is a financial interest involved with all of this. Worse yet, there might be a darker, more sinister occult purpose…

Getting back to the Illuminati agenda, one could argue that Crowley was actually presenting the entire program for the masses to hear. I believe this was done on purpose. Why would the Illuminati *want* us to know their devious plans? Because that is a requirement of magic, a concept that Crowley lived and died for. It's done for the same reason as they do all of the symbolism as well. Ritual magic requires the practitioner *and* an audience. This is why we were all subjected to Justin Timberlake and Janet Jackson with the infamous "wardrobe malfunction" at the 2004 Super Bowl halftime show. Over 143 million viewers saw this and it became the most searched for event in internet history. Everyone involved plays it as if it was an honest mistake, but if you look closely at "Nipplegate" you'll see that she was actually wearing a nipple pasty in the shape of a star. This star was quite intricate (more so than a standard stripper pasty) and had eight points on it. In Crowley's magick system this is the "8 of Wands", essentially the Symbol of Chaos which represents the Star of Ishtar/Venus; a feminine goddess principle. These tie us right back into Crowley's Whore of Babylon who is the feminine incarnation of evil. From an energetic standpoint, there were millions of people focused on Janet's Star of Ishtar/Venus, and occult beliefs think they can harness this sort of energy for a particular purpose. Don't ask me what the purpose is, I'm just presenting the theory. Perhaps it is to feed these reptilian shape shifters who exist in another dimension; who knows.

Crowley also followed the Kabbalah teachings, going as far as to attempt to traverse the Tree of Life, a concept I explained in the chapter on alter egos:

Perhaps this is from the attempt to cross the Kabbalah Tree of Life's "Abyss"; a Kabbalah practice that Aleister Crowley admitted would make one go crazy. A succinct explanation for this crossing of the Abyss would be that the practitioner is seeking to pass through Da'at; a realm where fallen angels exist in an attempt to attain spiritual bliss in Heaven (the sephirot point on the Tree of Life known as Keter) directly from Earth (Malkhut).

Although this concept is confusing to most (myself included), one depiction of it that we can see play out in entertainment is a concept of going to the "Other Side." The Other Side is a term used to describe a shadow-dark side of the Tree of Life. It is the evil twin of the sephirot that has evil spirits known collectively as the Qlipoth. The Hermetic Qabalah tries to make contact with these spirits in order to reach self-realization (recall that Crowley said the Aeon of Horus is a time of "self-realization"). There are various evil spirits that have certain attributes and they each could arguably be presented to us through various film plots and music videos. One example is the demon Golachab that is known for destruction, burning, ruins and fire. It is known for tyranny and execution of those who oppose it. Could this be why the second *Hunger Games* film was called *Catching Fire*? We saw the attempted public execution of some of the main characters when the tyrannical forces infiltrated their sector. Or perhaps the Capitol of Panem is the actual embodiment of this Golachab tyrannical demon.

There are several songs that incorporate the talk of going to the Other Side. Perhaps they are referring to the next life, but given the occult beliefs of most entertainers I beg to disagree. For instance, Aerosmith has a song called *The Other Side* that talks about love being like a 'devil in the sea' and having their conscience lead them to the Other Side. Other artists like Red Hot Chili Peppers (who have an album named after Crowley sex magick: *Blood Sugar Sex Magick*) have a song called *Otherside*, Macklemore has *Otherside*, and Jason Derulo has *The Other Side*. Rock band Arcade Fire has a song called *Reflektor* that uses lyrics about the other side before using a term known by Theosophists *"it's just a reflector."* Nicki Minaj was in a film called *The Other Woman* and she told MTV the following (in regards to her appearance and dress):

"I went so far to the other side that there's only one place to go from there…"
–Nicki Minaj, MTV interview

Kanye West had a song with Jay-Z called *Never Let Me Down* that says the following:

"But I can't complain what the accident did to my left eye
Cause look what an accident did to Left Eye
First Aaliyah now Romeo must die
I know I got angels watching me from the other side"

The Doors had a song called *Break on Through (To the Other Side)* that had lyrics about going through a gate that is

134

straight, deep, and wide (referring to the Abyss of the Tree of Life).

The celebrities who partake in this belief system could be using magic to evoke demons to attempt to reach the Abyss, where evil resides in Da'ath (some claim the *Star Wars* villains are named after this; like Da'ath Vader). Da'ath is an area of the Abyss that normally can't be reached without losing one's sanity, so people try to attract demons in order to help guide them to it. Crowley believed that you could use excrement (feces), blood and semen in order to draw these demon spirits closer to you. Strangely enough, Lady Gaga released a perfume called Fame that was described as having these attributes. As mentioned earlier, Gaga said the following:

"(Blood and semen) is in the perfume, but it doesn't smell like it. You just get sort of the after feeling of sex from the semen and the blood is sort of primal. And the blood was taken from my own blood sample, so it's like a sense of having me on your skin."

Tupac Shakur was seen throwing up his hand with his fingers twisted into a 'W' which most people see today as a symbol claiming 'Westside.' This is allegedly a symbol used in Kabbalah known as the Triad Claw, or Marrano. Many paintings depict powerful leaders like Napoleon doing this exact gesture. Theorist Texe Marrs claims that the Triad represents the sacred, Jewish powers of king, priest and prophet; an opposition to the Holy Trinity of Christianity. While this is one of those symbols that appear to have much speculation, one could look at the many prominent people of history and see that they are shown with their hand placed in this similar fashion. We saw him making this gesture on the cover to his double album *All Eyez on Me* while he was

135

pointing to one of his eyes; apparently acknowledgement of the All Seeing Eye. He was also clutching his Death Row Records necklace simultaneously, perhaps a tip off as to Illuminati involvement with Suge Knight's record company.

Besides Tupac's Triad Claw, the other most infamous hand gesture is Jay-Z's Roc diamond (discussed previously in detail). I pointed out that this is what the politicians and elites use as the "power triangle" or "Merkel Diamond", and you can see it on the cover of the Warren Buffett's (one of the world's richest men) book *Management Secrets*. I believe someone as successful as Warren Buffett showing us the power triangle while one of the most successful rappers of all-time showing us the same hand triangle means something. It isn't clear to you or me, but it means something to them and the people they work for. The same symbols can be seen depicted on Jay-Z's Roc-A-Fella clothing line as well with All Seeing Eyes and Freemasonry symbols. Some theorists suggest that Jay-Z has insider knowledge to the Illuminati agenda; and I propose to add to that theory by pointing out that his song *99 Problems* is the 9th song on *The Black Album* (black being a color known for the dark side of polarity; as seen with Black Magic). Take notice that the three 9's make an inverted 666; which supports the theory that inversion is a tactic of witchcraft and Satanism to pervert meanings. The 11th song on *The Black Album* is *Lucifer*, which talks about letting the demons rule yourself as a matter of necessity when living on the streets:

"Lucifer, dawn of the morning! I'm gonna chase you out of Earth. Lucifer, Lucifer, dawn of the morning; I'm from the murder capital where we murder for capital."

Now, take these two aspects of *The Black Album* (the three-9's and the 11th track being *Lucifer*) and consider that one

136

of the largest human sacrifices/tragedies in history occurred on 9/11/2001. Jay-Z released his 6th album, *The Blueprint* on 9/11/2001 as well. On his song *Empire State of Mind* he says the following potentially-blasphemous lyrics:

"Hail Mary to the city you're a virgin, And Jesus can't save you, life starts when the church ends"

He implicitly talks about the destruction of New York and how life can only start *when the church ends*; implying Christianity is something to be destroyed; a Satanic concept. He might also be referencing the sacrifice of the goddess (with NYC's Statue of Liberty who emulates the Babylon goddess Semiramis); an occult ritual seen with sacrifices of the moon goddess, Diana (there are strong ties to Princess Diana's death with this type of thing). Do all of these imply Jay-Z has knowledge of a satanic master agenda by the elites?

Rapper Prodigy (from Mobb Deep) cited a book by Dr. Malichi York called *Leviathan 666* that broke down the agenda to him. He said he realized that everything in life was a sham and rappers like Jay-Z know about it but are too afraid to publically address it. On a letter he penned about the subject, he said the following:

"J.Z. knows the truth, but he chose sides with evil in order to be accepted in the corporate world. J.Z. conceals the truth from the black community and the world, and promotes the lifestyle of the beast instead."

In fact, Jay-Z wore the Aleister Crowley motto of *"Do What Thou Wilt"* on a shirt; and that is a perversion from the "Great Beast" (Crowley's nickname) of Christianity. St. Augustine of Hippo was a Christian theologian in the late 300s who made several philosophical proses; one of which was *"Love, and do what thou wilt"* referring to letting one's heart be filled with love in all that you do, that way no matter what you do it will have a root base in love, and living life in accordance with Jesus Christ's will. Crowley's *"Do What Thou Wilt"* seems to imply more of a connection with a different kind of deity. He would routinely do whatever the magically evoked spirits dictated to him. Who knows whether those spirits were good or evil, but one thing is certain; and that is love for one another isn't necessarily a prerequisite for his beliefs. While he did promote ideals of equality, he seemed to take the notion that one could elevate themselves to a God-like status from within and living from the ego.

This takes us into the next phase of this Aeon of Horus. It's the transition of man into the robot. This is the ultimate agenda of these occultists who seek to revolutionize man into machine. This is the ultimate expression of man's 'superiority' over God. They want to take man-made machines and augment our bodies so that we can live forever. Another explanation for this is their desire to have immortality. Besides the implied benefit of not having to die, they also might be trying to prevent themselves from having to cross over into Hades upon death. I'm not saying this from a Biblical perspective of judgment, but rather to point out that these artists believe they are signing a pact with Satan to trade their souls for fame and wealth. If they never die, they theoretically will never have to pay up to their side of the contract and put their soul in torment. They can go about this several ways and I've laid it all out in my book *A Grand Unified Conspiracy Theory* in which I describe the eventual digital upload of consciousness to an avatar living in a virtual Facebook world. We've seen this concept laid out in sci-fi movies like *The Matrix, Metropolis, A.I., Terminator, Battlestar Galactica, Alien,* and

Transcendence. Some of these films depict this plan to merge technology and man, a concept known as transhumanism. In my other book I explain it as thus:

> *Another weird manipulation that is occurring in the entertainment industry is the push for transhumanism. This is the belief that humans and robots should be merged into one new species. It is the evolution of man to combine with electronics as a bio-electro-organism of the future. The music industry pushes this symbolism through the visuals found in music videos and apparel.*
>
> *The process known as auto tuning is a way of the system to get us to respect machines by listening to these robotic voices and preferring them over the actual human voice. You can hear it through examples of the Black Eyed Peas and other electronic voices. Will.i.am dresses up as this image of a cyborg in many of his videos, and even had one of his songs sent out to earth from Mars (it's called* Reach for the Stars*). We will eventually have to augment ourselves in order to become relevant and competitive in today's workplace. You can see this type of concept displayed in films such as* Surrogates *starring Bruce Willis. Eventually humans will be an inferior race and will die out as a process of natural selection. All of this is part of an Illuminati agenda because the elite will have the money to augment themselves with the best cyborg materials, making their superiority even greater. All of this will come about through the implanting of "acceptable" themes from the entertainment industry.*

Other films and music videos glorify transhumanism by showing the superiority of these augmented humans over their traditional counterparts. The first full length sci-fi film was called *Metropolis* and this 1927 silent film featured a dystopia with elites living it up while the commoners suffered grueling conditions in order to provide energy to the rich. The main character tries to reconcile the disparity of wealth between the two by joining forces with one of the commoners, only to find that she is actually a robot covered in skin. During the film you see symbolism of the Whore of Babylon, the Tower of Babel, and one of the machines the people toil to keep going is called the Moloch Machine ("Moloch" referring to the ancient horned God deity). This seems to imply the film was produced by people who followed the occult belief system (and financed by similar folks; it was the highest budget ever for a film at the time). Even Nazi propaganda minister Dr. Joseph Goebbels was captivated by the film, and we all know how dearly the Nazis held the occult belief system of Theosophy.

Fast forward to modern pop music and you'll see performers like Beyoncé and Lady Gaga dressing up in garb to emulate the robotic character (named 'Fake Maria') from the *Metropolis* film. Fake Maria manipulated the city and drove the men wild with lust for her to the point they would abandon their own children to pursue her. Similar to Nazi Joseph Goebbels, the music industry has taken a particular fondness to this film and the Fake Maria robotic character. The Queen song *Radio Ga Ga* had a music video that featured scenes from *Metropolis*, and this makes me wonder if it bears any influence on Stefani Germanotta's Lady Gaga character. Lady Gaga also referenced *Metropolis* and Fake Maria in her videos for *Alejandro, Born This Way,* and *Applause*. Whitney Houston's *Queen of the Night* video had clips of *Metropolis* and she wore the Fake Maria costume and sang lyrics about driving men crazy with her sexiness, while Kylie Minogue also paid homage to the character in her concert series from the 2000s. The video for Madonna's *Express Yourself* was directed by David Fincher and it featured themes of the film with the dystopian city and workers. As a side note, David Fincher directed *Fight Club* which had producer Arnon Milchan tied to it (he worked on films like *12 Years a Slave* and *Pretty Woman*). Milchan would later reveal that he was a double agent that set up arms deals for Israeli intelligence, Mossad, and tried to recruit others in Hollywood to do the same, including Sydney Pollack.

So where did this idea come from? Aleister Crowley wasn't the first to push a transformative agenda; he just publically talked about it. The Illuminati beliefs trace back in time through a man named Sir Francis Bacon (depending on how much you want to believe this stuff you could argue back to the ancient Egyptians or even to the beginning of time and the Garden of Eden). Francis Bacon was an English philosopher from the 1500s-1600s eras and influenced the scientific revolution. Many theorists believe that he was the actual ghost writer for William Shakespeare. Bacon was known for hiding ciphers in his works while many believe he had occult ties with secret societies like the Freemasons. He was alleged to have faked his own death and travelled by way of this network of secret societies to get around without being seen (apparently he was in debt and sought to avoid repayment). Some even believe that not only did he not die at that point, but he never died at all.

The occult group of Theosophists believe in a concept of Ascended Masters who are able to achieve a status of immortality and ascending into the next plane of existence (as opposed to the rest of us who they believe will continue to reincarnate until we "get it"). This belief system is professed in various works, including the I AM University in San Luis Obispo, CA; an acronym that stands for Integrated Ascended Masters University (does 'I AM' bear any influence on

Will."*i.am*" or perhaps the Nas album "*I Am...,*" or maybe even the Yo Gotti album "*I Am*," or how about the Earth, Wind and Fire album "*I Am?*"). A 2010 documentary film by director Tom Shadyac explores the meaning of life, similar to the uplifting and subtlety New Age film *The Secret*. The documentary is called *I Am* which makes one wonder if he's tied into this occult belief system. He was the director for *Ace Ventura*, *Liar Liar*, and *Bruce Almighty*; all films starring Jim Carrey, a known believer of New Age and occult philosophies. Alice Bailey also wrote about similar Ascended Masters concepts in her Theosophist book *Ponder on This*; a book that Tupac Shakur cited as a motivation for his life. This makes me wonder if there are any analogies we can infer from Tupac and Francis Bacon since both were allegedly faking their deaths…

Anyhow, back to Francis Bacon; he plays an instrumental role in this Illuminati/transhuman agenda because he allegedly had all these ties to the secret societies in question and showed them that you could use **entertainment as a form of manipulation**. You could capture an audience's attention with a play (or music and film) much easier than preaching at them. The entertainment speaks to us on a subconscious level as well, implanting a message or theme into our mind. It's a universal language that can speak to us through allegory and symbols. Bacon wrote a novel called *New Atlantis* and in this book he described the future of humanity, the ideal world in which the secret societies and Illuminati want us to live in. This land was depicted as having harmonious conditions and even had a college called Solomon's House that focused on science, which inspired the actual building of the Royal Society of London that has similar goals of scientific exploration. The point is that Bacon was giving us the insight into the Illuminati plans to push scientific processes and therefore the **transhuman agenda**. That's not to say science is inherently

142

evil; in fact it's obviously helped the human race immensely, but the theory claims that these elite secretive groups want to take science to the level of supplanting the human race with an immortal, digital robot.

Wu-Tang Clan rapper, Rza, is a known Five-Percenter; a religious group that broke off from the Nation of Islam because the Five-Percenters believe the black man is God personified (as opposed to Islam where they believe Allah is God- don't quote me on this, I don't know the specific details, only what I'm reading online so please research these subjects for yourselves). They call themselves the Five-Percent Nation because they believe that 10% of the population of the world knows the truth, while the elites keep another 85% of the population ignorant. The remaining 5% are those who not only know the truth but seek to enlighten the rest. They believe in a Supreme Alphabet and Supreme Mathematics to understand man's relationship to the universe (mathematics=science). This is why Rza's lyrics talk about this so often, including common Five-Percenter phrases like "dropping science", "overstanding" or "ALLAH=arm, leg, leg, arm, head" (implying man is God).

Other famous Five-Percenters include Busta Rhymes and Lord Jamar from Brand Nubian. Jay-Z was also seen wearing a Five-Percenter necklace at a basketball game (an 8-pointed star with a 7 in the middle), but when asked about it he doesn't admit full membership. However, in the lyrics to Jay-Z's *Heaven* he clearly recites one of the tenets of the group:

"Arm, leg, leg, arm, head- this is God body, knowledge wisdom, freedom, understanding we just want our equality"
– Jay-Z, *Heaven*

Rza released a couple of solo albums under one of his alter egos- Bobby Digital. This robotic-cyborg alter ego would rap using similar lyrics and content that is expected from a Wu-Tang rapper, but some of the lyrics talked about transitioning from analog to digital. It clearly depicted the superiority of going digital (as it would eventually play out in reality with the prevalence of CDs and further into pure MP3 digital files, as opposed to analog tapes of the 80s).

"Bobby Digital, keyboard clogged, bitch you analog"
– Rza as Bobby Digital, *Unspoken Word*

"Slimy savages, against the digital, Fuck you analog, this shit is critical"
– Rza as Bobby Digital, *Unspoken Word*

"All you analog cats from weak tracks and weak raps and weak video clips and weak stacks"
– Rza as Bobby Digital, *Bobby Did It*

"Fuck y'all analog niggas we be digital"
– Rza as Bobby Digital, *And Justice For All*

I believe all of these references are pushing the belief system of the Illuminati who want to turn man into God through a digital revolution of transhumanism. These lyrics and concepts all support this trend from the music industry. The artists and celebrities know they have massive influential power and they are trying to spread this message and theme in an attempt to "enlighten" the world. I explained this in *A Grand Unified Conspiracy Theory* as follows:

The real push for the transhuman social network will be the uploading up human conscious to a 'cloud' so that the soul can live eternally in digital form. There currently exists such a thing, and it is called a "mindfile." You can upload your mindfile to a website such as lifenaut.com in order to create an avatar that will live on eternally in this internet cloud. The web stores and preserves information about the user so that it can use an artificial intelligence program to replicate the consciousness. The replicated consciousness will be able to exist in this digital form and interact with other digital life forms. In yet another step further along, the mindfile will be able to fuse with a biofile that will allow an entire human entity to be recreated with the same memories and personality. The soul will effectively be transferred from one body to another. If you find any of this unbelievable, look up Bina48, she is the Terasem Movement Foundation's robot that has demonstrated the capability to perform such a feat. Bina48 is a prototype of an avatar body that can be used to upload consciousness information from the mindfiles. Bina48 took the mindfile from a real woman named Bina Rothblatt and successfully replicated her personality and memories provided.

The lack of discussion on transhumanism is concerning because these technologies are approaching us at a pace more rapid than we are aware. If you study Moore's Law (it states that computer processing power doubles every two years along an exponential curve) you can see that the increasing computational speed and demand for embedded consumer electronics will mean that Ray Kurzweil's Singularity theory isn't far off. It will be here before you know it and we'll all be faced with serious decisions about what we define our species as and what kind of fundamental beliefs we have for living. Mankind has always looked for the Philosopher's Stone or Fountain of Youth in order to achieve immortality, so I can't

145

see how cyborgs aren't the future of civilization and revolution of mankind. Ray Kurzweil said in an interview that he agrees that some of his ideas for the future don't seem possible, but that is due to the fact that technology is increasing at an exponential rate; not a linear one. Our brains operate by making predictions in linear, proximal fashion; not by projecting out an exponential curve that rises very sharply at a much higher rate.

Transhumanism in its darkest form could be considered the ultimate tool in the Illuminati's eugenics plan. Using artificial intelligence and augmented reality engineering, a cabal group of elites could provide the ultimate in distraction. No longer do they need to entertain us with an assault of sexual imagery on the television or reality shows to keep us sedated. They could provide a virtual reality world that lets you live out Facebook through an avatar body. Imagine interacting with high school classmates but without the drawbacks of "reality" where you put on a few pounds and settled for a middle management position. You could live out an alternate life similar to the Total Recall and Surrogates films. Once we're duped into these virtual excursions we'll find it hard to turn back to our regular lives. We'll volunteer to become permanent members of the matrix world. At this point the Illuminati group could succeed in sedating us and reducing the world population, as the Georgia Guidestones monument predicts. Perhaps it wouldn't be all that bad anyways, who knows. The planet earth could certainly use less people and pollutants, and it would also eradicate communal diseases and violence. However, if you believe in a higher power and grand creator, you have to question whether or not this is the experience intended for us. Transhumanists argue that adding these novelties to our lives will do nothing but improve the design; similar to the way an automobile helps us get around easier.

Another expression of transhumanism could be considered the Age of Aquarius. This is known as an Age of Technology with an ultimate goal of living as one harmonious consciousness of beings that have ascended into this plane of existence that only a God can achieve. Mr Gates released a podcast series called *Jupiturn* that explored the origins of the Illuminati and in it he discussed their adoration for the Zodiac system and astrology. The cycle (or "houses" as the astrologists call it) of Ages of man are based on star constellations. Changes in astrological ages correspond to changes on earth and humanity (echoing a concept known by occultists "*As above, so below*"). There are 12 ages, but we are most familiar with three of them: The Age of Taurus, Aries, and Pisces.

The Age of Taurus was the time period represented by the bull, and was the timeframe of the building of Pyramids of Giza. This was described in the Bible as the time when people worshipped the horned bull deity, Moloch. Moses descended from Mount Sinai with God's Ten Commandments and destroyed the golden bull idol. This ended the Age of Taurus and ushered in the Age of Pisces.

The Age of Aries was symbolized by the ram and sought to replace the worship of multiple pagan gods with a singular, monotheistic God. This was the same time of the ancient Egyptian Akhenaten who tried to streamline the Egyptian God system to one sun God- Aten. Some also claim the story of Abraham sacrificing the ram instead of his son was a correspondence between the constellations and the earthly realm (as above, so below).

Next up was the Age of Pisces, symbolized by monotheism and the fish. Jesus Christ is thought to be the realization of this time frame because of all the fish allegories He used (e.g. the disciples were fishermen, the feeding the multitude of 5,000 with two fish, and the Christian symbol literally being the fish).

That brings us up to this new Illuminati agenda era: the Age of Aquarius. This is a time characterized by a symbol of water and the water carrier. This is known as the Age of freedom and technology. It is also believed to be the time in which there will be a period of group consciousness thinking. It also claims that it will be a time of influence by the entertainment industry. There is much argument and speculation as to whether or not we entered into this Age or not, but songs like *Age of Aquarius* indicate that the music industry is itching to get there or to let us know we've arrived. To me it sounds a lot like this is the Age being forced upon us. The facts supporting this are the technology being at the level it is today and the influence of entertainment on our lives; both being unprecedented. You can often go on major news outlet websites and see celebrity-related headlines right next to actual world news, indicating the two are just as important.

So where do we take all of these conjectures and theories? I feel that there is an overwhelming amount of evidence to support the ideas here. There's so much evidence that I'm having a hard time *not* believing it. If you want to take it one notch deeper down the rabbit hole, follow along to the next chapter as we explore the disturbing concept of the Illuminati blood sacrifice.

Chapter 6- Illuminati Blood Sacrifices

Even though this entire book is full of provocative material, nothing is more controversial than the idea of Illuminati blood sacrifices. The reason this is taboo is obvious; it seems quite disrespectful to make bold claims against the dead who have no way of defending themselves. I agree with that, but it's still an avenue that needs explored. Just because a topic is inappropriate doesn't mean it doesn't exist. The action of killing another human being as part of a ritual is as old as humanity itself. Many people sacrificed children to deities like Moloch, only to transition over to the sacrifice of animals, and eventually abandon the practice all together. Or at least that's what the masses are led to believe…

"Man I gotta get my soul right
I gotta get these Devils out my life
These cowards gonna make a nigga ride
They won't be happy 'til somebody dies"
- Jay-Z, *Lucifer*

Sacrifices to the gods were performed in order to appease them and potentially allow the God's blessings to come upon the family of the victim or perhaps the entire tribe/village. The most famous sacrifice in recorded history was the Bible story of Abraham and Isaac. Abraham was instructed by God to sacrifice his son, only to have an angel of the Lord provide a ram as a substitute in the last moments. He was promised many descendants and prosperity, and he got just that because the three major Abrahamic faiths (Judaism, Christianity, and Islam) share beliefs in this event in common with one another.

The Phoenicians sacrificed infants to an idol of Cronus (aka Saturn), Hawaiians held sacrifices in temples called luakini, and Celtic Druids burned people in giant wicker men (like you'd see in the Burning Man festivals, or perhaps in the film with Nicholas Cage called *The Wicker Man*). The pagan Vikings of northern Europe were said to practice rituals called the "Blood Eagle" in which they'd take a warrior and sacrifice it to their chief God, Odin, who held similarities with the Greek God, Zeus. The ritual consisted of keeping the victim alert while carving an eagle design into his back and then tearing open his ribs and shoulder blade to form "eagle wings" before he died.

The Mesoamericans would also perform human sacrifices in order to prevent impending doom, often times during periods of disaster or drought with the thought that their gods could show mercy on them. The Mayan civilization collapsed and one theory behind their demise was that they were in the middle of a severe drought. To make the gods remove the drought they'd perform multiple human sacrifices. A high number of sacrifices were conducted towards the end of their existence, indicating that they were frantic to appease the gods and make the drought stop. The Moche of Peru also performed blood sacrifices at their Temple of the Moon (drawing analogies to the occult beliefs in the sacrifice of the moon goddess). During these rituals they would strike fear in the hearts of the victim before slicing their throat, and then the priests drank their blood in order to absorb their life force. Similar to the Mayan, they were believed to have met their demise due to weather forces; but not drought. Instead, they were believed to be victims of excessive rain during an El Nino, and during this time they desperately conducted sacrifices in order to make the gods stop.

      The Aztecs also sacrificed tens of thousands of people during ceremonies, while also performing retainer sacrifices of entire households in order to bring others with them to the afterworld upon death. Ancient Egyptian retainer sacrifices occurred where servants of pharaohs were killed in order to continue serving their master in the afterlife. Asian myths claim that there are people buried in the Great Wall of China and the Japanese have a legend of burying people at the foundation of buildings in order to protect the establishment from disasters ("Hitobashira"- "human pillar"). Strangely enough, the Freemasons practice a ritual where they ceremoniously place the first stone of a structure. The Freemasons claim the first recorded ceremony took place in 1738, but it's easy to see that this practice could've evolved from human sacrifice, into crops, and finally into just the corner stone; all rituals used to provide some kind of sacrifice that is believed to strengthen the building. A website called Bible-History.com has a claim that the ancient Canaanites used to sacrifice the children in order to fortify a building as well:

With the Canaanites, who preceded Israel in the possession of Israel, corner-stone laying seems to have been a most sacred and impressive ceremonial. Under this important stone of temples, or other great structures, bodies of children or older persons would be laid, consecrating the building by such human sacrifice. This was one of many hideous rites and practices which Israel was to extirpate. It may throw light on the curse pronounced upon the rebuilding of Jericho (Josh 6:26; see PEFS, January, 1904, July, 1908).

The paragraph references Josh 6:26 so let's take a look at that:

At that time Joshua pronounced this solemn oath: "Cursed before the LORD is the one who undertakes to rebuild this city, Jericho: "At the cost of his firstborn son he will lay its foundations; at the cost of his youngest he will set up its gates."

The Book of Joshua tells the tale of the Israelites and their conquering of Canaan. They witnessed the traditions of the Canaanites, who were placing first born sons as sacrificial offerings in the foundation of the buildings, in order to bring good fortunes upon its inhabitants. The region of Canaan would eventually transform into Phoenicia and Carthage, in which they were allegedly continuing this practice of child sacrifice, with the remains found in over 20,000 urns with messages to the gods. In the Stanford paper on this exact subject: *FROM INFANT SACRIFICE TO ABC'S: ANCIENT PHOENICIANS AND MODERN IDENTITIES,* author Brien K. Garnand discusses pop culture references that tie in with real life theory behind this idea. In it, there are Isaac Asimov's references to Carthage in *The Dead Past* novel:

The Carthaginians, it seemed, worshipped Moloch, in the form of a hollow,

brazen idol with a furnace in its belly. At times of
national crisis, the priests and the
people gathered, and infants, after the proper
ceremonies and invocations, were
dexterously hurled, alive, into the flames.

They were given sweetmeats just before the crucial
moment, in order that
the efficacy of the sacrifice not be ruined by displeasing
cries of panic. The drums
rolled just after the moment, to drown out the few
seconds of infant shrieking. The
parents were present, presumably gratified, for the
sacrifice was pleasing to the
Gods...

Even if you wanted to speculate on the validity of these things, the fact remains that there is solid evidence that the Carthaginian parents sacrificed their young to the gods in ritualistic burial grounds called tophets. The inscription on the tophet ended with a message that the gods were showing approval of the sacrifice: "(the gods) *heard my voice and blessed me.*"

Going back to the Freemason foundation corner stone ceremonies; one can see the similarities to the Canaanite rituals of child sacrifice. Many cornerstone ceremonies have taken place in America, including the US Capitol with Freemason George Washington in attendance. There is another pagan link with the US Capitol Hill being a replica of the Roman Capitoline Hill, an ancient site the Romans built temples upon. The legend is that a virgin was sacrificed from this hill and many others were executed here. When the Romans were digging the grounds at Capitoline Hill for the Temple of Jupiter

154

they found a human skull and named it Capitoline Hill because the word for skull in Latin is 'caput' (which is a term we use when something is dead). It's no surprise that there was also a Temple of Saturn at Capitoline Hill because the Saturn worship theme reoccurs over and over again with the pagan belief systems. The Romans believed Saturn ruled during the Golden Age and was the God of wealth (this is the same God of Cronus who Phoenicians sacrificed their children to). They stored the treasury at the Temple of Saturn, and this is another reason why we see rappers talking about the 'Rain Man' raining down dollars from the sky (there's more on that later).

Another conspiracy with sacrifice topics includes that of Jewish blood libel. Some theorists claim that the Jewish people desire Christian's blood and use it for various purposes, including religious ceremonies and the baking of matzos. This accusation has been used to persecute Jews and is usually cited as an anti-Semitic idea. However, this argument falls apart because the Torah forbids murder and Jews don't use *any* sort of blood in official kosher diets. I'd imagine the idea came about due to the specific banning of the practice in Leviticus and Deuteronomy where it details how the people would sacrifice to false idols like Moloch and Ba'al. The Bible says that the people were instructed to specifically *not* let their sons 'walk through the fire' which is a reference to the burning pits used to sacrifice humans to Moloch (or Molek). Moloch (aka Ba'al) was a bull headed king who was also believed to bring about rain during times of drought. This is strange because the Mesoamericans were also into sacrifices for their rain deities, even though there was allegedly no contact between the regions.

Greek historian Diodorus wrote about the history of the Middle Eastern regions and Europe, and he described the macabre process in which the people would place an infant in

155

the arms of a giant bronze statue of Moloch and begin a fire below him. As the fire heated up the arms of the statue they would expand and begin to lower the baby into the fire.

While I am an absolute novice when it comes to Jewish beliefs, I haven't been able to see anything that supports the idea of mainstream Jewish people continuing to practice this concept of 'blood libel,' so I'd have to side with the scholars who claim that this is a propaganda tool used to spread hate for the Jewish people. That doesn't necessarily mean that it doesn't happen (whether it be someone who is Jewish or not); it just seems pretty clear that the official stance of Judaism is to *not* practice this, so that is straight forward enough for me. The question is if any of the fringe "Illuminati" groups believe in this concept and if they continue to practice it in order to appease their gods.

The fact remains that there was a time when human sacrifices were conducted by cultures all over the world. We are led to believe that we've risen above these primitive beliefs, but what if not everybody has? The ritual aspect is obviously important to the followers of the occult and magicians, so it wouldn't be outrageous if they were secretly conducting these heinous things. If that is the case, the theory is that people help participate in these sacrifices by providing a victim to the Illuminati. It shows that they are committed to them and they now have a form of blackmail over them which keep them from revealing secrets.

Tony Montana might as well have blown up that car, killed those women and children, and stayed loyal to his team. Because he was gone already, already in hell. He had a limitation to his wickedness- he wouldn't kill any children. But that limitation was artificial, it was arbitrary on his part. And it was the end of him. The point is, you better go all the way.

You can't serve two masters. You better serve God or serve the devil.
– Rza, *The Wu-Tang Manual*

Some theorists claim there is a "20 million dollar club" which allows an artist the ability to earn that much money, so long as they provide a sacrifice of someone close to them. The theorists claim that people want to be in these higher positions of wealth but the gatekeepers prevent them from gaining access to the tools they need in order to make that happen. It's a way of keeping the royal bloodlines and the company they keep "pure." If you're not born into the 'family' then you will have to make a bold sacrifice in order to be brought in. This sacrifice would literally have to be someone close, preferably a family member. If you look around online you'll find a long list of rappers and R&B stars that are claimed to have been involved with this 20 million dollar deal: Eminem, Jennifer Hudson, Kanye West, Dr Dre, Jay-Z, Will Smith, Brandy, Snoop Dogg, C-Murder, Proof, and Bun B.

Another aspect worth noting is the concept of numerology tying in with these sacrifices. Some people died on dates of the solstice, indicating an offering to the sun God since the sun is at its highest (or lowest) point relative to the equator. Some people claim that there is numerology involved with celebrity deaths; noting that many of them die at the age of 27. Many famous rockers have died under this condition, including: Jimi Hendrix, Jim Morrison, Kurt Cobain, Amy Winehouse, Janis Joplin, Brian Jones (founding member of The Rolling Stones), Ron "Pigpen" McKernan (founding member of Grateful Dead), and most notably; Robert Johnson. He was a blues singer who allegedly made a genuine deal with the Devil and sold his soul at "the crossroads" in order to reach fame, as described in his song *Cross Road Blues*. Several websites and books have been written on this subject, including *27: A History of the 27 Club through the Lives of Brian Jones, Jimi Hendrix, Janis Joplin, Jim Morrison, Kurt Cobain, and Amy Winehouse* written by Howard Sounes. This book explores the various theories surrounding this mysterious coincidence, including numerology and astrology and the idea that perhaps the sacrifice is one they take on themselves:

> *Several of the artists on the 27 Club long-list who met apparently accidental, drug-related deaths may have intended to die. For example, the death certificate of Al Wilson, of Canned Heat, records that he died of an accidental overdose in 1970. But Wilson had a history of suicidal behavior, including suicide attempts, and at least one band member believes that he meant to take his life...*

Kurt Cobain left Courtney Love behind to have a successful career, as did Brian Jones with *The Rolling Stones*.

One more coincidence we'll explore in this chapter is the fact that many celebrities die on the 25th of the month. In numerology 25 is the number 7 (because reduction makes 2+5=7); which has been connected to occult beliefs as a number for God. The letter "G" is prominently featured on Freemason iconography, and is said to represent the Grand Creator, but theorist Marty Leeds explains that the letter "G" is the 7th letter in the alphabet, and that is symbolic because it is the sum of 3 and 4. In gematria (another name for numerology) 3 is a number that represents the material spirit realm of the Heavens, while the number 4 represents the material world we interact with. This is why the triangle is known as a symbol of manifestation with its inherent connection to the divine.

Another occult reference to the 25th includes the Hebrew Bible's Book of 1 Maccabees, which describes a pagan ritual of sacrifices every month in verse 59:

On the twenty-fifth of the month, these same evil people offered sacrifices on the pagan altar erected on top of the altar in the Temple.

The idea of symbolism and energy manifestation is also important in these secret groups of occult followers. They often times practice magic, especially those that worship Aleister Crowley and his various forms of energy manipulation known as sex magick. He believed that sex was the most powerful form of energy and was able to connect esoteric traditions through the use of Tantrism. Perhaps this is why we are subjected to hyper sexualization from all forms of entertainment and marketing:

The sexual act is a sacrament of Will. To profane it is the great offense. All true expression of it is lawful; all suppression or distortion of it is contrary to the Law of Liberty.
– Aleister Crowley, *The Law is For All*

Crowley believed that energy focused at the time of orgasm would be able to influence the universe towards ones "Will" and give them the power to evoke deities or accomplish a particular goal. He also believed one could focus their sexual energy into a talisman and 'anoint' the object with semen to achieve a desired end. This brings new context to the previously mentioned perfume Lady Gaga unleashed on the masses:

159

Lady Gaga released a fragrance called Fame *that was based on the molecular structure of blood and semen; two very important bodily fluids used in magic rituals. She even said that it was based on her blood molecules to have* "a sense of me on your skin."

When Crowley overhauled the Ordo Templi Orientis magical order's initiation rites, he added two degrees to the top of the list. The sexual acts required upon the initiate included homosexuality; as an article called *Unleashing the Beast* (found on esoteric.msu.edu) details:

Crowley's VIIIth degree unveiled... that masturbating on a sigil of a demon or meditating upon the image of a phallus would bring power or communication with a divine being... The IXth degree was labeled heterosexual intercourse where the sexual secrets were sucked out of the vagina and when not consumed... put on a sigil to attract this or that demon to fulfill the pertinent wish... In the XIth degree, the mostly homosexual degree, one identifies oneself with an ejaculating penis. The blood (or excrements) from anal intercourse attract the spirits/demons while the sperm keeps them alive.

So why am I subjecting the reader to all of this graphic detail? It's because Crowley found the sexual deviancy to be of utmost importance in this new Aeon of Horus. This is partially because he was rebelling from his oppressive upbringing and against the Victorian ideals of the time. However, it is mostly because he was a follower of occult teachings and I believe his influence is still pronounced in all of entertainment to this day.

*Just to clarify; I am in NO way putting down homosexuality, or even taboo sexual acts. Everyone should be

free to make their own choices of sexual preference or partner (should it be between two consenting adults). This particular occult belief system is NOT the same as true homosexuality where two people of the same sex genuinely love each other (or are attracted to one another). This is rather a perversion of heterosexuality used in defiance of society and for the purposes of magic and demon conjuring.

This leads us into a theory I've seen floating around various forums and websites, but put on my radar by Professor Griff. The claim is that world famous record producer Quincy Jones is involved with homosexual magick and Illuminati blood sacrifices. Jones has worked with a striking number of high profile musicians, including Marvin Gaye, Stevie Wonder, Tevin Campbell, Tupac Shakur, Aaliyah, Ray Charles, Trey Songz, El DeBarge, Will Smith and Michael Jackson. After what appears to be a deep dive into his ancestry, it turns out that he's related to the Royal Family as a direct descendant of King Edward I of England, possibly making him one of the reptilian shape shifters David Icke warns us about. His daughters are well connected with alleged Illuminati fronts-like Rashida Jones who was a star on NBC's *Parks & Recreation* and Kidada Jones, a fashionista who runs a line of Disney products called "Disney Couture." Kidada worked for Tommy Hilfiger to put on Aaliyah, Kate Hudson, and Nicole Richie as well. Kidada was also engaged to marry Tupac Shakur at the time of his death, but there will be more on that later.

Conspiracy theorists claim that Jones is connected to these inner circles of Illuminati members and therefore practices occult beliefs like astrology and Crowley's sex magick:

"I believe in astrology as much as I do in genetics."
– Quincy Jones

The claim is that Jones is the gatekeeper to success in the music industry, and artists must subject themselves to rituals that the secret cabal requests. This includes homosexual magick and blood sacrifices. Comedian Katt Williams tried to reveal aspects of what he's seen go down inside the business with claims that he saw homosexual parties in the entertainment industry, and he even went in on Jamie Foxx in a Los Angeles stand-up bit:

"Who's gay? Jamie Foxx, I can even tell you the name of the dude he fucked. His name is Marcus Anthony; he's the only dude signed to Jamie Foxx's label… Fuck Jamie Foxx and the Django Unchained check he cashed, they offered me the script and I said, 'Any nigga that do this deserves to die' and the next thing I heard, Jamie Foxx was in makeup."

Williams has made subtle claims of acknowledgement of an Illuminati group, and some of this is backed up by smear campaigns by the Illuminati in order to destroy his character. He's had multiple arrests for various charges and claims that he suffers from mental health problems. Some believe these are all attempts to assassinate his character because he's too close to the truth.

The hip hop duo of Kris Kross suffered a loss when one-half of the group, Chris Kelly, passed away on May 1st, 2013 (*May 1st is a pagan holiday known as Beltaine known for human sacrifices). He was only 34 years old and the official story is that he died from a drug overdose of heroin and cocaine. Jermaine Dupri originally founded the group and the claim is that he had homosexual intercourse with the underage

162

boys (*again- it's just an allegation, I have no *proof* to back that up; it's only what gets floated around as accusations). Gossip website DiaryOfAHollywoodStreeKing talked to an "insider" who made the following statement:

"Kelly did a lot of drugs. He was very depressed. Jermaine Dupri not only robbed Kelly and Smith, he also molested them when they were kids."

While that is a pretty wild and unfounded allegation, there are several similar ones being flown around in the hip hop industry. Keep all of this in mind as you read through the material because most of these artists have some kind of affiliation with ritualistic ordeals, insider knowledge to secret agendas, or Quincy Jones.

Quincy Jones produced three of Michael Jackson's biggest albums- *Off the Wall, Thriller*, and *Bad,* making him one of the wealthiest people in entertainment, worth over $310 million. When Michael Jackson died he released a statement addressing his loss of someone he considered a brother of his; only to sue the Jackson estate a few years later for unpaid royalties for *This Is It* and other allegations of breach of contract. This goes into the theory that MJ was worth more dead than alive and everyone was waiting for it to happen so they could get their cut.

Michael Jackson died from acute propofol, lidocaine, and lorazepam intoxication, which lead to cardiac arrest on June *25th*, 2009 in Los Angeles, California at the age of 50. I'm emphasizing the '25's you'll see throughout the material; recall the numerology importance of 2+5=7; the God number. There are many conspiracy theories online for why and how the Illuminati wanted to kill him, but I'll cover just a few here. The claim being perpetuated in the conspiracy community is that he was a sacrifice for the Jackson family as a whole, while lining pockets for the many people that stood to gain from his passing.

He started out in the R&B group comprised of Jackson family members called The Jackson 5 in the 60s before he broke out into a solo act in the 70s. He achieved unbelievable levels of fame with *Thriller* and continued to crank out hits until his death; even through allegations of sexual abuse of children. He was planning a comeback tour called *This Is It* with 50 shows at the London O2 arena, only to have his personal physician, Conrad Murray, provide a lethal dose of the medication Michael used to sleep at night.

The conspiracy and Illuminati affiliation claims come from various angles. One such angle is the attempted destruction of Michael's character. The first accusation of child molestation happened in 1993 when Jordan Chandler's father, Evan Chandler, claimed that his son was seduced and sexually abused by Michael Jackson. They would eventually settle out of court to the tune of $15M+, but the allegations of child abuse resurfaced in 2002 with the release of the *Living with Michael Jackson* documentary, in which he talked about sleeping with a young boy (not as in sex, but literally sleeping). Initial investigations from LAPD found no reason to bring forth charges, but in 2003 the boy and his mother told investigators that Michael had in fact improperly conducted himself with the boy. He was arrested and the case went to trial in 2005, but Michael was acquitted from all charges. The FBI was also helping the LAPD with investigations, but was unable to conclusively find evidence against Michael.

All of these allegations took a toll on Michael, and reasonably so. People questioned his sexuality and he lost favor to many of his original fans from the 80s due to his antics, allegations, and strange body modifications. He certainly had an odd 'child-like' behavior about him, including his infamous Neverland Ranch full of zoo animals and amusement park rides. He would eventually leave the Ranch because he said it was "...*contaminated by evil*". This supports the theory that Jackson's handlers wanted him to be a 'child-God' like Crowley told us would happen in the Aeon of Horus.

Another angle for conspiracy theories about Michael came from his own doing. He bought a chimp named Bubbles, and allegedly even released his own fake tabloid stories for publicity like sleeping in a hyperbaric oxygen chamber and buying the bones of the elephant man. All of these antics provoked some to claim he faked his own death and that he's actually still alive, or perhaps traveled through time. A 3,000 year-old Egyptian bust at the Field Museum in Chicago depicts Michael Jackson in a very similar manner, prompting us to look at his video for *Remember the Time* with a different angle. The bust even has a chiseled-off nose that resembles Michael's (Christians and Muslims removed noses from works of art to de-humanize them). He was also interested in promoting a show of his by building a 50 foot robot in his likeness to roam the deserts of Nevada near Las Vegas.

Support for a conspiracy around Michael's death includes coincidences around the time of Michael's death. For instance, the first child abuse lawsuit against Michael in 1993 came way by Los Angeles dentist Evan Chandler. He would commit suicide just five months after Michael's death. Actress Carrie Fisher (who played Princess Leia from *Star Wars*) detailed how Evan was her dentist in her autobiographical *Shockaholic* and claimed that he was very strange and even implied that his son was attractive to Michael when he told MJ:

"You know, my son is very good looking."

It wouldn't be surprising that Michael would be involved in such horrid offenses, considering that his brother, Jermaine, suggested that their father may have been shopping Michael around for similar abuse to elite cronies of his. Jermaine allegedly said that Michael joined in late night hotel room meetings with "important business people", only to come back and be sick for several days later. Of course, all of this is prefaced with "allegedly" because it was supposedly contained in a book called *Legacy: Surviving the Best and the Worst* that was never released. Jermaine talked about the book, only to later come back and say it wasn't true and the book was full of lies. Then the book publishers said they didn't release it because it wasn't juicy enough. Could it be that it was *too* revealing?...

        Investigative journalist Ian Halperin wrote a couple of articles for DailyMail.co.uk in which he detailed some disturbing coincidences with MJ's death as well. In one article he alludes to the greed of bankers, agents, doctors and advisers who wanted Michael's money so they pushed him to do the 50-date concert series, even though his health wasn't sufficient to do so. Ian Halperin accurately predicted Michael's death six months prior; in December 2008 (he was only *one* day off). He also highlights Jackson's financial troubles, and the fact that he was half-owner to the Beatles catalog, with the other half being owned by Sony. A source told Halperin that Jackson was in hock to Sony for hundreds of millions because they were paying all of his bills since banks wouldn't loan him any more money. The source claimed that Sony could've easily just taken Michael's half of the Beatles catalog but they didn't want to do it because of the inevitable backlash by his fans, with possible boycotts of Sony products. The source also pointed out that Sony has been dreaming of full ownership of the catalog for a good period of time. Perhaps this is why Michael publically stated that he thought Sony executive Tommy Mottola was *"the devil"* while also saying that *"the recording companies really, really do conspire against the artists."*

While Michael was reluctantly preparing for his final concert series, his health declined rapidly, including nightmares of being murdered. He even told a source that he thought he'd die before the concert series and that he'd be 'better off dead.' His sister, LaToya talked about how a group of people wanted him dead and how he in fact had handlers controlling his every move:

"People come into your life, wiggle their way in, control you, manipulate, control your funds, your finances, everything that you have."
– LaToya Jackson on Piers Morgan

In that same interview she revealed that Michael told her he was going to be murdered for his music publishing catalog and estate. He littered his house with notes saying to get *"these people out of my life."* She believes Dr. Conrad Murray was just a fall guy, and that there is a deeper pit of handlers that are involved with the murder.

Even after his death, allegations continue to fly against Jackson. In August 2014, the NYPost ran an article where they discuss a court filing made by a prior defense witness of Michael's who now claims *he* was in fact molested. Michael's maids are being utilized as witnesses and they've revealed some rather unsanitary and strange practices of his:

"He literally peed on the floor of the entryway, right where you saw Oprah walk in. It was surreal. He just stood there, unzipped his trousers and watered the floor."

167

– Maid #2

"Michael was a messed-up and depraved drug addict. He was twisted."
– Maid #3

"There were many times I had to sneak in and change his linen. I couldn't understand how he'd sleep in such filth. There'd be socks and underpants in the bed and half-eaten chicken and potato chips, empty bottles of wine and whiskey on the floor. And you knew he wet himself- the place reeked"
– Maid #2

The article goes even deeper into the psyche of MJ, explaining his hoarder tendencies and views on high profile industry insiders:

The most scurrilous item Jacko held on to?

"I'd say there were two," recalled Maid No. 2, who worked at Neverland from 1994 to 1996. "A soiled baby's diaper, and a pair of Fruit of the Loom that was obviously worn by someone who was either a teen or an early-age adult."

He also kept a dartboard in the foyer of his bedroom with pictures of DreamWorks founders Steven Spielberg, David Geffen and Jeffrey Katzenberg — who he believed had stolen his idea for the studio and even its boy-on-the-moon logo.

"Any of the children he played with who hit the bull's-eye would get extra ice cream or anything else they wanted," said Maid No. 3, who worked from 1996 to 1999. "He hated

those guys with a passion. He was surprisingly very anti-Semitic. He'd lead some of the kids in chants: 'Kill the bastards,' and 'Kill the bloodsuckers.'"

The article also seems to indicate trauma based mind control, or perhaps a trigger system brought on by the television show, *Twilight Zone*:

"It was crazy. He turned into his favorite 'Twilight Zone' character, and his eyes kind of bugged out, and he went into this crazy trance, pointing his finger at the television screen and saying, 'You're a bad man, a very bad man,'" she said, referring to the famed TV series' character of Anthony Fremont, a boy who "wishes away" anyone who displeases him.

"At first, I thought he'd bust out laughing or something or that he was playing around, but it changed his entire mood. He was dead serious."

Instead of banishing his foe to a cornfield, as Anthony did, Jacko would wish Spielberg into "Jew hell," the maid said.

Do these things indicate that Michael was mentally unhealthy? Or are they a smear campaign being perpetrated in order to feed on the lucrative estate he left behind? Perhaps it's a combination of these things. He might've been subjected to some awful forms of abuse as a child, and some could see that there are traits of mind control experiments. People claim that Joe Jackson coerced the family into persuading Michael to do the final concert tour; even though he was far too unhealthy to do so. This led to the idea that MJ was the blood sacrifice

169

because the family showed up at his house the very next day after his death with Atlas Van Lines moving trucks to claim his possessions. In fact, Don Lemon's CNN interview with Joe Jackson about MJ's death shocked fans when he segued into promoting one of his latest ventures:

"Marshall and I have- we own a record company. Talking about Blu-Ray technology. That's the next step."

Blogs blew up with nasty comments about Joe Jackson, including this one on Jezebel:

"A man seems pursued pretty much to the grave by the demons his father planted in him, and even in death the ghoul is still hustling."

Years later, Joe Jackson had the following to say about Michael:

"I havent shared this story before with anyone in the world but I think it is time I do so. Time and again in my sleep, my son visits me. When I was laying in bed sleeping, I dreamt he was in the same room with me, standing there and smiling. He started singing, his voice was echoing in my dreams and woke me up. I realized I was awake in a dream. He continued singing and his voice echoed out the door. In my dream, I woke up and walked to the door following the voice as it faded away. I woke up and realized I had been dreaming. I want to thank all the program directors, the fans and the DJ's for keeping his legacy going. "
-Joe Jackson, Las Vegas, 24th June 2014

Was he continuing the sales pitch? Or is Michael's ghost genuinely visiting Joe? These paranormal statements go by unnoticed by the public, but to me it seems that there is more going on than meets the eye.

Another example of possible manipulation evidence is when he said he hated his own reflection to the point that he covered mirrors in his house with sheets, which is indicative of mind control. That is because theorist Fritz Springmeier asserts that there are 'mirror' programs in which the Illuminati subject their victims to in order to hypnotize and give an experience of interdimensional travel (since they believe in inversions and this idea that there are reversals of the 'normal' world). This also explains why Michael was so interested in time travel, including lyrics from his posthumous *Xscape* album:

"Everywhere I turn, no matter where I look The systems in control, it's all ran by the book I've got to get away so I can clear my mind, Xscape is what I need, Away from electric eyes"

He was also interviewed by Martin Bashir and asked the following:

Interviewer: [When looking at a replica of King Tut's Golden Coffin at a Store in Las Vegas] Would you like to be buried in something like that?
Michael Jackson: No, I don't want to buried at all.
Interviewer: What do you want?
Michael Jackson: To live forever.

Another potential victim of the Illuminati blood sacrifice is Tupac Shakur. He was one of the most outspoken adversaries of Quincy Jones, because as I mentioned earlier, he was engaged to Quincy's daughter, Kidada, at the time of his murder. The issues Tupac and Quincy had with one another were stressed when Tupac said in an interview that all Quincy knew how to do was "*stick his dick in white bitches and make fucked up kids.*" Even bolder rumors show up on a YouTube video that claim Tupac was taken out because he was revealing too many of the business secrets, including a tale of how he was confronted by Quincy and asked if he could have sex with Tupac before he got with his daughter. The conspiracy theory that Quincy had Tupac murdered was so rampant that he actually replied to this claim in an interview:

"The people who say I wanted to have sex with him, man, this is the biggest age of haters I have ever seen in my life. I've been called a blonde-lover, a pedophile, gay, everything. I don't care, man. Imagine my daughter being engaged to Tupac and me trying to make love to him? And I'm not into no men, man. I'm a hard-core lesbian. Are you kidding? All my life, all my life."

The more rational theory on assassination is that Tupac was too influential and connected to the Black Panther movement. His mother, father, step father, step aunt, and Godfather were all political activists and ex-Black Panthers. A government program called COINTELPRO was run by the FBI in the 50s-70s that did surveillance, infiltration, and disruption of "subversive" groups including political activists and civil rights leaders (*previously discussed in this book). This illegal program was done in the name of national security, but what is more appalling is the fact that in 1969 Black Panther party leaders, Fred Hampton and Mark Clark, were assassinated as part of this program. J. Edgar Hoover was tasked with preventing the cohesion of the African American movement in the US, and he saw the Black Panthers as one of these "subversive" groups that needed broken up.

Recall the objectives of COINTELPRO that I stated earlier:

1.   Create a negative public image (e.g. digging up dirt on civil rights activists and political leaders with "subversive" ties)

2.   Break down internal organization (e.g. cause infighting)

3.   Create dissension between groups (e.g. the FBI wrote letters to related black activist groups alleging that the other was misusing resources allocated to them by the other group; more infighting)

4.   Restrict access to organizational resources (e.g. cut off funding to keep organizations going)

5.   Restrict organizational capacity to protest (e.g. psychological operations to keep activist groups from maintaining organization)

6.   Hinder the ability of targeted individuals to participate in group activities (e.g. the FBI released the criminal record of John Franklin to the New York Daily News in order to create negative publicity for this Manhattan Borough Presidential candidate in 1961)

Could Tupac have been *too* influential? I've heard that assassinations occur when someone has two things going for them at the same time: 1). A voice that goes against the "agenda", and 2). A large audience that listens to this voice. A 1995 letter from Tupac to Public Enemy's front man, Chuck D revealed that he was attempting to start some kind of "program" with Chuck D that he wanted to explain in further detail later on. He ominously mentioned that he was signed to Death Row Records, which surely steered his "program" away from its original purpose before he was gunned down at the age of *25*.

Supposedly Tupac reunited the Crips and Bloods with his THUG LIFE movement, sometimes explaining that THUG LIFE meant The Hate U Give Little Infants Fucks Everyone, but Suge Knight worked to start the feud back up again. The claim is that the FBI was very capable of disrupting these two street gangs (they managed to break up the well-organized Black Panthers; yet the low level street gangs proved to be too elusive…), but somehow didn't. Apparently the theorists believe Knight was involved with a master agenda and was used to roll it out. To look at this further we have to examine some of the roots of the Death Row Records label. Note that this will be an amalgamation of various videos and theorists that I've compiled this information from.

Ted Fields (*"Fields" is supposedly an Illuminati family name) started Interscope Records. This connected family has ties that go back to JP Morgan. Interscope was the label that introduced us to Marky Mark as another hardcore white rapper. This didn't take off with black people so they grabbed Tupac. Now, this is where Death Row Records comes into the story, with conspiracies that it was funded by the CIA, drug dealers Freeway Ricky Ross and Michael Harris. Supposedly Suge Knight approached Michael Harris and he connected Suge with David Kenner; Harris' attorney in order to setup Godfather Entertainment. Michael Harris also ties into the CIA because he was revealed to be part of a CIA contra scandal by investigative journalist Gary Webb. I talked about Webb earlier, so here's a refresher:

174

Journalist Gary Webb wrote a book called Dark Alliance: The CIA, the Contras, and the Crack Cocaine Explosion where he details allegations that the CIA supported drug smuggling of cocaine to support Nicaraguan rebels who opposed the Sandinista government. Gary Webb was subsequently found dead with two gunshot wounds to the head in 2004 and labeled a suicide. That's right, a suicide with two bullets in the head. I'm not sure how someone manages to shoot themselves in the head twice but apparently he did.

Death Row Records already had Dr. Dre and Snoop Dogg on the label, but wanted to add Tupac to the roster because he had all of this gangsta imagery and credibility due to his role as Bishop in *Juice* and time spent in prison. Allegedly Suge Knight was given the connections in order to 'somehow' got Tupac out of prison and he proceeds to release *All Eyez On Me*. This album noted a revolutionary switch to his music being almost all gangsta raps versus his past albums which had more conscious and black empowerment lyrics. Tupac would later get fatally shot in Las Vegas on the corner of Flamingo and Koval; only one block before their destination of Suge's club '662.' What's odd is that there was a hospital right by his club but apparently he went back towards the freeway to try and get Tupac to a hospital, where he would eventually succumb to the gunshot wounds.

So let's take a step back and see what Tupac was trying to convey to us via symbolism. His album *All Eyez On Me* was originally planned on being called *Euthanasia*. Did he change the name to say that the Illuminati All Seeing Eye of Horus was watching him? On the album cover he is shown with his hands in the Westside "W" which could be a version of the Triad Claw known to be employed by prominent Illuminati members, like the House of Medici. Supposedly this is used by

175

Freemasons and Jesuits in order to convey hidden knowledge of a reptilian race.

Another strange coincidence is the obsession Tupac had with death on his last album. His last album was called *The Don Killuminati: The 7 Day Theory* and he recorded it under an alter ego he called Makaveli who was depicted on the album cover being crucified on a cross. The term 'Killuminati' was rumored to symbolize Tupac's hatred of the system that was keeping black people down (the Illuminati). He believed that THUG LIFE was meant to overcome these negative reinforcements and uplift black people. Of course, Makaveli is a play on Niccolo Machiavelli, the Italian Renaissance writer whose name is used to invoke someone's dark side or evil alter ego. Conspiracy theorists claim that Niccolo Machiavelli faked his death at age *25*, and came back at 43 (which would be equivalent to the year 2014 if Tupac went this route). This isn't quite true as far as I can see; but the idea comes from Machiavelli's *Art of War* in which it is said that you can fool your enemies by faking your own death. "Makaveli" for Tupac was going to be a new record label he planned on creating after this third and final Death Row contracted album. He disliked Death Row Records and also supposedly even said that Dr. Dre was into these homosexual rituals. A forum post claims that he said the following about Dr. Dre:

"...couldn't make up his mind between pussy and dick. While he's upstairs eating and sucking he's supposed to be producing my album."

Now, that's a fairly boisterous and undocumented reference (it's a forum post about a YouTube video that was taken down), so I wouldn't necessarily take that and run with it quite yet. Tupac was known for being over the top so it is just believable enough that I wanted to throw it in there. There are more conspiracies about Tupac than I care to rattle off here, but it seems to me there is an overabundance of evidence that points to foul play here. As a final note on Tupac, take a look at some of his quotes from the book *Tupac Resurrection* and see if you don't see all of the red flags that point to disruption of an Illuminati agenda:

"Jail is big business. Believe me, I see the big business. They charge you for your telephone calls. They charge you for disciplinary problems. Jail is big business. You know, you could feed a whole town of one jail."
- Tupac Shakur, *Tupac Resurrection*

"I believe that I'm a natural born leader. I can take orders cuz I'm a good soldier, but I like to give orders, like to follow my own heart."
- Tupac Shakur, *Tupac Resurrection*

"We'll try to get a community center in every ghetto in the country that has the same things as they have in the Beverly Hills Community Center. They have a pool table, a VCR, a library. The kind of library you have at Yale. If they want the ghetto to have brains, give us the books! This is the type of thing young black males can do. We can do anything if you just give us a shot and stop trying to beat us down."
- Tupac Shakur, *Tupac Resurrection*

Another aspect of Tupac is the rivalry he had with Notorious BIG. The East Coast vs West Coast rivalry was supposedly staged in order to sell records, and some supporting evidence of this is found in Randall Sullivan's *Labyrinth* book about the involvement of Tupac, BIG, Death Row Records,

Suge Knight, and the LAPD. A lead detective named Russell Poole from LAPD was assigned to BIG's murder and said the following in a *Rolling Stone* interview:

"To me it was obvious this wasn't a gang shooting," *says Detective Russell Poole, who, with partner Fred Miller, would become a lead investigator on the case when it was finally assigned to Robbery-Homicide in April 1997. "Biggie's murder was much more sophisticated than anything I've ever seen any gangbanger pull off. This was professionally executed."*

In that same article, there is another theory behind Tupac's attempt to break from Suge; saying that he tried to start a production company named *Euthanasia* (previously I stated that was the first name for his *All Eyez On Me* album):

In October 1995, Shakur signed a three-page handwritten agreement drafted by Kenner, and within a week he walked out of prison to the white stretch limousine where Kenner and Knight waited for him. But within a year, Shakur would try to break away from Knight. First he formed his own production company, Euthanasia, *to develop movie projects. And later that summer, the rapper fired Kenner as his attorney -- effectively signalling his independence. It was a move that a lot of people predicted would get him killed. At the MTV Video Music Awards held in New York a week later, Knight approached Shakur to insist he had no hard feelings; as a gesture of friendship, he invited Shakur to join him in Las Vegas for the Mike Tyson-Bruce Seldon heavyweight title fight the following weekend. When Shakur confided to his fiancee, Kidada Jones, that he felt uneasy about the trip, she advised him to wear his bulletproof vest. But Shakur said Vegas was too hot for that.*

In the book, he lays out the theory that an LAPD officer named David Mack helped conspire with Suge to take out BIG and Tupac and make it appear to be a bi-coastal feud:

Poole's refusal to abandon his interest in the Biggie Smalls murder was making his position on the task force, and his assignment to the Robbery-Homicide Division as well, increasingly untenable. "I was complaining that we had had a series of incomplete investigations and that it was orchestrated to be that way," Poole explained. "I had become convinced that LAPD officers affiliated with Death Row Records had been involved in the conspiracy to kill Biggie Smalls and none of the brass wanted to hear that."

Notorious BIG's murder remains "unsolved" and you can comb through countless theories and allegations of who did it; but let me stay on the theme of Illuminati blood sacrifice and just say that there is obviously a conspiracy and well-orchestrated cover up with the deaths of both Tupac and BIG. Biggie Smalls was killed after leaving a Vibe magazine after party in Los Angeles (recall that Vibe is an entertainment magazine founded by none other than Quincy Jones). Tupac was gunned down on a *packed* Las Vegas strip with no apparent witnesses. Also, take a look at some of their albums that seemed to have aspects of predictive programming when they foreshadowed their own deaths. For example, BIG only had two albums while he was alive: *Ready to Die* and *Life After Death*. Tupac's last album, *The Don Killuminati: The 7 Day Theory* had a song called *To Live and Die in LA* which was produced by QDIII; which is an alias for Quincy Jones' son;

179

Quincy Jones III. In March 1994 Tupac was on a PBS show called *Blank on Blank* and they asked him where Tupac sees himself in the next 10 years. He replied:

"Best case, in a cemetery. Not in a cemetery, sprinkled in ashes smoked up by my homies. I mean, that's the worst case."

Tupac's homies in question were a band of rappers called the Outlawz, and sure enough, they smoked his ashes:

"Yes, it's definitely true... Had a little memorial for him with his mum and his family. We had hit the beach, threw [in] a lot of shit he liked at the beach. Some weed, some chicken wings, he loved orange soda... Pac loved that kind of shit, so we were giving him our own farewell...If you listen to "Black Jesus," he said, "Last wishes, niggas smoke my ashes." That was a request that he had. Now, how serious he was about it? We took it serious."

A song Tupac did with rapper Richie Rich called *Niggaz Done Changed* was released just two months after Tupac's murder and in it, 'Pac foreshadows his own death:

"What they tell me I'm makin these muthafuckaz hop on they toes like
Calvin Bally I've been shot and murdered cant tell you how it happened
Word for word but best believe that niggaz gonna get what they deserve"

BIG also spoke about his death on *Suicidal Thoughts*, the last track on *Ready to Die*:

"I swear to God I feel like death is fucking calling me"

You honestly can't make this stuff up. At some point you have to believe these rappers had the foresight to know what was going to happen to them. Another rapper who knew his fate was Wu-Tang Clan's Ol' Dirty Bastard ("ODB"). He publically talked about how Tupac and BIG were taken out and how the FBI and President Bush were going to get him next. This includes lyrics to the song *Diesel* where he specifically is crying out for help:

> *"I need help, because the black man is God,*
> *The government is after me*
> *And the worst is, black man is the Devil...*
>
> *They already did 2Pac, my children, all six billion humans,*
> *Biggie Smalls on the planet Earth,*
> *Somebody help me! "*

In his hit song *Got Your Money* he talks about how the FBI is watching him:

> *"I'm the ODB as you can see, FBI don't you be watchin' me"*

In an interview he had with Method Man and Zedd TV, he talks about similar concepts I've laid out before with COINTELPRO and the deliberate assassinations of influential people:

> Interviewer: *Do you think those kinds of killings will go on? (referencing Tupac and BIG).*
> ODB: *Well, If it does then it does. Hey, that's life...*

181

Method Man: *Them killings been going on since day one. It's just people aint recognize until somebody famous y'know? We've been crying out since fucking day one.*

ODB: *Somebody famous? Malcolm X, you want me to name about 1,000 of 'em? Jesus…*

Meth: *You know how many Biggie Smalls and Tupacs there is out there? That fell victim? We was brought up in a system that didn't give a fuck about us.*

In that same interview, Method Man lays out the agenda within the music industry and how they extort rappers when they use samples. He says that these samples are from older, washed up artists, and the record companies help sue the rappers in order to take what little profit they've carved out from album sales. He also makes a light jab at what could be telling of how the music industry is controlled by ancient Illuminati bloodlines:

"Money is older than I am in this industry."

Method Man also talks about how the hip hop audience tends to let the most unconscious and corny songs to get the most airplay. A prophetic ODB replies to this by saying:

"It's the government. The government brainwash our people with the mind control theory, that's what they do, so they make sure people like it. They keep playing that same song, that same song keep playing 'til you start to like it. You start to get probed with it, you start to get cloned with it. So therefore the clone exists and it starts to take over. It takes over the whole body. It takes over the spirit. It takes over the soul. And therefore behold, that's what you got. That's what Dirty is here for. Dirty is here to keep it dirty, (*repeats "Dirty" multiple times), where we all come from. You know what I mean you can't forget that and keep running up into astrology, and trying to run up into the Moon and into the Mars to build these cities. That already been built for trillions of years. "

What's strange about his comment is that there was a study that started in 2011 that exposed how the music industry works (see earlier when I reference the article on *The Music Industry Is Literally Brainwashing You to Like Bad Pop Songs- Here's How*):

Research suggests that repeated exposure is a much more surefire way of getting the general public to like a song than writing one that suits their taste. Based on an fMRI study in 2011, we now know that the emotional centers of the brain — including the reward centers — are more active when people hear songs they've been played before. In fact, those brain areas are more active even than when people hear unfamiliar songs that are far better fits with their musical taste.

This happens more often than you might think. After a couple dozen unintentional listens, many of us may find ourselves changing our initial opinions about a song — eventually admitting that, really, Katy Perry's "Dark Horse" isn't as awful as it sounds. PBS' Idea Channel's Mike Rugnetta explains, it's akin to a musical "Stockholm syndrome," a term used originally by criminologist Nils Bejerot to describe a phenomenon in which victims of kidnapping may begin to sympathize with their captors over time.

ODB said that Bush had a personal beef with him and that the government was out to assassinate him. Similar to other artists and their downfalls, his last few years were spent in jail stints, legal issues, and eccentric behavior. Some claimed that the government micro-chipped him because he made his way onto a list of one of the influential people that was outspoken enough to cause too much commotion. Officially, he died from an accidental drug overdose of cocaine and tramadol, but others claim foul play. They say that he fell on his knee at a show and asked for a painkiller; which a mysterious stranger gave to him, but he never woke up again.

A few years after his death, it was revealed through a Freedom of Information Act request that the FBI did in fact have a file on him, which included statements that the Wu-Tang Clan was "*heavily involved in the sale of drugs, illegal guns, weapons possession, murder, carjacking and other types of violent crime.*"

Many of the conspiracies about these deaths link into the east coast rap scene, with some people alleging that Jay-Z was the man who stood to gain the most from the murder of the two rap icons of Tupac and BIG. In 1995 while Tupac was on his way to being tragically murdered, Jay-Z was still selling CDs out of his car with Damon Dash on their independent Roc-A-Fella Records label. In 1996 Jay-Z released his debut album *Reasonable Doubt* which saw moderate success. His next album noted a different sound, this time being produced by Sean Combs (aka Puff Daddy). Combs was known for grooming BIG on his Bad Boy Records company; a label that was depicted as the antithesis to Suge Knight's west coast Death Row Records. One of the artists on the Bad Boy label named Mark Curry released a book called *Dancing With the Devil: How Puff Burned the Bad Boys of Hip-Hop* where he lays out allegations of the dark side of the industry, and connections Bad Boy had with the Crips (and Death Row's connections with the Bloods). He covers a lot of the insider information that was going on behind the scenes, implying that money was *always* the bottom line:

Although I was flattered at first at how much Puff imitated me and depended upon me to teach him how to rap, other Bad Boy artists warned me that I was making a big mistake. They would tell me about what Puff did to a dude known as Sauce Money. Sauce Money (real name: Todd Gaither) was working with Jay-Z in mid-1970s. In fact, he's the cat who introduced Jay-Z to the business. He was featured on "Reasonable Doubt," Jay-Z's first album.

Jay-Z tried to get Sauce to sign with Roc-A-Fella, but Sauce was leery. He was in college at the time and a bit more astute than most rappers, and something about Damian Dash's business operations troubled him. However, the constant cheerleading of the label by Jay-Z after the success of his album finally convinced Sauce that the label was cool. Shortly after he signed, his apprehensions about Dash kept haunting him, and he left Roc-A-Fella after less than a year.

When Puff heard about this, he tried to lure Sauce to Bad Boy. At the time, Faith was trying to compose a song to commemorate Biggie's death but was too grief-stricken to focus. At the same time, dozens of writers were composing tributes to Biggie and sending them to Bad Boy. None of them seemed to interest Puff or Faith.

He continues on to describe the manipulation and legal-shuffle game Puff played in order to avoid paying royalties to Sauce and other producers who helped build the final product; the hugely successful, 7x platinum selling *I'll Be Missing You*:

With the song making so much money, it was only a matter of time before some reporter got wind of the fact that most of the money was going to Puff. To avoid a dogfight with Biggie's mother over proceeds from the song, Puff told reporters that he was giving $3 million to Biggie's family. Anxious to capitalize on the song's success, Puff added the song to an album that he was working on called "No Way Out."

This album wound up winning the Grammy for best rap album of 1998, and getting Puff the distinction of *Rolling Stone's* "Artist of the Year."

Jay-Z was friends with BIG, and was shaken up over his loss. Theorists claim that Puff helped Jay-Z make a deal with the Devil and put BIG up as a blood sacrifice in order to help his career out. Again, this is one of these arguments that I haven't seen any solid evidence for; I'm merely throwing it out there as one of the ideas being floated around conspiracy circles. The only thing I *could* use as support for that would be the unbelievable levels of success Jay-Z has had, meanwhile using various forms of symbolism previously mentioned. If you take a look at the history of rap music, Jay-Z absolutely came through the winner of the last 20 years with a net worth over $500 million and over 75 million records sold. He also secured well-connected positions like President of Def Jam Records and starting successful ventures like 40/40 club and the Roc Nation label.

The 'evidence' being used to support the claim of Jay-Z's Illuminati involvement include the idea that he snitched on Dame Dash in order to support a secretive agenda of the Boule. This secret society comprised of black men is allegedly willing to do the bidding of the Illuminati, who is comprised mostly of white men. They wanted Jay-Z to break up black owned labels, so they forced him to start a beef with Dame Dash. Jay-Z's new 'buddy' was Def Jam Records and they bought out Roc-A-Fella in its entirety (with the help of Jay-Z). In return for this favor, Jay-Z was granted the keys to the kingdom, while Dame Dash would struggle and even take another blow when Jay-Z bought out the rest of the Rocawear clothing line (a multi-million dollar organization at this point).

Damon Dash was also known as the man who Aaliyah was dating when she passed away on August *25th*, 2001. She was also linked with Quincy Jones, because she was friends with his daughter, Kidada, as I mentioned earlier who was engaged to Tupac at the time of his death. Some claim that she was a blood sacrifice, but there could be multiple culprits. She had affiliations with Tupac, Damon Dash, Quincy Jones, R. Kelly, Sean Combs, Beyoncé, Timbaland, and many more artists; so it's hard to tell. All of these artists have affiliations with Jay-Z in one form or another, so it's pure speculation that we can use six degrees of separation and implicate him as well. The actual cause of death was due to a plane crash when its pilot, Luis Morales III tried to take off with an overloaded aircraft, only to have it crash a short time later. Investigations into the accident found that the airline company he worked for, Blackhawk International Airways, had hired Morales and let him take this trip as his first official day of employment. Morales was not certified to fly for Blackhawk, and the production company for the video she was shooting, Instinct Productions, had provided the transportation services. Some theorists claim that the aircraft was controlled remotely (a common conspiracy among theorists-citing 9/11 and the assassination of a Panamanian General as evidence). Her last piece of work to be released was a film called *Queen of the Damned* where she had a lead role as a vampire named Akasha, who ends up getting her blood drained and consumed by other vampires. Could this be a fitting analogy of her passing? Were real life reptilian shape shifting vampires from the constellation Draco involved with her death? Mary J. Blige talked to Oprah and had this to say about Aaliyah:

Oprah: What brought you to that point? I know 9/11 was traumatic for you.
Mary: Yes. And Aaliyah had just died. [Recording artist Aaliyah's plane crashed on August 25, 2001.] My life was her

187

life. She was surrounded by people who weren't telling her the real deal. We weren't close friends, but I'd talked with her a couple of times. I very well could've been the woman on that plane.
Oprah: *It was your wake-up call.*
Mary: *Yes.*

In 2010 Jay-Z helped a rapper named Jay Electronica by signing him to his Roc Nation label. Electronica is also a Five Percenter and would eventually go on to have a relationship with Kate Rothschild; an heiress in the Illuminati affiliated Rothschild Family. This German-Jewish royal bloodline established a banking system and has been alleged to be the wealthiest family in the world, and prominent members of the Illuminati with their hands in multiple industries (implying world domination by theorists like David Icke).

Jay-Z married Beyoncé and some claim this was an Illuminati arranged marriage. Even wilder claims are made about their baby, Blue Ivy; with some saying she was a modern day version of Rosemary's Baby. I've already covered some of the occult connection between Jay-Z and color of blue, so perhaps there is some traction to the theory (although I'll admit it's pretty far out there). An idea that supports the occult agenda is that Jay-Z and Beyoncé announced the birth of their first child, Blue Ivy, at the 2011 MTV Video Music Awards; a show known for containing ritualistic performances, like Nicki Minaj exorcising demons and various other forms of symbolism rituals. The pregnancy announcement was in the Guinness World Records for 'most tweets per second recorded for a single event' on Twitter, indicating a focus of energy on this event. In 2014 Jay-Z changed the lyrics to *Beach is Better* to say "*Cause she pregnant with another one*" alluding that they're expecting another child. This was done at their *On The*

Run concert series while in Paris; a place known for its rich occult history. This is where the alleged Illuminati - Merovingian dynasty set up shop, and also the location where Princess Diana was taken out in occult fashion.

Another protégé of Jay-Z is rapper-producer Kanye West. He has been alleged to be into the occult and Illuminati because of various lyrics talking about selling his soul to the Devil, clothing with satanic imagery on it, and his appearance on the *Cleveland Show* episode about the Illuminati (called *Menace II Secret Society*). The blood sacrifice allegations come into play when theorists say that Jay-Z convinced West to perform a sacrifice in order to take his career to the next level (like Jay-Z did supposedly). Kanye West's mother, Donda, died on Nov. 10th, 2007 in Marina del Rey, CA at 58 years old. She passed away from complications in post operation cosmetic surgery. Theorists tied her death to Illuminati sacrifice allegations due to his other loose affiliations, but let's take a closer look…

One of the arguments to support this theory is the abrupt change in artistic expression from Kanye since his mother's passing. On his 2004 debut album *The College Dropout* he covered topics like consumerism (*All Falls Down*) and the gospel of Christ (*Jesus Walks*), but most interesting is that he covered blood sacrifices as well, if you want to take that angle. Kanye had a track with Jay-Z called *Never Let Me Down* where he says:

"Nothing sad as that day my girl's father passed away
So I promised to Mr. Rainey I'm gonna marry your daughter
And you know I gotta thank you for the way that she was brought up
And I know that you were smiling when you see the car I bought her
You sent tears from heaven when you seen my car get balled up
But I can't complain what the accident did to my left eye
Cause look what an accident did to Left Eye

189

First Aaliyah now Romeo must die
I know I got angels watching me from the other side"
- Kanye West, *Never Let Me Down*

Now compare that album with his 2013 album, *Yeezus*, where he talks about what the music industry is capable of doing to a person and about how he is still under their control:

"Fuck you and your corporation
Y'all niggas can't control me
I know that we the new slaves
I know that we the new slaves
I'm 'bout to wild the fuck out
I'm goin' Bobby Boucher
I know that pussy ain't free
You niggas pussy, ain't me
Y'all throwin' contracts at me
You know that niggas can't read
Throw 'em some Maybach keys
Fuck it, c'est la vie
I know that we the new slaves
Y'all niggas can't fuck with me
Y'all niggas can't fuck with 'Ye
Y'all niggas can't fuck with 'Ye
I'll move my family out the country
So you can't see where I stay
So go and grab the reporters
So I can smash their recorders
See they'll confuse us with some bullshit
Like the New World Order
Meanwhile the DEA
Teamed up with the CCA
They tryna lock niggas up

They tryna make new slaves
See that's that privately owned prison"
- Kanye West, *New Slaves*

One thing that's for certain is that he's gained more knowledge in his first decade of affiliation with the music industry. His music got much darker starting with his 2008 album, *808s & Heartbreak*, after Donda passed away. *808s & Heartbreak* was *drastically* different from his previous albums. This new album used auto tune and more abstract, melancholy sounds over Kanye singing (instead of rapping). A year later in 2009 he infamously interrupted Taylor Swift during her acceptance speech at the MTV Video Music Awards. Some claim that the Illuminati used Kanye as a tool to promote Taylor Swift, because at the time the hip hop community had no knowledge of who she was, which supports my theory that rap and pop are being merged as one in order to simplify the processing of an Illuminati agenda.

The website Gawker.com obtained a recorded rant from Kanye at a New York City restaurant (from that same night in 2009) where Kanye talked about how unjust it was for Swift to win over Beyoncé. In the rant, he said:

"Because my mother got arrested for the fucking sit-ins. My mother died for this fame shit. I moved to fucking Hollywood chasing this shit. My mother died because of this shit. Fuck MTV."
– Kanye West

The rational argument is that he is referring to his mother fighting for civil rights, only to be overlooked because of her skin color. The conspiratorial argument is that he is actually revealing the truth behind the Illuminati directed sacrifice of his own mother. If you take all of these things and put them together you could perhaps see why there might be claims of Illuminati sacrifice with Kanye West. The darker lyrics, crazier antics, and alleged admission are all pointing to the possibility. Something that doesn't support these arguments would be the record sales. If someone sacrificed their own mother in order to make an offering to the Illuminati you might expect them to sell more records *after* the deed. Kanye's record sales have steadily been dropping since his debut album released. The death of his mother in 2007 seemed to have no effect at all on the charts. Of course, if you ask a conspiracy theorist they'll tell you that he was repaying the debt of allowing his debut album to make over three million sales, so who knows.

Lisa "Left Eye" Lopes was one third of the R&B music group TLC; the bestselling American female group of all time. She was known as the eccentric one who would provide the rap verses on several popular songs like *Waterfalls* and *No Scrubs*. The most infamous event that she was tied to was when she burned down Atlanta Falcon's football player Andre Rison's mansion in 1994. The media outlets portrayed her as an alcoholic with mental issues, which may or may not be true, but in reality she claimed she was suffering from some domestic violence with Rison right before it happened.

There were some versions of the songs released that you could hear her rap verse; while others had it cut out; suggesting she was, in a sense, the outsider of the group. In 2013 TLC (the remaining members of the group) released a remake of *Waterfalls* that replaced Left Eye's verse with a verse by a Japanese pop star named Namie Amuro. Needless to say, Left Eye's family was upset with this new "Japanese version" of the song. This just goes to prove that the group had some serious strife that remained unresolved with Left Eye's passing.

The trio suffered much turmoil towards the latter portion of their career, including bankruptcies and feuds amongst each other. At one point Left Eye challenged the other two members of TLC (T-Boz and Chili) to each release solo albums in a three-way contest to see who could sell the most albums. T-Boz and Chili didn't play into the contest and seemed to try to keep the drama away from public view for the most part, aside from a few jabs like on MTV's *TRL*. When the group was recording the *Fanmail* album Lopes made a public claim that she was the best member of the group and she started venturing out and collaborating with groups like 'N Sync and Toni Braxton.

Her rap nickname of "Left Eye" is enough to draw theories as to Illuminati involvement. The symbolism of the All Seeing Eye is important enough that you see it on the Great Seal on the reverse side of the US Dollar bill and elsewhere. It all traces back to the ancient Egyptians and their worship of the sun and sky gods like Horus, Ra, Osiris, and Thoth. One myth claims that the God Osiris died and his son Horus and brother Set battled for the throne. Set removed Horus' left eye, but Thoth was able to use magic to reattach it. Horus then offered the left eye to Osiris in the hopes of bringing him back to life, leading many to this day to believe the left Eye of Horus represents sacrifice, healing, and rebirth. Another myth suggests Horus offered up the eye to Osiris in order to help him rule the underworld, and Osiris ate the eye and was brought back to life. This started an idea of making an offering to the gods, or a sacrifice because an offering can be made divine upon receipt of the gods.

Another ancient Egyptian myth claims the right eye is associated with the sun God, Ra; while the left is the mirror image, representing the moon; or Thoth. If you can take a step back and combine these myths, you could argue that the left eye is symbolism for sacrifice of the moon goddess (because the moon is associated with the female goddess, while the sun is for the male God). This is important to the alleged Illuminati group because they are into rituals and devoting energy to their gods. Princess Diana was allegedly murdered in a ritualistic fashion in the Pont D'Alma tunnel, which means "passage of the moon goddess", while the name "Diana" is literally an ancient name for the moon goddess. Could the death of Left Eye have been a ritual for sacrificing the moon goddess? The coincidences are truly astounding when you look at all of the evidence that suggests an occult belief system might've been involved. For instance, what are the odds that she would be filming herself at the time of her death?

If there is truly a thing such as Illuminati sacrifice, it would definitely include a ritual. Rituals were included in many of the ancient practices of human sacrifice, including the Aztecs who would perform a ritual at the top of the temple before removing the human sacrifice's beating heart. The Illuminati are rumored to conduct secretive rituals and study occult practices. This could include magic and sacrifice; both of which require an energy exchange between the practitioner and the audience. I propose that Left Eye might've fell victim to such a horrific thing.

The Last Days of Left Eye is a VH1 Rock Docs episode that shows footage obtained while Left Eye was spending time in Honduras, attempting to cleanse herself and others in her entourage. Her cleanse consisted of eating certain herbs, hiking, yoga, and reflecting on her life while the cameras captured it all. One must wonder what precisely she was seeking to cleanse herself from, but in all reality it was probably the standard stresses of life, or perhaps she knew her time was coming for the sacrifice. Some online forums suggest she was possessed by evil spirits and was attempting to cleanse herself of them. She had in fact been accused of having an alcohol problem, and during the documentary she addresses it briefly while describing an alter ego of hers called Nikki. As I mentioned earlier, the concept of aliases and alter egos seems to run rampant in this entertainment industry; most particularly in the realm of music.

Before the documentary filming period ended she was involved with a car accident that would tragically end her life. She was driving an SUV down the road when she swerved to avoid some other vehicles and their SUV flipped; killing her while leaving all the other passengers alive.

What does seem odd is the astounding amount of occult symbolism we find her taking part of during her time in Honduras. For example, she spent time performing yoga, which is an ancient practice that was/is used by many occult practitioners, like Aleister Crowley. There is a claim that the yoga and meditation go hand in hand to allow a person to reach towards enlightenment and perhaps even let a spirit enter one's body. She also studied numerology, an occult belief system that assigns certain attributes or characteristics to numbers. Throughout the documentary you can see that they divided it up into the days that she was there. For instance, on the first day of filming it scrolls a message across the screen that says the number 1 is about knowledge and birth. And it continues through each day, and at one point in the film she explains that she was born on the 27th, which is the number 9 in numerology (you simply add each number until you're down to a single digit value). She explains that 9 is the highest number next to God, and this is significant because it indicates that she was into the Kabbalah and the Tree of Life. This is an ancient Hebrew mystic belief system that uses a visual diagram of 10 circles, called sefirot. The 10th and final sefirot (God) is the manifestation of man into God. Practitioners of Kabbalah believe they can communicate with God by using these sefirot as a path to incorporate different lessons in life. There are various paths they can use to reach the manifestation, and the left line is known for being the line of the feminine. This is yet another similarity with the occult where we see Left Eye traveling down the feminine-left line of the Tree of Life.

Since she was into numerology and the documentary presents the importance of each day and its numerological characteristic, we can take a look at the day of her passing; the *25th*.

Some theorists speculate that she could've been triggered to actually wreck the SUV through an elaborate mind control program, similar to the film *Manchurian Candidate* where the victim has a small section of the mind take over and perform an automated action without the conscious ability to stop it. The support for this theory is that she appears to have a calm, trance-like demeanor just prior to the crash, and perhaps during (although I disagree with all of that because the documentary seems to show otherwise). If she actually wrecked the car on purpose, the only thing that would support the theory would be the fact that she believed she was possessed by a spirit named Nikki (the alter ego I mentioned). During the documentary she says:

"Anytime I got drunk this girl Nikki would show up. When I got drunk I was just a different person. When these two started battling it out I had to create a third person to straighten them out."

She later details an evil twin named Nina as well and that she was creating all of these different personalities and that's when her problems started. This sounds like the problems that occur when people start dabbling in magic and evoking other people's spirits. This also happens in ghost hunting or Ouija board séances where people try to contact the spirit realm and become possessed. It's possible that Left Eye was plagued by these spirits before she went to Honduras and was truly trying to cleanse them away. Her mother, Wanda Coleman said in a Philadelphia Weekly article:

"She said she had a split personality. I don't know if I believe it, but she said she would be another person."

Her mother also had this chilling statement, as website PanacheReport claims:

"Her death was pre-destined. The Lord had already prepared me for Lisa's death two years in advance."

That same article discusses how some of the others who went to Honduras with Left Eye sensed something disturbing before the fatal accident. Her cousin, Jasmine Brodie said:

"The air out there was thick. We were staying where people who were sick went to get well. They would take the herbs to get better, and if they didn't get better they died there. A few people died in the room, and when I was in the room, I felt them ... 'Haunted' is a pretty strong word. But I would say there were spirits in the room."

Left Eye was also in touch with the spiritual realm which included attempts to contact her dead father's spirit, or even Tupac Shakur (who again, also died on the 25th). Her relatives explained that she would sometimes disappear up to days at a time to try and communicate with spirits, and she sometimes claimed she succeeded. Some of the relatives were concerned about her experimenting into the occult. Two years before Left Eye's death her mother had a vision in which she saw her in a casket and felt that she was going to die young. In the final footage before her death, you can see that she's holding a large tin that was allegedly used to hold a set of Tarot cards. A passenger in the back seat clearly asks for "*the cards*" and Left Eye hands them off right before you can hear the SUV skidding out of control.

To make things even worse for Left Eye, she was involved in another car accident just two weeks prior to the fatal car accident that took her life. Left Eye was inside of a van that accidentally hit and took the life of a 10-year old Honduran boy by the name of Bayron Isaul Fuentes Lopez. The accident didn't appear to have any foul play and occurred because the boy was walking alongside a dangerous road. Left Eye and her crew stayed at the hospital with the boy and his family, and even went as far as to pay for his medical expenses and funeral. In the documentary she says she felt a presence of a spirit following her and it may have been a mistake that the boy lost his life and not her. She notes the coincidence of his last name being the same as hers (his was Lopez; while she was Lopes). She believed that a spirit was chasing her:

"*I have premonitions, dreams, I think it's the energy in the air.*"

The final few scenes before the day of filming Left Eye's fatal accident included a chilling shot of Left Eye in her room saying that whatever you fear gets manifested when you're in Honduras. She said it's like going down a hill in a car and not hitting the brakes. Meanwhile, on the wall of the room you can see that she spray painted a giant All Seeing Eye of Horus.

She was also seen holding the dead boy's shoes and says that she felt the spirit that is haunting her had killed the child by mistake. She also said she doesn't believe in death, but rather transformation. "*When someone passes away, look up; a*

198

new star is born." The fact that she was in possession of the boy's shoes is of concern because this is a practice known in the occult as sympathetic magic. Practitioners believe that this use of a material world object would physically link a person to it. This is also used in with voodoo dolls when they inflict pain upon the doll and the person feels it in a similar manner. In fact, this concept holds even more value when you consider that Honduras has a population known as the Garifuna who practice a religion that some compare to Haitian Voodoo. Left Eye's Aunt had suspicions of voodoo involvement because not only did Left Eye die in an odd sequence of events, but her uncle Anthony Lopes also died. He accompanied her to Honduras and stayed after the fatal accident, only to succumb to congestive heart failure just months later.

Even if you don't consider all of the occult coincidences involved with her death, you could also consider that she was a major figure in disrupting the Illuminati money machine known as the music industry. The publicity around the bankruptcy of TLC brought out this side of Left Eye and she wasn't bashful about explaining her side of the story. At the Grammy Awards she told the press that you can sell 10 million records and still be broke if you have greedy people behind you (perhaps referring to the handlers within the music industry). In the documentary you can watch her break down the formula of record companies. She said they made about $5.6 million from selling 10 million records, but the record companies paid about $3 million to record the album and they charge the band that amount in order to cover the costs of videos, recording, etc. They pay half of the remaining income to taxes and split the rest; about $300K a piece. TLC claiming bankruptcy was bad publicity for music industry and her explanation of what was going on behind the scenes made it even worse. This included outing producer Dallas Austin, saying he wanted to charge them $4.2 million for beats.

After much infighting between her other members of TLC, in January 2002 she signed with Suge Knight and his Death Row Records (renamed Tha Row at this point). She was supposed to release a solo album under a new alias with the name N.I.N.A. (New Identity Not Applicable). Now you can see six degrees of separation with her channeling of Tupac's spirit and a new relationship with Suge Knight, who Tupac was allegedly indebted to from scandalous deals made while with Knight's Death Row Records shortly before *his* early death (one more time: on the *25th* of the month).

Some theorists claim she was taken out like Aaliyah; just outside of the continental United States. The support for this is that it's easier to kill someone in another country because there is too much media attention and police scrutiny (as is evident by the Tupac and BIG murders). Honduras' police were scouted as potential candidates who would be able to fumble enough facts and keep from meddling too deep into things.

Jennifer Hudson rose to fame through the television talent contest *American Idol*. She would not only win a Grammy for her debut album, but also an Academy Award for her role in *Dreamgirls*. Things were going smooth for her until October 2008 when her mother, brother and nephew were all killed by an ex-husband of Jennifer's sister, Julia. Even though this was a horrific tragedy; theorists claimed that this was part of a package deal she made in order to achieve fame and success. Singer Nicole Scherzinger from the Pussycat Dolls once warned about winning Grammys and Oscars in a deal with the Devil in an interview on Independent.co.uk:

"This is such a tough industry, you know. To make it, you really have to sell your soul to the devil." And has she? She turns back to face the mirror, and closes her eyes. Her make-up artist resumes her work. *"No, I haven't. That's probably why I haven't quite reached the top of my mountain. I mean, where's my Tony Award, my Grammy, my Oscar? Why don't I have any of those things yet?"*

The allegations against Jennifer Hudson and the sacrifice of her family were so pervasive that she was asked by fans on a U-Stream about it:

"I'm so glad someone brought this Illuminati mess up because only a child of God would address it. That is the most ignorant thing I have ever heard in my life. And it's offensive because basically what? The people that are here today don't deserve to be where they are? What, we didn't work for it? So I find—and I hate to go there—but I find it's those that can't make it that would probably join Illuminati, or whoever that is, to get somewhere.

Don't listen to that type of stuff, don't follow that stuff because those people are only luring you in to become a part of some mess like that, so know that you're only falling victim. That's their way of gaining [followers]. I'd advise you to stay away from it. Those who are reading it are falling into it. It could not be more untrue."

She also addressed it on an interview with Washington DC's *Majic 102.3* (how appropriate the radio station is "Majic"...):

"I think people find a way to discredit people in everything you do. Nothing is ever what it really is. And at the

201

end of the day, we all work hard for what we get and what we do just like anyone else. And it's unfair that some people would be that cruel to impose such negativity on things that is done from a positive place and perspective. And t's very hurtful and extremely upsetting. Especially coming from a Christian standpoint.

Every time I hear stuff like that, I'm like 'You will not take the credit for God's work and give it to Satan. Not on my watch. Not on my watch.' So again, it's extremely upsetting. There's so much to be said about that, but you don't have the time, and neither do I."

Some claim that the death of Run DMC's DJ, Jam Master Jay, benefitted Rev Run because it coincided with the success of *Run's House*. Jam Master Jay died on October 30th, 2002 (*a time period known for pagan sacrifice rituals during Halloween known as Samhain), which was three years prior to Rev Run's debut of *Run's House* which was created by Sean "Puff Daddy" Combs. This show was a launch point for Run's son "Diggy" who is now a rapper and started a clothing line with Pharrell Williams.

Before achieving fame, 50 Cent released a song in 2000 called *Ghetto Qu'ran*. On this song he talks about drug dealers from his local Jamaica, Queens stomping grounds and this led to a music industry blacklisting of 50 Cent at the advice of Kenneth "Supreme" McGriff who was allegedly the one who set up the shooting of 50 Cent. Jay ignored the blacklisting and brought 50 Cent into the rap game, only to be murdered a few years later.

Detroit rapper, Proof, came up with Eminem and he used the chorus from 50 Cent's *Ghetto Qu'ran* on his last album called *Searching for Jerry Garcia* that was released in **2005** (there's another 2 and 5; 2+0+0+5=7), precisely 10 years to the day after the death of Jerry Garcia; implying both that Proof is 'searching the afterlife' and also a ritualistic pattern. The album cover depicts Proof clutching death, represented by

202

a skeleton. Only months later, Proof would be murdered during an altercation at a club in Detroit on the now infamous 8 Mile Road. People claim Eminem had something to do with the blood sacrifice of Proof, citing his dark lyrical content and subtle hints of demonic possession and regret of Faustian bargains in his lyrics.

In a 2004 video for Eminem's *Toy Soldiers*, he shows Proof getting shot and killed outside of a club with an homage at the end to slain rappers Tupac, BIG, and Big L.

There are *many* more examples being thrown around with connections to blood sacrifice. In fact there are so many you could devote an entire book to this fascinating, yet morbid topic. Some claim that Whitney Houston was a goddess sacrifice used by Nicki Minaj to advance her career (citing the oddity that Houston's daughter was found unconscious in a bathtub in the *same* hotel, on the *same* floor just one night prior). Others say she was taken out by the Norwood family of R&B singer Brandy and her brother Ray J. Some go as far as to say Brandy was setup to take over Whitney Houston's role as the R&B goddess, but she was supposed to sacrifice her first born and couldn't bear to do it. Ray J allegedly stepped up and made the Kim Kardashian sex tape and somehow that all links into him getting the glory for Houston's sacrifice.

Other examples not written about in this book include The Game, Dr. Dre/Nate Dogg, Cam'ron/Big L, Jim Jones/Stack Bundles, Soulja Boy, Ludacris/Camouflage, TI/Dolla, James Prince/Pimp C, Lil Wayne/Static Major, Chief Keef, Lady Gaga with the eerily similar Lina Morgana, and many more. A theorist named James Downard claimed there was a process used by the Freemasons in order to assassinate JFK known as the Killing of the King ritual in his *King-Kill/33: Masonic Symbolism in the Assassination of John F. Kennedy*, an essay in the book *Apocalypse Culture*. Theorists cite this King-Kill 33 ritual as a process that continues to this day behind the veil of the music industry.

This concept of Illuminati blood sacrifices is *by far* the most controversial and unsubstantiated part of the conspiracy theory world. It's all wild and unrealistic stuff, but it's out there in the dark recesses of the web so I thought I'd enlighten the reader of some of the ideas that are floating around. I'd like to reiterate that I think *most* of it is irreverent and I am in no way advocating them to be true, even though *some* of them have a kernel of truth worth looking into. Most particularly the murders of Tupac and BIG seem to indicate foul play, because they were evidentially part of a conspiratorial cover-up that was successful since they remain unsolved after all of these years. The real question to ask is where all of these various sacrifices and occult practices are designed to lead us. By now the reader should be full of questions that I hope to resolve in the next section where we see the agenda truly unfold.

Chapter 7- The Unveiling of the Agenda

So what are true hip hop fans left with in the present time period of 2010s? Is it a music industry that has sucked the life from the creative force of an MC and a DJ and repackaged it as they see fit to make a profit? Is it the natural progression from a fun loving party environment of harmony, expanding into the various regions that artistically express the socio-economic factors they are dealing with? Does art imitate life or does life imitate art? One could argue that hip hop is *all* of these things.

"Reality is wrong. Dreams are for real"
- Tupac Shakur, *Tupac Resurrection*

Many have said that rap music would never last and it would die a quick death. That is being proven both true and false at the same time. Rap is 35+ years in the making and it doesn't appear to be going anywhere. The violent content raised its popularity to levels unheard of. The crossover into pop music has made rap music both a permanent fixture in the landscape of music, while also eroding away at its authentic traditionalist roots.

The bar for shocking lyrics has been raised so far there is nowhere to go from there but to actually live out these gangsta fantasies full of sex and violence as a way of emulating today's celebrities. The confused and attention seeking fans feel the need to follow suit and live these lifestyles out, promoting their own "brand" on Twitter or Facebook. The quest for obtaining street cred and being more misogynistic or appalling than the next person is the new formula that survived the test of time, whether we like it or not. The unfortunate thing is that 'we are what we eat' on an energetic level. The frequencies we absorb through music can take affect inside of us and mold our perceptions of the outside world. If you listen to enough music that glorifies drinking water, you'll find yourself thirsty for the water. If you watch enough television shows about cooking food, you'll find yourself hungry. That's because images and sounds work on us at a subconscious level.

Rap had only become a "problem" when white America became interested. And what was it that made the white audience listen? Violence. Hollywood and the west coast brought gangsta rap onto the scene, when rap actually started with a positive and motivational message on the east coast. During the 'gangsta rap golden age' of the 1990s, ¾ of all rap albums sold went to suburban, white, teenage customers. There is an insatiable desire for guns and violence and that is evident all around us with intense video games and films. The music industry is just another aspect of this twisted death-obsessed culture of ours.

"America is built on the gun. America is in love with the gun. It's a sick love affair. But it's just hard to break."
- Ice Cube

Even though the rap lyrics have negative aspects, the corporations still feed into it because there is a profit to be made. Civil rights leader Delores Tucker exposed a connection between Time Warner and gangsta rap during her campaign against the music genre. This connection was the fact that Time Warner owned 50% of Interscope Records; the financial backers of Death Row Records. Interscope was dropped by Time Warner due to the negative publicity of rap music, but immediately picked up by Seagram's for $200M. Seagram's also owned all sorts of ventures including Universal Pictures and its theme parks, alcohol, etc. Seagram's was trying to expand into the entertainment industry, but eventually had to sell itself to Vivendi.

"Seagram, which makes most of its money manufacturing alcohol, says they don't want to put out hard rap music because of the effect it might have on kids. But let me ask you this: What kills more kids each year? Is it rap music or is it alcohol?"

– Suge Knight (regarding the label drop from Seagram's)

It should also be noted that Seagram's is tied to the Illuminati by theorist Texe Marrs in his book *Codex Magica* and an article on his website called *Jerusalem, Blood and Dynasty: A Look at Edgar Bronfman, Sr.* He claims that the Seagram's founding family, the Bronfman's, are part of a Jewish Zionist agenda. He also shows an advertisement for Crown Royal whiskey (formerly a Seagram's brand) with a serpent wrapped around the bottle with the question "Tempted?" and claims that it is symbolic for Satan worship because of the serpent and its coiling like an 'S' around the bottle.

There are countless conspiracy theories that tie big corporations into the Illuminati. The financial interests are too great to ignore. David Icke goes through this in his presentations, showing how the pyramid is a perfect shape to reflect how it is all structured. Acts like Jay-Z or Kanye West are nowhere near the top of the pyramid. The apex is comprised of people you and I have never heard of. The ultra-wealthy that have so much money they want to pursue something else; control.

One aspect of the control perspective is the Hegelian Dialectic. This idea is the concept that you can create a circular logic to force reactions from the unsuspecting in order to push an agenda against their will. David Icke more eloquently points this out as the Problem-Reaction-Solution method. A problem gets fabricated, the public reacts, and a pre-determined solution is presented to alleviate said problem. It's a clever design used to keep people in a prison without bars. Slavery works better if the slaves don't know they're enslaved.

An example for this could be illustrated as such: the record companies push gangsta rap with lyrics about gun violence. The same company who owns the record company owns a media outlet, so they put all gun violence stories to the top (under the credo 'if it bleeds it leads'). The problem here is clearly gun violence. The problem comes to a head when it starts to affect the masses (we'll say the middle class suburban white demographic). This is done through a coordinated false flag event that is staged and we'll say that is a school shooting in the "heartland." The people are now in fear (there's your reaction) and demand a solution for safety. The people who own the record company and media outlet pay lobbyists to hook politicians up to PAC funds, and they propose the idea of gun control (your solution). Problem (guns)-Reaction (fear)-Solution (gun control).

   "80% of the media that we hear, read or see is controlled by six companies"
   - Steve McKeever, founder of Hidden Beach Recordings

   Of course that was a hypothetical scenario just to illustrate how the theory goes; I'm not advocating gun control laws, or the blocking of gun control laws. I'm just pointing it out with one of the most common situations that conspiracy theorists rave on and on about. Conspiracy theorists apply the P-R-S model to most "false flag" events as an attempt of the Illuminati to strip away freedoms.

   We've seen what happens when someone disrupts the master agenda of the controllers of media. Whatever you'd like to believe about the events surrounding 9/11 is debatable, but what is factual is the overwhelming response by the entertainment industry in helping paint the 'official story' of what happened. Here's an example to convey what I'm suggesting: In 2003 at a concert in London, lead singer of the Dixie Chicks, Natalie Maines, spoke out against the US invasion of Iraq. Radio stations stopped playing their songs, Lipton dropped their sponsorship, and fans bulldozed their albums. Whether or not these things were staged and planned out is another conspiracy one should consider. Were the corporations who stood to profit from the wars involved? It's not too far of a stretch to be possible. Country musicians like Alan Jackson proceeded to release songs like *Where Were You (When the World Stopped Turning)* and Toby Keith released *Courtesy of the Red, White and Blue*; all songs that drummed

210

up patriotism in this trying time. We also have songs about 9/11 that could potentially have a more occult basis. For instance, Jay-Z and Alicia Keys had the previously mentioned song *Empire State of Mind* that could've had an esoteric message:

"*Hail Mary to the city you're a virgin, And Jesus can't save you, life starts when the church ends*"

What does that mean? Is he talking about the "sacrifice" of the "virgin" being the destruction of the twin towers? The twin towers might've been desired targets of the occult because of their resemblance to the twin pillars of Freemasonry; Boaz and Jachin. These supposed symbols of Saturnian worship were found in the original Solomon's Temple and represent the entrance to a sacred and mysterious place. Smashing them might've been a desire by practitioners of occult belief systems. Fleetwood Mac released a song in 2003 called *Illume (9/11)* that could be coded to be saying "Illuminati 9/11" if you wanted to be overly paranoid about things. The word 'Illume' is referencing the light bearer of Lucifer. Luciferianists use symbolism and occultism on a regular basis in order to glorify human progression and enlightenment, attributing mankind's success to Lucifer. They use the morning star of Lucifer to represent free thinking and independence from things like organized religion. These ideals are all traits of the Illuminati secret society, and the fact that we see most of that word in the title *Illume (9/11)* makes one question whether or not there is a secret message being conveyed.

Another idea that lies further down the paranoia side of the spectrum is that of the Archons and reptilian shape shifters

211

that was highlighted earlier. The theory suggests that they feed off the negative energy as a form of sustenance and they are able to enter our dimension with it. David Icke claims that they seek to harness pre-puberty energy from children because it is of greater value and richness to them. He suggests that there are so many missing children because they get pulled into these rings of ritual abuse and are sacrificed to these energy absorbing Archon entities. While this is pretty far-fetched stuff, there is definitely an issue of missing children that staggers the mind (literally hundreds of thousands just disappear annually in the US). We hear of child pedophilia rings on an all-too regular basis, while seeing a trend of over-sexualization of the youth. It seems that the film and music industries want to activate the sexual energies of these young people at an increasing rate and perhaps that is to satisfy the Archon overlords.

The Archons are characterized as having an inability to be creative. This could support the theory of music industry-mind control because they would obviously need creative artists to get the message out since they're unable to do it on their own. Professor Griff spoke about the origins of rock and roll coming from black artists like Chuck Berry and Little Richard; only to be taken over by white artists. He alludes to the idea that black people have a trend of creating material, only to later abandon it and hand it over to other races (e.g. Asian people dominate the b-boy scene, white people like Kaws are now the famous graffiti artists, and R&B has been taken over by white people like Robin Thicke, Justin Timberlake, and Justin Bieber). R&B was a genre that used to celebrate femininity and make them feel good about themselves but it is now being turned into a more thuggish environment with the men covering themselves in tattoos and talking about using women for the night. These are traits of

Archon manipulation because they take things that are already in existence and invert/pervert them to fit their agenda.

The Archons are supposedly orchestrators of a higher level of trickery and are projecting a virtual reality world upon us. Icke claims that they project a frequency from the planet Saturn and this frequency is sent down to Earth in order to trap us into a certain low density energy that keeps us from becoming *truly* enlightened. This sounds like an exotic idea but in all reality many mainstream people echo it. For example, on Oprah's *Super Soul Sunday* show from April 29th, 2012, Deepak Chopra said the following:

"In the movement towards enlightenment where you are is the point of arrival. The way we are educated in the West there is always some point of arrival. so everybody is looking for the future and they're never in the present so when they arrive at the future it's not there for them because they're not present for it. If you get the idea that this is the moment that you have, it's the only moment that you have, then you live in the present and you move with the flow. Because this is the point of arrival, right now."

-Deepak Chopra, interview with Oprah Winfrey

We see symbolism in music videos and on rapper's albums that suggest they have allegiance to a darker side. When we see Drake wearing a necklace of the Owl of Minerva, or producer Mike Will Made It sporting a cap with the bull God Moloch while doing the Mano Cornuto hand gesture (the Devil horns) on it, we have to wonder if they aren't providing an energetic "shout out" to their true masters. We've seen the symbolism of the All Seeing Eye or even the 666 hand over the eye from multiple rappers and pop singers. That includes:

213

Lil Wayne
Jay-Z
Kanye West
Rihanna
Nicki Minaj
50 Cent
Dr. Dre
Pharrell Williams
Michael Jackson
French Montana
Bruno Mars
Future
The Game
Eminem
Waka Flocka Flame
Jason Derulo
Kid Cudi
Drake
Tyler
Wiz Khalifa
MC Lyte
Kendrick Lamar
Lady Gaga
Willow Smith
Ke$ha
Iggy Azalea
Justin Timberlake
Beyoncé
Justin Bieber
Ciara

The symbolism they are displaying is an energetic exchange the listener participates in. This is all part of the magic ritual; it requires an active and willing audience. Professor Griff mentions that rap music is constructed like nursery rhymes, which were used as a tool to teach and instruct infants. These things penetrate into our subconscious through the use of music. Witches perform incantations and magicians cast spells in a similar manner. All of these things focus on sending messages and energy into a realm of the unseen. An example of this would be the pervasive use of rap music and hip hop in advertising. They are using it as a tool for programming tastes and desires. Eminem worked with iTunes, soda companies like Sprite and Pepsi have had countless rappers like Nas and Fat Joe, and HP worked with Jay-Z and Dr. Dre to advertise products.

Another reason why we might be coerced into witnessing these magic rituals is to support a pact the artist made with the Illuminati or worse yet, the Devil. In Freeman Fly and Jamie Hanshaw's *Weird Stuff (Operation Culture Creation)* first book they explain a concept of satisfying a pact:

The foundation of black magic is the pact or contract. It is primarily focused on the art of conjuring up spirits from the lower planes by means of a secret process of ceremonial magic in order to gain their help. True black magic is a contract with a spirit, where, for a time, the magician becomes the master of the spirit he has summoned. The demon agrees to serve the conjurer for the length of his earthly life, and after death he will become the servant of the demon. The magician would sign the contract with his own blood according to the magic axiom: "he controls the soul who controls the blood of another." When the magician binds an elemental to his service, a battle of wits ensues, which the demon eventually wins. For this reason the black magician will attempt to prolong his life as much as possible.

This could explain why the rappers us their lyrics in this "battle of wits" to fight the demons.

"Tripping while I'm slipping, busy fighting off these demons."
– A$AP Rocky, *Lines*

"But it just dawned on me you lost a son, demons fighting you, it's dark, Let me turn on the lights and brighten me and enlighten you"
– Eminem, *I Need a Doctor*

"Is it truth or it's fiction, is it truth or it's fiction? Is Hova atheist? I never fuck with True Religion, Am I down with the devil cuz my roof come up missin'? Is that Lucifer juice in that two cup he sippin'? "
– Jay-Z, *Devil Is a Lie*

"I pray to God I ain't ever dying broke, If I ever owe you, you ain't ever going broke, Everything you seen been the realist shit you saw, What the business is keep minds on Allah, Devil want my soul, Bitches turn me cold, Bottle after bottle watching bitches on a pole, Promise never fold, Money never fold, Getting money fast, watchin' niggas dying slow. "
– French Montana, *Devil Wants My Soul*

"Ooh devil wants my soul, Self made millionaire! No nigga I owe"
– French Montana, *Devil Wants My Soul*

"I'm possessed by evil demons that torture me while I'm sleeping, I keep dreaming of death and I'm hearing people

screaming, The devil's spirit's trapped inside me and I want out "
   − Eminem, *Demon Inside*

  "Look at my scalp real close and you'll see triple sixes, There's no doubt I'm all about a dollar, I just signed a lifetime contract with the funeral parlor "
   − Big L, *Devil's Son*

  This concept doesn't exist solely in rap music either; here are the Rolling Stones describing it explicitly when referencing a troubadour, or "a poet who writes verse to music":

  "Let me please introduce myself, I'm a man of wealth and taste, And I laid traps for troubadours, Who get killed before they reach Bombay "
   − The Rolling Stones, *Sympathy for the Devil*

  But that's not to say that all rappers are promoting the Devil. Mobb Deep's Prodigy has been an outspoken critic of the evil ways of the music industry, including these lyrics:

  "I don't care if you the pope, the president, or prime minister, king, queen, prince or princess, You just fronting for the public and you fronting for the press, But behind closed doors, What really goes on is, Ritualistic, cannibalistic, sadistic, masochistic, Some real sick shit "
   − Prodigy, *Black Devil*

  Perhaps this is why we see rappers like Will.i.am featuring transhumanism promos in his videos and doing publicity stunts like blasting his song called *Reach for the Stars* from outer space. He supports this transhumanism movement that seeks to supplant the human body for a digital consciousness in an effort to live forever. If these people sign pacts with the Devil for their soul, they would want to stick around here as long as possible, and that requires an integration of technology. This is why we see Will.i.am and Beyoncé glorifying cyborgs and helping push that idea of human augmentation. It makes it acceptable and cool to the youth so that someday they can instill this "mark of the beast" and upload their souls to a digital medium and never have to pay their debt back to the Devil.

A self-proclaimed former witch and "Illuminati insider" named John Todd came out during the peak of Satanic Panic in the 70s-80s to warn the planet of the occult belief system inside of the music industry. Although many claim he was a right wing fraud, he did manage to drop some pretty interesting knowledge before he disappeared from the conspiracy theory scene. He claimed to be from a family of high priestess witches and a bloodline within the Illuminati. He said that he spent time as a manager of Zodiac Productions, a company that would allegedly go on to form virtually all of the other music outfits. He claimed that while at the record company he witnessed and helped enforce the mandatory enlistment of every rock band into a witch coven before they got a contract. He said that the master recording of every album was taken to a satanic temple room that had pentagrams and witches. They would perform rituals to conjure up demons to follow every single copy of this master recording. The reason they would do this is because witches can't cast spells on Christians so they must "accept the music" as a backdoor way of taking in the spell.

While I believe these claims are bold and most likely false (for example there was never even a recording company called Zodiac Productions as far as I could tell); the concept is very much possible. Even if you and I don't believe the spells are real, the people that practice this do. It doesn't even take a deep rooted belief in the occult to back this up either. This concept of magical words and the power of the voice can all be tied into actual scientific experiments. The philosopher and mathematician Robert Hooke studied these types of things in the late 1600s while he was in the Royal Society. Hooke studied a field of science called Cymatics in which he would study the formation of patterns in flour. A plate would be vibrated with a bow, and the flour on top of the plate would form into certain patterns. This field of Cymatics studies the movement of matter into an organized pattern with vibrations, and this could just be an extension of being able to affect the material realm through the vibration of the vocal chords (e.g. talking, singing, or rapping). In the Bible's Book of Genesis, it literally claims that God *said* "Let there be light" and there was light. The water experiment from Dr. Emoto showed us that there are inherent properties of harmonious characteristics that water molecules will align to for positive words or thought (or not so harmonious for the negative ones), so one could see that certain frequencies of the unseen have a real effect on the material world; whether positive or negative.

The spectrum of electromagnetism is the range of all possible frequencies that electrical and magnetic waves will propagate through, but scientists believe there may be more than that in existence. Visible light is only a small band of frequencies within this huge electromagnetic spectrum, effectively making everything we can see with our eyes merely just illusions defined as objects vibrating at a certain wavelength.

To sum all of this up: it seems that nonphysical things like thoughts, prayers, or the spoken word, are able to cause changes in the physical world.

Taking a look at the demon known as Rain Man again, one could see why these rappers are worshipping it. The rain is an analogy for water, and the Age of Aquarius is denoted as the time in which the water carrier reigns supreme. This links us right back into the occult belief systems I talked about in previous chapters where Aleister Crowley believed he was bringing us into the New Age, or the Aeon of Horus aka the Age of Aquarius. It also links into the Crowley beliefs in the Kabbalah where rain signifies the downpour of material blessings from the spiritual realm and into the physical. This might explain why we see a disproportionate number of celebrities sporting the Kabbalah beliefs; they want the financial blessings poured upon them. Lil Wayne says he's going to *make it rain*" and perhaps that's on a deeper level than just dollars flying through the strip club we've been led to believe in. This could also be a reference to the ancient deities of Mesoamerica and the Middle East like Moloch who the people would sacrifice humans to in order to gain favor and hopefully receive the rain and blessings from.

The Mayan people believed that underground caves with networks of rivers (called "cenotes") were pathways to the underworld. They thought the waters were somehow pulled up by the gods and dropped as rain, so they would hold rituals and sacrifices at places like the Sacred Cenote at Chichen Itza to the rain God, Chaac. The Maya would take a child sacrifice and paint his face blue before taking him to the deepest underground point before the priest would sacrifice him and toss him into the rivers as an offering to Chaac.

We can also link all of these things back into the theories of Saturn being the basis of all occult beliefs due to some hidden secret with its origins. For example, a commenter inside of the IlluminatiWatcher.com community named Fleurdamour made a very interesting correlation between the planet Saturn and the sign of Aquarius:

"It also mentions that in the old astrological system (before the outer planets were discovered when the telescope was invented) the **sign Aquarius was associated with the planet Saturn** *instead of Uranus as it is now. Which gives a whole new spin to the concept of the Age of Aquarius..."*
- Fleurdamour on Illuminati symbolism on Michael Jackson's *Xscape* album

In Stephen Flowers' *Lords of the Left-Hand Path* book he describes the zodiacal sign of Aquarius being ruled by Saturn and how the Fraternitas Saturni (Brotherhood of Saturn, aka F.S.) magical order subscribes to the notion that we are in fact transitioning into this Age. However, they paint a picture of the New Age in stark contrast to what the hippie movement advertised. The F.S. believe this time will be one in which the spiritually enlightened will grow in power, referring only to their occult brethren. The F.S. (and other occult practitioners) will be able to use magic as a tool for transforming others into followers through the 33 degrees of the Saturnian system, to the point where everyone will be able to reach 'self-deification' at the culmination of the left-hand path. Of course, Flowers also details how these groups of magicians worship Saturn because they believe it embodies Satan, or Lucifer (for various reasons; one being the 6th planet in the solar system, and even further back it was believed to be the outer most planet; hiding in the darkness).

In the Bible there is also an interesting verse that some claim talks about the ancient worship of Saturn as well:

"You have taken up the tabernacle of Molek and the star of your God Rephan, the idols you made to worship. Therefore I will send you into exile' beyond Babylon."
- Acts 7:43

While that might seem fairly innocuous to those who don't really understand what the verse is saying, Wikipedia claims that the Greek forms of this translation changed the original Hebrew language and switched out the letters for 'k' with 'r', and 'ph' for 'v'. That means instead of Molek (or Moloch) being the star of the God Rephan, Molek would be the star of the God Kewan. This could be the truncated form of the Old Babylonian Kayawanu, which was the **planet of Saturn**.

In the last few paragraphs we've connected Moloch, Saturn, Satan, Kabbalah, Aleister Crowley, and the Age of Aquarius. For years on IlluminatiWatcher.com I've been presenting the argument that music videos and films are inundated with symbolism from each of these realms of occult beliefs. With added speculation using this symbolism, we can see that the music industry could very well be under the controls of a sinister force. Many people enter into the music industry and end up making radical changes in their outward behavior or mannerisms, suggesting that they've been exposed to something frightening and all they want to do is revert back to their former selves and give up all of the fame and fortune. We've seen complete metamorphosis happen from rappers like DMX. For example, here are lyrics to DMX's *Let Me Fly* from 1998:

"I sold my soul to the devil, and the price was cheap, A yo it's cold on this level cause it's twice as deep, But you don't hear me, ignorance is blissing and so on, Sometimes it's better

to be taught dumb, Shall I go on, You don't want no real, what the deal is a mystery, How is it I can live and make history? If you don't see it then it wasn't meant for you to see, If you wasn't born with it then, it wasn't meant for you to be"
    - DMX, *Let Me Fly*

It seems he was professing the arrangement that allowed him to go on to sell millions of records and reach the top of the charts. Over the course of the next 15 years he would prove to live a tumultuous life while releasing hit records. This included multiple run-ins with the law including weapons charges, drug possessions, stints at rehab and mental health, and bankruptcy.

In 2006 DMX released a single from the album *Year of the Dog... Again* called *Lord Give Me a Sign* in which he seems to be confessing his turning away from the same evil force that sped him to stardom:

"Devil I rebuke you for what I go through, And trying make me do what I used to, But all that stops right here, As long as the Lord's in my life I will have no fear"
    – DMX, *Lord Give Me a Sign*

That was his first album to **_not_** debut at number one the Billboard charts.

In 2013 DMX appeared on the *Dr. Phil* show and told him that the Devil propositioned him, which is why you hear his conversations with the Devil on his albums.

"To make a fair decision you have to be aware of both sides, and I was approached so of course I had a conversation." – DMX, *Dr. Phil* show

It seems that once you decide to break free from the choke hold of the music industry and not push their agenda, you find yourself falling into obscurity and being on the wrong end of the law. Other prominent rappers have tried to switch sides as well, including Mase, who came up during the reign of Puff Daddy's Bad Boy label during the Tupac-BIG manufactured "feud." In the previously mentioned book by Mark Curry: *Dancing With the Devil: How Puff Burned the Bad Boys of Hip-Hop* he reveals why we saw Mase switch from flashy gangsta rapper to a minister preaching the gospel:

"When Mase got busted in 1998, it dawned on him that he had fallen for the hype about hip hop. He wasn't the hard-core thug that he rapped about, and he was smart enough to realize that young dudes were trying to do the things that he rapped about. Being incarcerated opened Mase's eyes just like it does for a lot of young cats."

Reading on, it makes known that Mase saw the video for *Hate Me Now* with Puff and Nas on crosses and told fellow rapper Foxy Brown that "*Rap music is the devil*" and invited her to abandon the scene and pursue gospel. She didn't accept his offer, citing that she thought he was losing his grip on reality.

Another rapper by the name of Amil was the female voice that can be heard on Jay-Z's *Can I Get A...* song from the *Rush Hour* soundtrack. She landed a career with Jay-Z's Roc-A-Fella Records but was dropped shortly thereafter. Some claim that she left the industry because she didn't like what she was exposed to, with some websites claiming she specifically said she was being forced to make deals with Satan:

"The more money she made, the more deals she had to make with Satan"

In her album, *A.M.I.L.* she makes some pretty bold statements in her lyrics that support this whole theme and perhaps reference the propositions made to her by Jay-Z:

"You said, "Amil I want you to meet a good friend of mine
His name is Money and we partners till the end of time"
Introduced me to your clique, hate, envy, lust and greed
Said you want the whole world in ya custody
And if I give you my soul you'll give me luxuries
Said you could hit me up wit power, it's just up to me
I turn you on when I'm in short skirts and tight jeans
You want my kids to write Santa and celebrate Halloween
Told me sell my people crack and get rich off fens
You love the number six but hate the number thirteen"

And there is much more implying Illuminati knowledge on the track with even more references to the All Seeing Eye of Horus, prison conspiracies, and the New World Order:

"...I see your eye watching me on the dollar bills...

...You used to smile every time I pledge allegiance to the flag...

...When we was cool you used to tell me all your visions
Like how you gonna rule the nations under one religion
You got this New World order, it's like a big prison
You said you wanna be worshipped from noon to noon..."

The Fugees released an album in 1996 called *The Score* that sold over 17 million copies and toned the gangsta image of rap music down quite a bit. In a 1996 *Newsweek* article on the Fugees being the "New Conscience of Rap", Lauryn Hill stated:

"We're trying to do something positive with the music because it seems like only the negative is rising to the top these days. It only takes a drop of purity to clean a cesspool."

After the success of *The Score*, the members of the Fugees branched off and started solo projects, with Lauryn Hill being the first to really blow up as a solo artist. Her 1998 album *The Miseducation of Lauryn Hill* successfully blended elements of rap, R&B, soul, and pop in a revolutionary way, selling over 12 million copies in the process. She won five Grammys and was credited for having the first hip hop album to be named Album of the Year at the 41st Grammys.

Shortly after the success of *Miseducation* would sink in, groups came forward and sued her for allegedly not citing them on her works (New Ark- an outfit of music producers). She fought the allegations but wound up allegedly paying close to $5M to settle it. This marked the beginning of her "unraveling."

An article in *Rolling Stone* titled *The Mystery of Lauryn Hill* attempted to put the pieces together and notes that her 2001 *MTV Unplugged* album had some signs of disturbance:

In 2001, she recorded her MTV Unplugged 2.0. Few bought the album, but many talked about how she could be heard on the record breaking down in tears and saying, "I'm crazy and deranged . . . . I'm emotionally unstable," and repeatedly rejecting celebrity and the illusions that make it possible. "I used to get dressed for y'all; I don't do that anymore," she said on the album. "I used to be a performer, and I really don't consider myself a performer anymore . . . . I had created this public persona, this public illusion, and it held me hostage. I couldn't be a real person, because you're too afraid of what your public will say. At that point, I had to do some dying."

After *Miseducation's* success, the industry had plans of turning her into the next multimedia star with movie role offers for *The Matrix, Charlie's Angels, The Bourne Identity,* and *The Mexican,* but the experience she had with the New Ark lawsuit seemed to change her outlook on the industry, while perhaps also exposing her to something evil, as that *Rolling Stone* article describes:

Friends say she wanted to get out but didn't know how. "It was tough for her to admit all that to someone," a friend says. "So I think she spoke to God, and maybe it wasn't God, but **somebody showed up.***"*

She started spending more time with a spiritual mentor named Anthony Hill, yet nobody was certain what precise religion he followed:

"I don't think he had a religion," a friend says. "I think he was more like, 'My interpretation of the Bible is the only interpretation of the Bible. I'm the only one on earth that knows the truth.'"

She was also showing signs of the MKULTRA-type mind control:

Several of Hill's friends and associates are clearly worried about her. "She's Dr. Jekyll and Mr. Hyde," one says. "But not,

227

like, two faces but, like, eight faces of that. You don't know who you're gonna get from one hour to the next. Not just one day to the next but one hour."

Her Fugees bandmate, Pras, also suggested she was 'fighting demons':

"Sometimes people gotta find themselves, man," Pras says. "I don't believe that's crazy. People go through certain things, they gotta fight certain demons, and she's entitled to do that.

Granted, the term 'fighting demons' is used as a metaphor for someone battling internal struggles; not necessarily evil, but looking at all of her other signs of trouble I wonder if there isn't more to the story than what we know. She's caused quite a stir in the eyes of the Illuminati by having children with Bob Marley's son (some theorists allege that the CIA tried to take Marley out for being a revolutionary; akin to Tupac), alleging the Vatican was covering up molestation of children, and releasing songs like *Fearless Vampire Killer* with lyrics that potentially spoke out against this entire Illuminati agenda I've been laying out:

Watch yourself up in the realm
Watch yourself up in the front
You didn't come up with nothing
These are fuckin' liars
Holes in your pocket, and
now you're a department store buyer

You never had money now your whole Op's about cash
Come on find a new topic

You got kids in the street listening to this SHIT
You going to kill them just to make a profit

Months after the release of that song, she was charged with tax evasion, and eventually sentenced to three months in prison.

Later on, she released a song called *Neurotic Society (Compulsory Mix)* that also seemed to be relaying a message of the Illuminati agenda of vampire sacrifice, supporting the notion that blood sacrifices are conducted by an evil cabal:

They're just looking for a sacrifice
They've been doing this since before Bobby Darrin sang Mack the Knife
Before James Dean's car did a jack knife
Never confuse the head with the butt
Opinions are like assholes and most of them stink
I was told by a woman so rethink
Don't ever let them lead you to drink
Lead you to doubt
Lead you to fall
"Get up stand up/ (And) cast Lucifer out"

In 2012 she released a lengthy diatribe on her Tumblr page that explained why she's been in exile. Among other things, she made some statements referring to the greed, corruption, and manipulation involved with the music industry:

Learning from the past, insulating friends and family from the influence of external manipulation and corruption, is far more important to me than being misunderstood for a season!

229

As this, and other areas of issue are resolved and set straight, I am able to get back to doing what I should be doing, the way it should be done. This is part of that process. To those supporters who were told that I abandoned them, that is untrue. I abandoned greed, corruption, and compromise, never you, and never the artistic gifts and abilities that sustained me."

When she was charged with tax evasion the judge in Newark also ordered her to undergo counseling because she was too outspoken on conspiracy theories and artists being oppressed by the military and media (*note that the original lawsuit that started her down this path of paranoia and mistrust came from a group of producers by the name of New Ark; who hailed from Newark, NJ).

These rappers seem to have a message they want to desperately disseminate, but the industry has no room for it. Part of the overall conspiracy is that if you're not towing the line you're susceptible to the destruction of your public image, with examples being DMX and Michael Jackson. They want to prevent a major comeback if you decide to truly break free and spread a message that goes against their agenda. Malcolm X once said the following prophetic quote:

"If you're not careful, the newspapers will have you hating the people who are being oppressed, and loving the people who are doing the oppressing."

Another rapper that went through a radical transformation is Kanye West. He seemed to change his entire behavior and image, albeit in the opposite direction from DMX, et. al. In 2004 he released his debut album *The College*

230

Dropout and on it was the hit single *Jesus Walks*. The lyrics were as one would expect from a song with that title:

> *"God show me the way because the Devil trying to break me down, (Jesus Walks with me), The only thing that that I pray is that my feet don't fail me now (Jesus Walks) "*
> – Kanye West, *Jesus Walks*

In 2010, he released *My Beautiful Dark Twisted Fantasy* and it featured a song called *Dark Fantasy*:

> *"We stopped the ignorance, we killed the enemies, sorry for the night demons still visit me"*
> – Kanye West, *Dark Fantasy*

Then, in 2011, Kanye was on Snoop Dogg's *Doggumentary* album and said the following:

> *"I sold my soul to the devil that's a crappy deal, Least it came with a few toys and a happy meal"*
> – Kanye West, *Eyez Closed*

Kanye would continue to go further down the eccentric path, including a stint on the radio show *Sway in the Morning* where he got into a heated argument with Sway on what appeared to be a subtle cry for help from the industries that he is involved with- music and fashion. His self-professed "visionary stream of consciousness" included a statement that we're born free, creative artists, only to eventually be controlled by symbols like the Nike sign or Mercedes logo. It appears that he is becoming aware of the ultimate end game of symbolism and Archon control…

In one of Professor Griff's lectures he points out the fact that Kanye West made the cover of TIME magazine in 2005, when the reality of the situation is that the demographic who listen to Kanye West don't read TIME magazine. Why are they doing this? It's a message for the people who read that magazine; politicians and CEOs (aka the Illuminati elite). Rappers don't typically make the cover of TIME; it's generally reserved for politicians and CEOs. The story was teased on the cover with the message *"Defying the rules of rap, Kanye West goes is own way. Why he's the smartest man in pop music."* He was being paraded as the latest experiment in the Illuminati control of hip hop in the article by trying to dilute the message of rap music into pop.

And that leads us up to the overarching plan of the Illuminati. They have successfully infiltrated the hip hop culture and hijacked rap music. What used to be a political movement and symbol of freedom is now being perverted into a bubblegum pop genre used to manipulate the youth and usher in the occult Age of Horus. This is to be expected from the Archon shape shifters who have no creative ability, but rather wait in the shadows and seek the opportunity to take something mankind puts into existence and pervert it to the point of it being unrecognizable from its original concept. Instead of listening to messages of love from Marvin Gaye or The Temptations, the hip hop community is being bombarded with messages of infidelity, sleaziness, violence, drugs, and other negative messages meant to keep spirits down.

The magical rituals are being subjected upon all those who listen and in turn allowing a voice for the Illuminati messages of negativity to support the low vibrational revenue system to exist. The Archons feed off the negative energy while the terrestrial Illuminati enjoy the riches made off the backs of the people who fuel it. The music and imagery supports the concept of child worship; a key attribute of the Age of Horus. Many people are paying for plastic surgery or even getting body hair laser removed in an attempt to capture a more youthful image. Celebrity news conflates in with real world news on the home page of virtually every news website. Many people obsess with the transition of entertainers from childhood stars into adulthood. Artists like Justin Bieber, Selena Gomez, and Ariana Grande have all held the public's fixation when they reached the vital age of 18. Why is this? Is this part of the master agenda of worshipping the new "gods?" I posit this as such, and the agenda will roll on as we see the mainstreaming of rap music and curtailing of messages that will be aimed at the youth, only to later shift into a darker purpose and attract them into the Aeon of Horus.

I still listen to rap music on a regular basis, although I'm finding it slightly more difficult to find acts I can enjoy due to the eye opening process of investigating these conspiracies. I'm not trying to say I'm above this problem of perpetuating violence and supporting these things I've been laying out. I am, however, trying to point out the illusion that is distorting reality and taking advantage of the masses. It really is putting us under a magic trance.

Does this mean listening to this type of music *will* have a negative impact on your life? It's hard to tell. Many people say 'garbage-in, garbage-out' and maybe you could take a step back and look at your life and explore if it has affected you negatively. Do the messages in the music cause you to act in a manner that is incongruent with you true personality? Notions of fear, violence, objectification and overall negativity will take its toll on your psyche if you don't keep it in check. Realistically, all you can do is try to keep an open perspective of what you're listening to and stay above the low vibrational weapons being used to wage the war against the common man and woman.

Afterthoughts and Bonus Material

Since I originally researched and wrote this book I've seen validation of my hypothesis from the hip hop industry. I've decided to include a post-analysis section to the book in order to further illustrate some of the ideas I've presented in *SACRIFICE: MAGIC BEHIND THE MIC*. It came at a time where I decided to correct a few errors in the book (I'm a one-man show, so I've researched, written, AND edited the book; so a few slips squeaked their way through to the final print).

Writing this book has given me some strange publicity… In fact, I was invited to appear on SIRIUS/XM's "*All Out Show*" on Eminem's SHADE45 channel. For those of you that aren't familiar; the show is hip hop themed with hosting duties by "Rude" Jude Angelini (the same "Rude Jude" from the 1990s *The Jenny Jones Show*) and Harlem-based DJ Lord Sear. I'm a long time listener of the show so I half-knew what to expect before I showed up in the Los Angeles studio…

I was in the "green room" waiting for Jude to call me into the SHADE45 studio (Jude is in L.A. while Lord Sear is in NYC). I heard Jude interviewing UFC President Dana White in the meantime but I knew the tone would change once I stepped into his territory. You see; the audience of the *All Out Show* is pretty intense. If you're trying to tell them that the music they love *may* have bad intentions, you might be in for a moderate sized whooping!

Jude called me into the studio on a music break and chatted it up with me on the topic at hand. He told me he was going to let me do my thing since he wasn't well versed in the theories and asked if I would be able to field some questions from the audience. Knowing that I was going to be covering a controversial and hard to grasp concept- I anticipated a rough time, but to me it's all in good fun because that's generally how the show is. The audience of the *All Out Show* like to be argumentative and dismiss anything that is too far out of the bounds of their reality; including the amateur rappers on the *Hate It or Love It* skit who submit songs only to be trounced by the callers and literally told to "go kill themselves." It's all in good fun and feedback, but not for the faint of heart.

After Jude let me talk about a couple of subjects he opened up the phone lines to the audience. *Immediately* they hounded me with irrelevant questions, like asking me if I was ever forced into a mental health facility (*I haven't*), or trying to tell me that Aleister Crowley *wasn't* in the O.T.O. (*not only did he lead the British arm of the O.T.O.; but he added ritualistic degree initiations to it*).

We took a quick music break and Jude tried to coach me through how I should better present my material (which I appreciate greatly- don't let his street talk and slang fool you; he's a smart guy). He suggested that I was going way too deep into the theories for the audience and I should try and give some examples of what I was referring to. I attempted to pull it back together and actually received a call from someone who agreed with me, along with several people on Twitter who were professing that I was speaking the truth. All in all, it was a great experience and it was awesome to sit in the studio with Jude and to appear on one of my favorite radio shows. I believe

I reached a few people, although I had to take several shots to do so. It's bound to happen in this sub-culture of conspiracy theories so I take no regrets with it; in fact I rather find it one of the most valuable experiences I've ever had.

The show left me with new insight into the mind of the masses. I've been on several podcasts and radio shows that explored the fringes of society, but this show was much different. The audience was definitely more of a "proper" proportion of our society as a whole, where most people find these conspiracies silly or not worth their time. They've committed to believing the "official" story that has been spoon fed to them, and they're the ones that continue to keep others in line.

David Icke talks about this phenomenon when he explains that it's much easier for the puppet masters to train us to police one another than it is to try and keep everyone in line. This is exactly what happened when I tried to provide some rational thoughts about what might be happening in hip hop-only to be shouted down with nonsensical accusations. If nothing else, it helped sparked my interest in spreading the word and trying to reach out to those that won't even hear the evidence- similar to David Icke's Terry Wogan incident.

After the show I started to transition into research of the occult on a much deeper level, but that doesn't mean I've forgot to keep an eye open for hip hop symbolism. In fact, I've seen so many symbols and conspiracies in the last year that I would like to briefly cover a few that supports a lot of the ideas presented in *SACRIFICE: MAGIC BEHIND THE MIC*.

I talked about the concept of the blood sacrifice and unfortunately there have been more examples to add to the list. One such example is the rapper named Chinx. He was a member of rapper French Montana's Coke Boys record label

238

and passed away as a victim of a drive-by shooting in Queens, New York in May 2015. Chinx was introduced to French Montana by way of fellow rapper Max B who is now serving a 75 year sentence for a multitude of crimes, including murder.

The theory being floated online is that French Montana set Chinx up for the blood sacrifice with support coming from multiple lines of French's raps including talk of the Illuminati:

> "*I done came from that black hole,*
> *and I popped up in the black robe,*
> *BET awards, Versace black robe,*
> *Four heaters up n*gga that's a hot stove,*
> *Illuminati for the new Bugatti,*
> *Self made who they ask when they ain't got it,*
> *Ten-mill' shield for this holy war...*"
> – French Montana, *Trouble*

> "*...Illuminati? I'm from the streets,*
> *Never sold my body, we takin' bodies*"
> – French Montana, *Work (Remix)*

Earlier in this book I mentioned the fact that Whitney Houston was found dead in a bathtub only one night after her daughter, Bobbi Kristina, was found unconscious in a bathtub in the same hotel. This seemed *more than* strange, so imagine how surprised I was to hear that Bobbi Kristina was found unconscious in a bathtub again in 2015.

Bobbi was engaged to marry a man named Nick Gordon who many thought of as a big brother to her since he was a close associate of the family for several years. Gordon and a friend were the ones that tragically found Bobbi unconscious in their home's bathtub in January 2015 near

Roswell, Georgia- drawing analogies to Roswell, New Mexico where the infamous UFO crash happened in 1947.

The bathtub scene is important to occultists because some claim this is the place where one can be cleansed of their sins before passing into another realm. In ritualistic Kabbalism there is a Supreme Invoking Ritual of the Pentagram which utilizes the top right corner of the pentagram as a symbol for water in order to keep evil at bay. Recall that we saw A$AP Rocky dabbling with magick inside of a pentagram in his video for *Wassup*; because we also see some occult symbolism in his *Long Live A$AP* music video which features the bathtub between black and white pillars (symbolism of the twin pillars of Boaz and Jachin- labeling the entrance to a mystical place).

Could it be that Bobbi was being held in there as some kind of sick ritual?

The Fulton County Medical Examiner determined a cause of death, but the details were kept from the public due to a court order dated September 25th, 2015. The story gets even stranger when we find out that a nurse taking care of Bobbi while she was in hospice turned out to not even be a nurse! She was charged with impersonating a nurse and financial identity fraud; and many question how the outcome of Bobbi's life would've been had it not been for this fake nurse watching over her.

A friend of Bobbi Kristina named Debra Reis Brooks spoke out about her belief that Bobbi wouldn't have got into the bathtub on her own because she has been afraid of bathtubs since her mother's passing:

"Krissi never took a bath, ever never! She was deathly afraid of bathtubs. No way Krissi would have drawn a bath, no way." –Debra Reis Brooks, RadarOnline interview May 22nd, 2015

Bobbi Kristina's alleged drug dealer, Steven Stepho, has also died since the incident, and her cousin Jerod Brown has been taking to social media to make ominous claims like:

"When the smoke clears you'll know everything there is to know."

Bobbi Kristina's viewing was held at the New Jersey Whigham Funeral Home- a location literally *covered* in Egyptian symbolism and owned by a noted Freemason…

Another oddity of 2015 is the February charges of murder against Death Row Records CEO Suge Knight. You may recall that earlier in this book I spoke of Suge's alleged connections with the crack epidemic and various organizations like the gangs of Los Angeles and even the CIA.

The allegations against Suge are that he ran over two men in his Ford Raptor truck after an argument on the set of the NWA film *Straight Outta Compton*. Since his imprisonment he has had a slew of odd medical problems, including passing out in court and talk of a brain tumor. If all of that isn't odd enough; *Rolling Stone* published an article called *The Endless Fall of Suge Knight* where they detailed his associations into the world of gang banging. Knight said that the only one he ever lies to is the police- further pushing the "stop snitching" message I spoke of earlier as well. Here is where the article takes a strange turn when they allege that he truly had close ties to the police:

(One former Knight associate, however, believes the Death Row boss had unusually close ties with law enforcement. "I always [thought Knight was] an informant," says Lake. "The

FBI knows the hip-hop industry, entertainment and drugs on the streets are all intertwined, so you can't find a better informant for the government than Suge Knight – he can infiltrate almost any camp." Knight's lawyer Mesereau calls Lake's assertion "absolute nonsense," and Jones also disputes the idea: "There's a code in the streets. If you don't have real proof, don't call nobody a rat.").

It seems that we may not know the truth of Suge Knight's legacy- especially if his medical problems are true. There seems to be an abnormal amount of power that he wields along with plenty of rumors that connect him with those he clearly tried to distance himself from publically.

The film *Straight Outta Compton* took on some peculiarities besides the Suge Knight situation. There were a couple of symbols embedded that wouldn't have been picked up by the "untrained" eye. For example, there is one part where Eazy-E is contemplating a life changing decision and on either side of him are lamps of opposing colors. One lamp shade is white while the other is black- a classic esoteric symbol conveying the entrance to the unknown. This means the initiate (Eazy-E in this case) is about to be enlightened to higher callings, which is what we find Eric Wright doing before the film's closing.

Conspiracy theories about Eazy-E's acquisition of HIV swirled the internet around this time as footage of Suge Knight revealing that he may have injected Eazy-E with a contaminated needle went viral. Could it be that Suge was blocking Eric Wright's entrance into the "Illuminati?"…

Another symbol from the film worth mentioning is the use of the term "RISE" by one of the rappers. This is akin to Charles Manson's delusions of a Helter Skelter race war because he had his "Family" write the word "RISE" in blood on the walls of victims' homes (at the LaBianca residence). Charles Manson heard this word on The Beatles' *White Album* on tracks *Revolution 9* and *Blackbird* and he believed it was a signal for the black man to rise up and kill white people. There will be more on this in my pending Charles Manson book- so be sure to check that out if you're interested in this topic.

Another newer rapper that didn't make the book was Young Thug. I've written up a full analysis on this rapper and the mystery continues to build. Young Thug and Lil Wayne had a public beef and it came to a head when someone shot at Lil Wayne's tour bus. What is interesting is that there was some predictive programming at hand because the man accused of being the shooter was in a Young Thug video holding the *same* assault rifle while calling someone on his cell phone (which was how the Lil Wayne shooting went down with the recipient of the phone call alleged to be Birdman- although no charges have been made). From Rolling Stone's November 20th, 2015 article:

Jimmy Carlton Winfrey was sentenced to 20 years – 10 in prison followed by 10 on probation – after reaching a plea deal with prosecutors. Winfrey was initially indicted on 30 counts stemming from the April shooting, but as per the deal, he only pleaded guilty to six gang-related charges,

No one was injured in the incident. Winfrey is the only one so far to face charges for the April 26th shooting, even though Cash Money CEO Bryan "Birdman" Williams and rapper Young Thug were named as Winfrey's associates. The shooting occurred just months after Lil Wayne's very public beef with Cash Money, his longtime label, an acrimonious split that resulted in Wayne suing the label for $51 million in January. Birdman denied any involvement.

In the State of Georgia's indictment against Winfrey in July, prosecutors claimed the Young Thug associate opened fire on the tour buses and then attempted to hide the Camaro he was driving at the time. The indictment noted that, five days before the shooting, Young Thug posted an Instagram video that appeared to threaten Lil Wayne; Winfrey and weapons were seen in that video. Similarly, the video for Young Thug's "Halftime" features Winfrey toting an assault rifle that was similar to the firearm used in the tour bus shooting.

After the shooting, Winfrey placed a call to a cell phone owned by Birdman.

One of the key interests surrounding Thug is that he appears to be gay. As of this writing he hasn't come out as gay, but he certainly isn't opposed to letting people believe he might be. There have been images of him wearing female clothes and even watching gay adult films that support the theory. All of this came at a time when Bruce Jenner revealed that he wants to be referred to as a woman named Caitlyn Jenner. I'm not saying there is anything wrong with Young Thug being gay or Bruce Jenner claiming to be a woman; I'm just suggesting that the timing is suspect.

Much like the theory I built in this book about the influential crossover of rap into pop music; it appears to me that there is interest in pushing the image of the androgynous being, or even the hermaphrodite. It makes me wonder if there isn't a coordinated effort to plant this idea into the subconscious because it is in fact occult in origin. While most people know that the liberal elite of Hollywood campaign for equal rights (which I also support); I find it odd that there is such a strong and sudden push for this acceptance.

I'm absolutely supportive of the acceptance of the LBGT movement (I have loved ones in my family that are part of it) - I just want people to understand that occultists believe in an alchemical transformative process that seeks to unite male and female into one being. The alchemical process seeks to merge both hemispheres of the brain as much as it does the feminine with the male. The twin pillars of Boaz and Jachin depict the two polar opposites with the rising middle pillar being the perfected form rising between the two.

Does this mean Caitlyn Jenner is wrong or evil? Do Young Thug's feminist ways void his masculinity?

Absolutely not.

The question I'd like to ask is if there is a coordinated agenda behind them. Keep in mind that Bruce Jenner's entire family is filthy rich for no apparent reason besides their social media presence. Do you think Bruce/Caitlyn is above selling a lie for a quick buck? This is the same thing that I've talked about with Miley Cyrus somehow being the voice of the LGBT community all of a sudden. I don't believe that she's gay at all- in fact up until 2014 the tabloids were always providing updates on her latest boyfriend. Now she has somehow been put on the forefront of the movement as the voice of the LGBT group. If I was a member of the LGBT movement I'd be a bit upset since she's apparently a publicity seeking fraud; or worse yet- a puppet for the Illuminati...

In this book we talked about sex magick and some of the notions that hip hop artists may be taking part of rituals that utilize this occult practice. A song has come out from Ciara and Justin Timberlake called *"Love Sex Magic"* which I find ironic since I also talked about Ciara wearing a jacket with the words "Hermetic Order of the Golden Dawn" in her *Keep On Lookin* music video. So here we see an R&B singer advertising for a magick order which had Aleister Crowley as a member; only to come out with a song that could be referring to the practice of sex magick. I seriously can't make this stuff up.

We saw several music videos continue the effort of the Illuminati by soaking the subconscious realm with more symbolism and mentions of the Illuminati. For example, Drake and Migos released a video for the song *Versace* in which they both reference the Illuminati:

"*Versace Versace, Medusa head on me like I'm Illuminati*"

Further on in the set of lyrical bars we also hear mention of Fritz Lang's influential film *Metropolis* which was of great importance to the Illuminati and occultists due to its messages and portrayal of the Whore of Babylon:

"*Drowning in compliments, pool in the backyard that look like Metropolis*"

Missy Elliott and Pharrell Williams released a video for their collaboration for *WTF* in which Pharrell leaves us with some interesting lyrics as well…

"*I come into this bitch like liquid*
Drip drip, then the business
Click click, get the picture
Hermes Trismegistus
Witness and get lifted
Basic, n*gga I was born in the basement
Shape shift, n*gga I think like a spaceship"

What we see here is Pharrell's expressing his knowledge of the occult by mentioning Hermes Trismegistus who authored the sacred texts that were the foundation for Hermeticism- an esoteric tradition much like the other beliefs that have been handed down through underground secret societies to new initiates deemed worthy. Hermes was in tune with the ancient teachings of alchemy and supposedly was a reincarnation of the Egyptian god Thoth, who was also alleged to be one of the sorcerers of Atlantis.

We also see Pharrell make mention of shape shifters and UFOs; but further down we hear another topic that most would gloss over:

> *"The way that I balance the bars*
> *I never fall*
> *And if I do I just call*
> *The almighty yellow star- God"*

The yellow star he is referring to is also known as Sirius, which brings up a host of ideas in the realm of conspiracy theory. One such idea is the belief of some that our true creator comes from Sirius.

In Theosophy, there are Seven Stars of the Pleiades that transmit energy from the creator to Sirius; which is eventually channeled down to Earth. The Freemasons venerate this "blazing star" by putting it in every Freemason temple. This constellation is also called the Dog Star and is used as the logo and name for the satellite radio company "SIRIUS." I mention this because I find it quite odd that SIRIUS's creator, Martine Rothblatt, is involved with many talking points of the Illuminati. For instance, Rothblatt is a transgender woman who started the Terasem Movement which is a belief in the transhumanism future of the world. Those of you that read my first book know that the path the Illuminati are paving for us includes the revolution of mankind into transhuman robots; so

247

it appears that Rothblatt is one of the pioneers of this. In fact, her spouse (Bina Aspen) was the model for an android named BINA48 that experimented with the idea of downloading a person's consciousness into a robotic form (which I also referenced unknowingly in *A Grand Unified Conspiracy Theory*).

Lil Wayne released a mixtape called *Sorry 4 the Wait 2* in which he mentions a topic we've heard of many times:

> *"I go down and kiss her Pearl Harbor,*
> *She's so down with this New World Order"*

Lil Wayne also got a tattoo of the All Seeing Eye on his face around this same time…

Drake will be releasing an album called *Views from the 6* which supposedly references Toronto, but nobody online can seem to figure *why* it references Toronto. My stab in the dark is that it's a reference to 6-6-6 because he had a concert which flashed three 6's in between flashing images of Rihanna (which stirred up a theory that he's calling Rihanna the Devil).

Diddy and Cassie joined forces to release a fragrance called *3A.M.* which is obviously a reference to the witching hour. Devil worshipers prefer this hour because it is the inversion of 3P.M. which is when Jesus Christ was put on the Cross. Concepts of inversion are of high importance to these practitioners- just like inverting the cross. The videos also shows us Cassie and Diddy romping around in bed choking one another which was another push towards BDSM since this commercial came out around the time of the theatrical release of *Fifty Shades of Grey*.

Big Sean made some big moves in 2015 as he hit the cover of Complex magazine, posing with the All Seeing Eye while dating Ariana Grande. I compiled some of the esoteric symbols behind Big Sean's Complex appearance in an article that examined a promotional video released for the issue. In this video we see symbolism for the Mark of the Beast (the "X") which may be considered equivalent to 666 if you consider that in Greek the letter X (Chi) is the numeric equivalent of 600. If there are three X's we get 666- the number of the perfected 'new world' in Kabbalah.

In Revelations Chapter 13 we hear that people worshiped "the dragon" and "the beast." The beast was *"given a mouth to utter proud words and blasphemies"* which is what we see Big Sean doing when he is rapping about having sex in the missionary position while in a church for Ariana Grande's *Right There* video (*later on Ariana Grande would release a video called *Break Free* in which she takes the Kabbalistic Tree of Life with her to another planet).

At the end of the Big Sean Complex promotional video we see the dissolution of ego and the black sun- a symbol that represents the alchemical transformation. He is the latest initiate to enter into this hidden world of hip hop. Perhaps this is the end result since he and Lil Wayne released their video *My Homies Still* that featured the Batman symbolism and skeletons inside of a movie theater just prior to the actual tragic Aurora Colorado shootings.

There was an effort by several "connected" musicians to start a new music streaming service called TIDAL. This service boasted lossless compression to streaming music as well as exclusive videos. The list of artists with buy-in includes: Beyonce, Nicki Minaj, Rihanna, Kanye West, Madonna, and of course; Jay-Z. The effort wasn't received too well because the promotional videos included audio clips of the artists talking about how the power would be in their hands and showed them making pretentious toasts to one another (*aren't these the *same* rappers bragging about how much money they already have?...).

If you examine the symbolism behind the TIDAL experiment, you'll see the black inverted pyramid and even the All Seeing Eye over Willow Smith. Even deeper into it we can see that the name "Tidal" belonged to a king in the Bible who was a ruler of ancient Mesopotamia. Could it be that these artists believe they are kings of pagan tribes?...

"This is the beginning of the new world." –Kanye West, TIDAL commercial

When Prodigy said *"Illuminati want my mind soul and my body, Secret societies tryin to keep they eye on me"* in *I Shot Ya*, he wasn't far from the truth. In fact, he remains one of the few voices in hip hop that tries to wake the rest of the planet up to the agenda that persists behind the scenes. I believe that there are several pieces of evidence to support this idea, and if you consider the connections I've presented in this book; it could mean that the pace of the agenda is accelerating.

Given my time spent staring into the abyss it appears that the Illuminati (should they truly exist as one cohesive organization) think they're actually doing us a favor. They're pushing the "evolution of consciousness" in an attempt to remove our old ways of thinking and replace it with a new world that will be filled with their beliefs. Some of these beliefs are reasonable- for example equality for all. Others are a bit more sinister- like the destruction of all organized religions; particularly Christianity.

The only way for them to create this world of the "super human" and evolved man is to completely tear down the old one in a nihilistic fashion and pave the way for this new one. I believe that they could use paradigm breaking discoveries like alien life forms to do so. Considering that NASA has made claims that we'll find extraterrestrial life by 2025; it could happen much sooner than expected. Studies indicate that there is a rapid increase in the disbelief of life after death and this is a byproduct of nihilism and the persuasion of the dark arts employed by certain forms of rap music that spread the idea that life is meaningless and without consequence.

Like I mentioned earlier- there is an agenda to make mankind believe they are capable of becoming god or even finding god on their own. This is the final stage of evolution because it marks the end of the human race when we begin to supplant our bodies with robotic elements and computational devices- all in the name of self-improvement and mastery of efficiency. One must ask which path they want to be on before it is too late. The trajectory has long been set by those in power and reinforced by the artists that are selected to become superstars…

"Who wishes to be creative, must first destroy and smash accepted values."
- Friedrich Nietzsche

Appendix

Decoding Illuminati Symbolism

Psychiatrist Carl Jung once said about symbols that their purpose was to *"give a meaning to the life of man."* Catapulted into the mainstream by Jay-Z's infamous Roc-diamond (which only *looks* like a triangle, although he has said that it's a four sided diamond for the 'Roc' in Roc-A-Fella records), the symbolism of the triangle and pyramid are key players in the realm of conspiracy theories and Illuminati symbolism. You can find these symbols in most any big-industry; music, film, corporate logos, etc. But why do we see these symbols so often? What do they truly mean?

Illuminati symbolism is arguably all around us. While one could argue that the symbols of the triangle, pyramid, or All Seeing Eye are merely self-seeking paranoid delusions, it also begs the question why we see the same forms of imagery in corporate logos, films, and music videos. This section is attempting to explore the various symbols representing the sun, pyramids, All Seeing Eyes, the cube, and why they're considered Illuminati symbolism.

First, we must understand how the Illuminati operate. The "Illuminati" is an alleged group of the top elites who seek to control humanity through various avenues of control (e.g. media, film, music, etc.). Without going too far in depth, the Illuminati holds occult beliefs that are hidden from the common man and woman. As to what these beliefs are, and perhaps *why* they hold these beliefs; there are various theories which I won't get into here. If you want to get more into that check out my book *A Grand Unified Conspiracy Theory: The Illuminati, Ancient Aliens, and Pop Culture*.

The Illuminati uses various symbols in pop culture in order to implant themes and ideas into the public's subconscious. This may seem innocuous, but it has a rather sinister and darker purpose. Depending on whom you ask, certain signs indicate Illuminati ownership, magic symbols, or energetic sacrifices to other worldly deities. What's the harm in a symbol you may ask? From *The Secret Language of Symbols* by David Fontana:

Symbols and colors are the building blocks of all visual symbols and have been used since the dawn of man to represent divine energy (e.g. the direct depiction of God is not allowed in several religions). Colors can be used to influence the mind, as is evident in foods that are colored differently from their natural version to make them more palatable, or even in sales marketing. Carl Jung was one of the forefathers of modern psychology and had a deep interest in colors. He believed there was a connection between alchemy and the psychology of the unconscious mind, most likely because of the ability of images to influence our internal thoughts.

    The book *Symbols of the Goddess* by Clare Gibson says that Carl Jung and Sigmund Freud recognized how a symbol has the power to evoke and influence our actions on a conscious and unconscious level. Take a moment and let that sink in. You've got possibly two of the most influential psychologists of all time telling us that a symbol can influence our actions. The author goes on to discuss how Jung noticed similarities of symbols used by all ancient cultures (even though they didn't have any direct knowledge on one another; kind of like the elongated skulls mystery referenced on *Ancient Aliens*).

    An example given is how early Greek and Roman psychiatry type sessions had clients drawing "trees and mandalalike circles." These universal symbols represent the tree of life (the axis mundi), and Jung attributed it to some kind of genetic mental blueprint. He subsequently made a theory of the collective unconscious that defines universal archetypes of symbols. He believed there are three strata of the mind: the conscious, personal unconscious, and collective unconscious. This collective unconscious is the universal one that all of us somehow understand on a subconscious level. These ideas manifest through universal symbolism (e.g. triangles, horns, All Seeing Eyes, etc.). He believed that symbols such as the moon and the sun are subconsciously understood by us as father and mother, or warrior and princess, or god and goddess archetypes. He said it was *"an attempt to explain the reasons behind the creation and future direction of both the cosmos and humanity."*

Here's some direct quoting from the book (which I highly recommend if you're interested in symbolism of the female and goddess):

"Symbolism is, then, a truly international form of communication, for it bypasses the barriers of language, race and culture, speaking directly to each level of the human psyche, but most meaningfully to the collective unconscious. When we view a symbol, say, an image of the moon, we recognize it on a conscious level, equating it to the astral body that shines at night; our personal unconscious may also recall a particular night with which, for whatever reason, we associate the moon strongly. Our collective unconscious, however, transcends such superficial connotations: in accordance with a more profound, metaphysical response, it associates the symbol with the tides, water and feminine fertility, but also with coldness, death and the underworld, and thus, since all of these are her attributes, with the Goddess."

Conspiracy theorists Jamie Hanshaw and Freeman Fly detail symbols in their book *Weird Stuff Vol. 1* and says that symbols are magical seals or 'signatures' thought to be the…:

"…cross stiches in the fabric of reality. The language of symbols works on the subconscious level of the mind as they are easy to grasp and meditate upon. The only magically effective symbols are those charged with the peculiar vitality of the subconscious."

Carl Jung said in *Man and His Symbols*:

Thus an examination of Man and his Symbols is in effect an examination of man's relation to this own unconscious. And since in Jung's view the unconscious is the great guide, friend, and adviser of the conscious, this book is related in the most direct terms to the study of human beings and their spiritual problems.

And later:

When the medical psychologist takes an interest in symbols, he is primarily concerned with "natural" symbols, as distinct from "cultural" symbols. The former are derived from the unconscious . . . the cultural on the other hand . . . used to express "eternal truths", and . . . still used in many religions

As you can see, the concept of symbolism is far more than the surface level idea that one might believe they are. People often times joke about the triangle being a paranoid delusion of conspiracy theorists, but they are the ones that are ignorant to the true purpose and influence the symbol can have over a spirit.

The All Seeing Eye and 666 Hand Gesture

The symbolism of the eye is referenced by practically every conspiracy theorist on the planet. Its prevalence in the world of entertainment and various forms of media begs for an interpretation and explanation. I've attempted to produce a succinct, yet thorough guidance into the various forms of the eye and the symbolism it represents.

I'll start off with one of the most ancient interpretations of the eye and the concept of a deity watching over us. The idea of an omnipresent being watching over us is referenced the Bible several times (1 Peter 3:12 and Proverbs 22:12) and this also includes the Biblical reference to The Watchers, aka the Nephilim. These were the hybrid offspring of extraterrestrials who were called the 'sons of God' in Genesis and the daughters of men at the time on Earth (*Ancient Aliens* had an episode in season 6 called *Alien Breeders* that covers some of this). The Nephilim were said to be giants, approximately 300 cubits, or 450 feet tall, based on the translation of the Hebrew Bible and the Book of Enoch.

Now it came about, when men began to multiply on the face of the land, and daughters were born to them, that the sons of God saw that the daughters of men were beautiful; and they took wives for themselves, whomever they chose. Then the LORD said, "My Spirit shall not strive with man forever, because he also is flesh; nevertheless his days shall be one hundred and twenty years." The Nephilim were on the earth in

those days, and also afterward, when the sons of God came in
to the daughters of men, and they bore children to them. Those
were the mighty men who were of old, men of renown.
- Genesis 6: 1-4

The tie-in with The Watchers is found in the Book of Daniel and again in the Books of Enoch, as they are described similar to the Nephilim in that the Watchers were sent to Earth to watch over the humans, only to succumb to lust for the women and procreate with them and create the Nephilim-giants. At this point God decides to get rid of this undesirable race so the Great Deluge occurs, with Noah being the one held responsible to maintain the human race while the flooding occurs.

The Bible references the right eye multiple times as well. Zechariah 11:17 says:

"Woe to the worthless shepherd, who deserts the flock!
May the sword strike his arm and his right eye! May his arm be
completely withered, his right eye totally blinded!"

Some translations of this verse claim that it is speaking of the Israelites being subjected to poor leaders who do nothing for their people (the Pharisees) and how they should be taken out with a sword for not watching over their flock with their right eye.

Here is a different reference in 1 Samuel 11:2:

"But Nahash the Ammonite replied, "I will make a
treaty with you only on the condition that I gouge out the right
eye of every one of you and so bring disgrace on all Israel.""

In this case they are conveying the importance of one's right eye and how it is more important to live without sin than to have this essential body part. The physical incarnation of God, Jesus Christ, said in Matthew 5:29:

"*If your right eye causes you to stumble, gouge it out and throw it away. It is better for you to lose one part of your body than for your whole body to be thrown into hell.*"

Again, this is a similar argument as in 1 Samuel 11:2. So why do they reference the *right* eye throughout the Bible? Using modern technology we know that the majority of humanity is right eye dominant (from a perspective of ocular dominance). So it appears the writings of the Bible knew about the importance of the right eye over the left long before scientific methods existed. Looking at it from a more ancient or occult perspective, the right eye is symbolic of the solar power, or masculine traits. This is why we often see symbols of masculinity tied in with symbols of the sun, because the sun rises, as does the phallus of the man. The phoenix rising from the ashes and the eagle are both representing the same thing; the power of the right eye or the masculinity of the sun and its rising power. The eagle is used in American iconography, as was it used in Nazi Germany. All of these things could be referencing the same ancient deity of the sun. The right eye is also controlled by the left brain; this is the same reason why most people are right handed. Most people are left brain dominant, so their right hand and eye are their most important appendages. In my book *A Grand Unified Conspiracy Theory* I explain how the Illuminati agenda seeks to strengthen the left brain because it reinforces concepts of logic and structured rules. The right brain is known for harnessing more abstract concepts, associating it with free will and creativity. The

Illuminati want us to think solely from our left brain so that we quickly assimilate to the rules they've presented.

When holding a conversation with someone, we typically default to looking into their right eye. In The Science of Soul Mates by William Henderson, he discusses how unnatural it is to try and look into someone's left eye because you are actually looking into their soul through this esoteric 'window.'

Theorists such as David Icke hint that the Watchers and/or Nephilim are part of the Illuminati shape shifting reptilian bloodline (and I can't forget to mention L.A. Marzulli; arguably the most 'expert' theorist on the Nephilim). The symbol of the eye is actually satanic in nature since the reptilian bloodline is evil (reptilians are also known as the Archons in Gnosticism). Many cultures believed in a malevolent 'evil eye' that was able to place a curse on another person. This evil eye is the antithesis of the 'third eye' (which is discussed later). The Greek Medusa mythological character was known for turning people into stone upon seeing her, and this was because she was the physical incarnation of the evil eye.

You can find jewelry to this day that has an eye on it, which actually represents the talisman to ward off the curse of the 'evil eye.' One of these talismans is the Italian horn, referred to as a cornicello. The word 'corno' means horn and we also see the mano cornuta (horned hand) being used in the entertainment industry as symbolism of Moloch. All of this is covered in my post about *Occult & Illuminati holiday traditions*:

The unicorn's horn was attributed with healing powers, and was considered one of the most valuable things on earth.

The Inquisition would torture those that wouldn't acknowledge the strength and existence of the unicorn and its horn. The unicorn horn spirals (just like the ziggurat of the Tower of Babel), and is yet another reference to Moloch. The horn gives you blessings if you could acquire it as well (again, same logic for the Moloch sacrifices). The leprechaun shillelagh was just another representation of the horn of Moloch with its powers.

Infowars.com posted a similar idea about the evil of the eye from John Daniel's *Scarlet and the Beast*, Vol. III:

The Serpent promised Adam and Eve that their eyes would "be opened" if they ate of the fruit of the tree of knowledge of good and evil. The key word in this passage is eyes, which in Hebrew can be translated "knowledge." Opened can be translated "broadened." What the Serpent promised Adam and Eve was that knowledge would be broadened if they ate of the forbidden fruit.

But the most foreboding aspect of this scripture emerges from the fact that the Hebrew word for "eyes" is not plural, but singular. What the Serpent actually told Adam and Eve was that their "eye" would be broadened by knowledge. The "eye" that Scripture wants us to consider is not the physical organ of sight, but the eye of the mind or the soul. This singular "eye" is called the "third eye" of clairvoyance in the Hindu religion, the eye of Osiris in Egypt, and the All-Seeing Eye in Freemasonry.

Whether you want to believe that these were literally angels, giants, reptilians, or the offspring of Seth & Cain; the point is that the concept of a big eye in the sky watching over us is a common thread, lying subtlety below the radar to the uninitiated. The ancient Egyptians had the Eye of Horus (the right eye), which is also known as the Eye of Ra. This 'wedjat' is a symbol of life because in Egyptian mythology, the god Horus had his moon eye (the left eye) torn out by Set, only to have Thoth invoke magic spells of the falcon to restore it (again, here is the sun symbolism with eagle or the phoenix, this time a falcon). The Eye of Horus would continue to be used as a symbol of a protective amulet, including its use on the tombs of Egyptians to assist in the afterlife. This is also what gives rise to theorist claims that the right eye is the 'darkened' eye; as opposed to the left eye which is the 'light' eye. These two opposites form the basis for concepts of polarity and dualism that is so prevalent in Freemasonry and occult systems like Satanism. The checkered pattern floors found in all Freemason temples (called 'Moses Pavement') depicts this dark versus light concept, and initiates are trained in the importance of these concepts. It makes the initiate reflect on the concept of opposites and how they can contradict, yet complement each other.

The third eye was a conceptual symbol used by the ancient Egyptians and Hindus as a reference to the pineal gland. This chakra is believed to be the gateway to higher consciousness and sense of enlightenment. You've surely heard the phrase "open up your third eye" which means to become aware of the world around you. Theosophists believed that the pineal gland was literally a third eye with a physical and spiritual purpose, but evolution worked it back into our heads into a present day pineal glands (as did the ancient Egyptians; according to some Egyptologists- see *The Pyramid Code*). It's no wonder that Theosophist Helena Blavatsky had such a powerful influence over Adolf Hitler and the Wizard of Oz's creator Frank L. Baum. You can see connections of Theosophy and the Eye of Horus being presented in my post about Lady Gaga's Wizard of Oz performance of *Applause*:

This society was based on a philosophy presented by Helena Blavatsky, who is sort of infamous for being the one who Adolf Hitler used as motivation for his racial and occult beliefs. He was known to keep her book called The Secret Doctrine close by his side. So anyhow, Gaga did up the single in the likeness of The Wizard of Oz and gave us a shot of the one all seeing eye of Horus.

The US dollar bill has the Great Seal on its reverse which was designed by Pierre-Eugene du Simitiere in 1776, who also included the Latin phrase E pluribus unum ("Out of many, one"). Pierre was a member of the American Philosophical Society along with Benjamin Franklin. This social club included many of the American founders who all supported this theme of liberty, freedom, and justice for all. While these ideas are great and all; it's important to consider the root of the concepts when delving into this realm of conspiracy theorizing. I summed this up previously in my post about Arcade Fire's *Reflektor* Illuminati symbolism:

The 'Age of Reflection' refers to the Romanticism period (1800-1840) of thought, both scientifically and intellectually. It essentially sought to unify man and nature through science; an opposition to the Age of Enlightenment that sought to divide out the two. Granted, the Age of Enlightenment had prominent Illuminati-Freemasonry ties and historical connections, considering how the two had roots through prominent intellectuals like Isaac Newton (known Freemason), Robert Boyle (known Freemason), John Locke (probable Freemason), and Francis Bacon (rumored

Freemason). So one could say the Age of Reflection is in
opposition to the practices of the Age of Enlightenment, and
therefore the Illuminati. But I'm not going to. And the reason
why is because the Age of Reflection believed in a concept of a
'Golden Age'. Romanticism had four basic principles: "the
original unity of man and nature in a Golden Age; the
subsequent separation of man from nature and the
fragmentation of human faculties; the interpretability of the
history of the universe in human, spiritual terms; and the
possibility of salvation through the contemplation of nature.

The Age of Enlightenment gave birth to the scientific process and with it, the ideals of liberty and independence, as we can see on the Seal of Delaware (also created by Pierre-Eugene) which has the words "liberty" and "independence" written across it.

Getting back to the Great Seal on the dollar bill; we can see Latin phrases that could take an ominous tone if you wanted to believe in some of the paranoid schools of thought that are presented here. Annuit Coeptis means "He approves our undertakings", or even more nefariously "it is favourable to our undertakings". We can also see Novus Ordo Seclorum which means "New Order of the Ages." The "New Order of the Ages" is the 'New World Order' that the Illuminati is believed to be orchestrating, and has been revealed to us through many speeches by prominent politicians.

The eye on the Great Seal is featured on top of a pyramid with thirteen steps, which represent the original 13 colonies. The pyramid is significant here, as I've explained in the section about the symbolism behind the triangle/pyramid:

The upright triangle represents solar power, or in the
Hellenic tradition, the element of fire. The ancient deities that

were affiliated with the sun were done so in order to convey the symbolism of strength and power (e.g. the Egyptian gods Horus and Ra, or the goddess Isis). The association of power and the sun eventually finds its way into a symbol for male power. This is appropriate since patriarchal-dominated societies are known for wars, primal urges, aggression and instantaneous flare ups. The lunar association with the goddess is tied into the inverted triangle; but we'll get into that later.

There is also the year 1776 written in Roman numerals underneath the pyramid, which is implied to mean the year of America's independence, when one could actually argue that it is referring to the secret society of the Bavarian Illuminati, which was also formed in 1776. Shortly after this time, the Freemasons (which were also many of the prominent founding fathers) also started using the logo of the eye. There are various interpretations of what it means, including the idea that it represents the All Seeing Eye of God (whom they call the "Great Creator" or "Great Architect"- the 'G' you see on the compass & square), who is always watching us. The Freemasons believe the Supreme Being represented by the eye symbol is a reminder that he watches over their every deed. It is often times encased in a triangle, which is covered in the section on triangles and the significance of the number 3 in Freemasonry:

As an example for the use of 3 and 4 in symbolism, we can take a look at the infamous Square and Compass of Freemasonry (again, I'm using material from Marty Leeds; check him out). A triangle is Freemasonry symbolism for a representation of the higher power; the 'G' in Grand Creator. The trowel used in Freemasonry symbolism is also triangular, while the 32nd degree initiates are symbolized with the

triangle. The symbols can be explained as the duality of our
purpose in life. The compass represents the spirit realm, or our
soul, and this is purposefully drawn above the square to show
its importance.

Thomas Smith Webb's *The Freemasons Monitor* wrote
in 1797:

"...although our thoughts, words and actions may be
hidden from the eyes of man, yet the All-Seeing Eye, whom the
Sun, Moon and Stars obey, and under whose watchful care
even Comets perform their stupendous revolutions, pervades
the innermost recesses of the human heart and will reward us
according to our merits."

Officially, nobody on the design committee was a
Freemason, so to claim the pyramid and eye on the Great Seal
is of Freemason origin is technically false. The root of this
debunked theory comes from 1884 when a Harvard professor
named Eliot Charles Norton, wrote:

"(it) can hardly look otherwise than as a dull emblem
of a Masonic fraternity."

Although, I'd like to counter argument and say that
even if the Seal was designed before the Freemasons started
using; they certainly embraced it well. The LDS church has
roots in Freemasonry, with Joseph Smith's membership and
conducting of black magic rituals to find the golden tablets,
and you can see the All Seeing Eye on the Salt Lake Temple in
Utah.

Aleister Crowley became the figure of attention for pushing the Illuminati-occult agenda into the 20th century. I wrote more detail of his agenda in the Aleister Crowley & the Illuminati magick trance on the entertainment industry post online:

After his stint at college he further pursued his interest in alchemy and the occult, joining the Hermetic Order of the Golden Dawn, which performed magic and drug rituals. The Golden Dawn's three founders were Freemasons, and their masonic influence is present in Golden Dawn because it follows a similar initiation and hierarchy before gaining any true insider knowledge. Crowley identified himself as a Freemason, and followed the teachings which were based on the Kabbalah, astrology, tarot and geomancy. Golden Dawn temples were established in London, Scotland, and Paris; all key points of interest for Illuminati rituals

Crowley was always a prominent member of the Ordo Templi Orientis (OTO), and introduced homosexual sex magick initiations for high degree members. He was promoted through the ranks very quickly because of his ritual experience and contacts made with the spiritual world in Egypt. Shortly after buying the Boleskine estate, Crowley and his wife spent time doing rituals in Egypt and believed they communicated directly with the Egyptian god Horus A few weeks later he was contacted by his Holy Guardian Angel named Aiwass ("Aiwass means "Lucifer" in Gnostic terms) while in Egypt, who dictated to him the document that would later form the Thelema religion, The Book of the Law. This book is where Crowley discusses the "Aeon of Horus," a time in which the people will "Do what thou wilt" (reinforcing the concept of freedom). Crowley believed that Horus wanted him to be the prophet that was to inform the human race of the entrance into

269

this Aeon of Horus era, ushering in the 20thcentury. Thelema religion says human history can be divided into eras of different magical and religious expressions. The first era was the Aeon of Isis; the second was Aeon of Osiris, and the third is the Aeon of Horus (what we're experiencing now; since Crowley's introduction into it). Here's where we can see the tie-in between the Ancient Egyptians, the occult, and the modern day "Illuminati": Aeon of Isis: This was known as the era of Goddess worship (e.g. Egyptian goddess Isis). The emphasis at this time period was on matriarchal values, and the balance of human nature. Aeon of Osiris: This occurred during the medieval times with male god worship (e.g. Egyptian god Osiris). The emphasis during this time was on patriarchy and male dominated values. Aeon of Horus: This is the modern time with child god worship (e.g. Egyptian god Horus). This current Aeon of Horus that Crowley believed he was intended to usher in is why we see the musicians doing the symbol for the all seeing eye, or the Eye of Horus (on the US Seal on the dollar bill pyramid). This symbol for the eye is found in Freemasonry as the Eye of Providence as well.

There's also a variation of the eye symbolism known in various circles as the '666' hand gesture (it is also more familiarly known as the 'ok' hand symbol). I mentioned this in the post *Is Khloe Kardashian in the Illuminati?*:

Chapter 24 of Texe Marrs' Codex Magica book goes into detail about this controversial symbol. He says the 'OK' sign has the 'O' which is symbol for the sun, while it also symbolizes the female genitalia. In tantric yoga this gesture shows spiritual and physical ecstasy. I already showed how Aleister Crowley was into yoga in my post devoted to his magick trance on the entertainment industry:

Getting back to Crowley, his interest in the occult and magick continued and he proceeded in seemingly innocuous activities such as yoga and Tantra. These activities are practiced by celebrities and are viewed as some kind of New Age, peaceful actions; but their roots are more evil than that. Even though yoga is good for clearing the mind, it pushes an anti-Christian concept of finding God within you, which abandons Christian teachings of following the true Creator and glorifies the person themselves. The Tantric practices are another form of sex magick, which is simply a ritual. These themes will come up again, since Crowley was able to push this agenda of promoting the importance of "self" over religion.

The three extended fingers are claimed to represent the connection to the divine, or the feminine triple goddess. The Satan worshipers are believed to think the three fingers show the unholy trinity between the horned god (aka Moloch, or Ba'al), the goddess (aka Semiramis or Whore of Babylon), and their offspring: the Antichrist. The Satan worshipers would view the circle as the symbol for their sun deity; Lucifer, or the illuminated one. They call this the symbol of the Divine King, and make reference to it on the dollar bill with the Latin phrase 'Annuit Coeptis', which means 'He approves our undertaking.'

And of course, you can see that the image appears to show us three overlapping 6's, perhaps giving it more cred as a satanic symbol. Now, generally you'll see this '666' hand gesture placed over one, or both of the eyes; giving it an appropriate placement in this post since we're talking about eye symbolism.

Now we've come back to present day where our culture is inundated with symbols of the eye from various

271

entertainers in music and film. We continuously ask why they would do such an out-of-place gesture, but when you consider the historical path of the occult and Illuminati symbolism, it becomes quite clear; the symbol is not intended for the masses to understand, but rather to become a part of the ritual and a pawn in the grand scheme of the Illuminati.

Triangles, Pyramids and the Sun

The symbol of the triangle is commonly held to have a much deeper and esoteric meaning than the basic geometric shape us common-folk see. The symbolism, or meaning, of the triangle is usually viewed as one of spiritual importance. The Christian faith views the three sides of the triangle as the Holy Trinity: God the Father, God the Son, and God the Holy Spirit. Ancient Egyptians believed the right sided triangle represented their form of the Trinity with the hypotenuse being the child god Horus, the upright side being the sacred feminine goddess Isis, and the base is the male Osiris. This concept was kept in a sort of 'chain of custody' when the Greek mathematician Pythagoras learned much from the ancient Egyptians and then applied it to geometry. He even went as far as to set up one of the first schools of mystery with a religious sect that practiced his philosophy, mathematics, and conferring of esoteric principles. In theory, the secret societies, cults, occultists, and other nefarious groups, collectively known as the Illuminati, maintain all of this knowledge and use it in a much different manner.

To understand why all of this matters, you must learn about the belief system of the occult. A researcher named Marty Leeds wrote books on mathematics and the universal language that nature uses to communicate to us. He believes that various languages are sacred and have a basis in ancient symbols through mathematics. I find his argument compelling, and I've tried to incorporate some its logic into this post, as I find it important to the argument.

The three sides of a triangle represent the number 3, and this concept is used in gematria, the ancient Babylonian/Hebrew numerology practice that assigns numbers to words or letters (and also other mystical schools of thought). The number 3 is representative of the spirit realm (or the Heavens), while in contrast, the number 4 represents the physical realm (the material, three-dimensional world we can relate to). The number 3 is a number of the divine, showing the union of male and female that create a third being. It's the number of manifestation; to make something happen.

Another analogy to consider is that the upright triangle points towards the Heavens, while the inverted points to the Earth (or Hell if you want to get all 'fire and brimstone' with it). As an example for the use of 3 and 4 in symbolism, we can take a look at the infamous Square and Compass of Freemasonry (again, I'm using material from Marty Leeds, so check him out). A triangle is Freemasonry symbolism for a representation of the higher power; the 'G' in Grand Creator (there are several supposed words that this 'G' represents, including "Geometry"). The trowel used in Freemasonry symbolism is also triangular, while the 32nd degree initiates are symbolized with the triangle. The symbols can be explained as the duality of our purpose in life. The compass represents the spirit realm, or our soul, and this is purposefully drawn *above* the square to show its importance.

The number 3 and the number 4 can be coupled to form the number 7, which is a mystical number representing man's connection to the divine (why do you think 7 is so lucky?). This is why the letter 'G' is the 7th letter of the alphabet and is displayed in the Freemason compass/square symbol. The number 7 is also seen in many forms we know as the days of the week, deadly sins, levels of hell, colors in the rainbow, days to create the world, Hindu chakras, Buddhist steps, and music notes (to name a few). *Officially*, the compass/square symbol in Freemasonry emphasizes trust and loyalty, while also symbolizing the sun because the compass provides the light for self-realization. From the book *The Freemasons* by Jeremy Harwood:

"The Compasses are Freemasonry's most prominent symbol of truth and loyalty. It is believed that while the Volume of Sacred Law sheds light on a Mason's duty to the Supreme Being and the Square illustrates the duty he owes to his fellow Masons and to society, so the Compasses provide the extra light necessary to understand the duties he owes himself- to circumscribe passions and keep desires within bounds."

The upright triangle represents solar power, or in the Hellenic tradition, the element of fire. The ancient deities that were affiliated with the sun were done so in order to convey the symbolism of strength and power (e.g. the Egyptian gods Horus and Ra, or the goddess Isis). The association of power and the sun eventually finds its way into a symbol for male power. This is appropriate since patriarchal-dominated societies are known for wars, primal urges, aggression and instantaneous flare ups. The lunar association with the goddess is tied into the inverted triangle; but we'll get into that later.

When researching Witchcraft ('the craft of the wise') you can see that the upright triangle is a symbol for the 2nd Degree initiate, in the process of a Witchcraft salute that follows the path of one breast to the other, and then the mouth and back down to the first breast. Conversely, the 1st degree initiate gets a salute of an inverted triangle with breast-breast-genitalia. The principle behind making and closing a triangle with a salute is because of the worship of the feminine triple goddess through a non-Christian version of the trinity. This is believed to follow the Egyptian trinity of Isis-Osiris-Horus, and the Greek Artemis-Selene-Hecate trinities. This concept is explained further in *Occult &Illuminati holiday traditions*:

> *It's important to understand that the connections are made and they allow this circular repetition of holidays to observe a ritual pattern. This ritual pattern is all revolved around astrology and Paganism. The Semiramis (or any goddess who represents Semiramis) is believed to go through the same cycles of life over and over. She is believed to be three different forms, referred to as the "Triple Goddess." These three forms are: fertility goddess, aka the Maiden; the Earth Mother, aka the Mother; and the old lady, aka the Crone. These forms are believed to be based on the phases of the moon, which is why we get concepts such as the "moon" goddess.*

Since the triangle ties into the number 3 and solar worship, we can see in alchemical and hermetic mystery schools that the sun is symbolized with the dot inside of the circle. You've seen this in corporate logos; particularly the one that's read and white with the bull's eye on it… The circle with the dot in the center also represents the serpent swallowing its tail; symbolism from the Babylonian times for the sun god Ra. It also corresponds to masculine characteristics such as sulfur (sulfur being equated to fire, or the sun) and the divine spark of man. It's also the Church of Satan logo, or the Leviathan cross.

One of the reasons we see the sun and solar worship so often is because some of the ancient mystery schools worshiped by the Illuminati believe they are rooted through the Atlanteans and the myth of Atlantis. The people of Atlantis were sun worshipers and had a solar deity who personified youth and had long golden hair to represent the rays of the sun. This sun god would be killed in order to show the evil that exists in the world, but then resurrected to show man's power over physical limitations. Manly P. Hall described it as:

"symbolized those cultures by means which man is to overcome his lower nature, master his appetites, and give expression to the higher side of himself. The Mysteries were organized for the purpose of assisting the struggling human creature to reawaken the spiritual powers…"

-Manly P. Hall *The Secret Teachings of All Ages*

Sticking with the sun symbolism for a bit more, the Black Sun or Dark Sun is also occult in nature. The Black Sun is considered to be the first stage of the 'The Great Work' or the 'Magnum Opus' which is basically a term for the alchemical process of creating the philosopher's stone. This philosopher's stone theory is the idea that you can make something out of nothing; or turning lead into gold, as Isaac Newton pursued (which helped him derive calculus, the theory of gravity and laws on light). Ironically, Newton was opposed to the mechanical view of the natural world, even though his Newtonian physics seems to mechanize functions like planetary motion, which he made a point to mention that only God could've set the planets in motion. In a way Newton was one of the O.G. conspiracy theorists, as he was obsessed with finding links between Biblical prophecies with actual events, and also predicting the Apocalypse wouldn't end before 2060 based on the Book of Daniel.

"It may end later, but I see no reason for its ending sooner. This I mention not to assert when the time of the end

shall be, but to put a stop to the rash conjectures of fanciful men who are frequently predicting the time of the end, and by doing so bring the sacred prophesies into discredit as often as their predictions fail."

–Isaac Newton

Red Ice Radio published an article on Newton being a scientist and a sorcerer:

Then there was Newton's biblical prophesy. In almost the same years that he was working on the Principia, he also wrote a treatise on Revelation in which he talked about souls burning in lakes of fire. With talk like that, he could have been the lyricist for Iron Maiden. (He had the hair too.)

Tempting as it is to dismiss all of this as somehow removed from Newton's science, his belief in spirits and what the alchemists called active principles almost certainly allowed him to conceive gravity in the mathematical form that we still use today.

In Newton's time, the natural philosophers had turned their backs on astrology and with it, the idea that influences could simply leap across empty space. Instead impulses had to be transmitted through things touching one another. So, if there was a force coming from the Sun that moved the planets, then it had to do so through a medium.

The occultists of the time were the alchemists, and the philosopher's stone was an attempt to achieve immortality; (or as I argue in my *A Grand Unified Conspiracy Theory*, the push towards transhumanism, reaching enlightenment and a new stage of evolution). We can see pop culture references to the first stage towards this immortality through its use of the Black

Sun symbolism, with songs such as Soundgarden's Black Hole Sun with lyrics about immortality:

In my shoes,
A walking sleep,
And my youth
I pray to keep.
Heaven send Hell away,
No one
Sings like you anymore.

Black hole sun,
Won't you come
And wash away the rain?
Black hole sun,
Won't you come?
Won't you come?

The Nazis also used this Black Sun symbol in the Wewelsburg Castle to channel the Aryan race of Atlantis, not to be confused with the more familiar swastika symbol which is also symbolism for the sun. The swastika is basically a spinning cross with light streamers at the ends. If it's spinning clockwise, then it's a symbol of male power, and if counter clockwise; female power. Hitler used the swastika in the counter clockwise fashion, which is supposed to unwind the spirit, and he thought he was doing that through his Nazi/Aryan movement.

The quest for immortality and youth is all around us, with entire industries devoted to makeup and plastic surgery. The entertainment industry helps push the desire for these things in a coordinated effort of music, film, and television imagery of sex and obsession with the youth. These things were told to us by Aleister Crowley who claimed to be introducing us to the new age of man in the early 1900's. Crowley dubbed this the "Aeon of Horus" and this new period of time for the world would revolve around child-god worship and worshipping the youth. I went into detail on Crowley in my IlluminatiWatcher.com post about his Illuminati magick trance on the entertainment industry:

> *A few weeks later he was contacted by his Holy Guardian Angel named Aiwass ("Aiwass means "Lucifer" in Gnostic terms) while in Egypt, who dictated to him the document that would later form the Thelema religion, The Book of the Law. This book is where Crowley discusses the "Aeon of Horus," a time in which the people will "Do what thou wilt" (reinforcing the concept of freedom).*
>
> *What I find most interesting about all of this, is that the Aeon of Horus that Crowley prophesied about is coming through in the entertainment industry through their use of the symbolism of the one eye and also the rising popularity of younger aged stars which supports the worship of children as gods found in the Aeon of Horus. Acts such as Justin Bieber, Miley Cyrus, and Willow Smith are all common household names, and this isn't without reason. The entertainment industry is riddled with occult worshippers and Crowley followers embedded in groups such as Freemasonry, OTO, Thelema, A.:A.:, etc. and the evidence is all around us.*

Getting back to the triangle symbolism, we also see concepts of the inverted triangle. Satanic images are often just inversions of the 'regular' symbols (like making a cross inverted), but here we see that an inverted triangle is a symbol for female goddess moon power. In the Hellenic tradition it is the element of water, which is related to the sexuality of the female, which is more fluid than a male, and needs "warmed up" before reaching boil. As opposed to the male sexual energy which is more solar in nature because it can be ignited quickly. The inverted triangle represents the womb, or even the crotch region of a nude female, while the male/upright triangle represents the erected phallus. Here is an excerpt from a GnosticTeaching.org article about the Kabbalah and similar discussions:

Obviously, when man (upright triangle) and woman (inverted triangle) unite, the result is the same symbol: ✡. This is why all the religions have chastity as the first requirement to enter the Daleth. To really enter religion and become a serious practitioner, a person always takes vows. In every religion, the traditional vow includes to not spill the sexual energy. In Buddhism even lay practitioners take this vow "I vow to cease sexual misconduct". If you have been initiated into Kalachakra Tantra, then you take the vow "I will never emit the Jasmine flower drops", which is the Thig-le, the sexual energy. Interestingly, in the Tibetan language, the word for door (sgo, which looks like a daleth) is also the first letter for egg and for testicle.

The number three is the number of fertile sexual union; one and two, male and female, joined together to form a third. This is pointed out in the book *Symbols and Their Hidden Meanings* by T.A. Kenner:

By extension to the concept of fertility and birth, three is also the number of manifestation, of making something happen. It indicates creative power, moving energy, resolving the conflict of duality, growing and developing. Wishes, petty misfortunes, witches and many more things are all said to come in threes.

The triangles can be placed in opposite directions to symbolize the union of male and female, which is also the union of spiritual/physical in the esoteric traditions. This is a Hermetic principle translated '*As above, so below*' that shows that decisions made in one realm will effect another. Many New Agers are also familiar with this concept, with positive thinking and projections of positive thought being placed into the universe; only to come back in a positive way to the person (e.g. Karma).

The hexagram combines the two unionized triangles with the Star of David and Seal of Solomon (which used it as a magical sigil for the control supernatural creatures). When talking about magic, the occultists believe a single triangle can be used as a method for summoning spirits. They'll stand inside of a circle while a spirit is conjured into a triangle during rituals to allow the demons to channel through from the underworld and appear within the triangle. The hexagram also displays the unity and balance of all things with the upright triangle being the elements of Air and Fire, while the downwards is Earth and Water.

Naturally, the triangle has the same meaning in symbolism as the three dimensional version; the pyramid. In its three dimensional form it is meant to symbolize the world's axis, with the highest point representing the enlightenment, or the highest point of attainment one can get to. These are seen on the Great Seal of the dollar bill; again, mentioned in the Decoding Illuminati Symbolism: All Seeing Eye section:

The US dollar bill has the Great Seal on its reverse which was designed by Pierre-Eugene du Simitiere in 1776, who also included the Latin phrase E pluribus unum ("Out of many, one"). Pierre was a member of the American Philosophical Society along with Benjamin Franklin. This social club included many of the American founders who all supported this theme of liberty, freedom, and justice for all.

The pyramid demonstrates that the power is concentrated at the top and as you go down towards the base (the main population) it gets distributed out. The power is in a corporation or even military type structure with each level flexing as much power on the level below it, all based on the premise that they will move up to the next tier above them someday. Another example is the Tower of Babel being a pyramid structure, which makes one wonder if that has any kind of analogy meaning beneath it. The symbolism behind the pyramid and triangle is most famously known for showing up in the entertainment industry; particularly by Jay-Z...

Saturn and the Black Cube

The occult beliefs of the Illuminati are believed by some theorists to be magical in nature. This is why the knowledge is kept secret from the masses; because they are the ones who want to be the sorcerers controlling everyone else's destiny. They employ symbols and various rituals in order to accomplish this. One such symbol is the cube. The most basic form of the cube is the two-dimensional square. This represents solidarity: a perfection that is static, earthly, and material. It suggests dependability, honesty, shelter, safety. As the most frequent shape in Hindu symbolism, the mandalas with gates represents order in the universe and the balance of opposites.

The lineage of the Illuminati traces back to mystery schools of the east. The cube represents earth in Pythagorean, Indian (Indian deities standing on cubes), Egyptian (Pharaohs sitting on cube thrones), and Platonic traditions. It's even realized as a sacred symbol today by the Freemasons (believed to be Illuminati affiliated) when they stand on an oblong square (cube) during particular rituals to the Worshipful Master. The cube is the building block of all nature, and the five solids of the ancients labeled as the "Pythagorean solids" include a tetrahedron (pyramid), cube, octahedron, icosahedron, and dodecahedron.

Another reason the cube is considered the building block of nature is because the ancient Greeks believed that the element of Earth was comprised of cube shaped particles; given their stability of the shape. There is also importance in the numerology (gematria) of the cube, as I allude to in the section on triangles, pyramids, and the sun:

The three sides of a triangle represent the number 3, and this concept is used in gematria, the ancient Babylonian/Hebrew numerology practice that assigns numbers to words or letters. The number 3 is representative of the spirit realm (or the Heavens), while in contrast, the number 4 represents the physical realm (the material, three-dimensional world we can relate to). Another analogy to consider is that the upright triangle points towards the Heavens, while the inverted points to the Earth (or Hell if you want to get all 'fire and brimstone' with it).

As an example for the use of 3 and 4 in symbolism, we can take a look at the infamous Square and Compass of Freemasonry (again, I'm using material from Marty Leeds; check him out). A triangle is Freemasonry symbolism for a representation of the higher power; the 'G' in Grand Creator. The trowel used in Freemasonry symbolism is also triangular, while the 32ⁿᵈ degree initiates are symbolized with the triangle. The symbols can be explained as the duality of our purpose in life. The compass represents the spirit realm, or our soul, and this is purposefully drawn above the square to show its importance.

The cube is merely the three dimensional version of the four-sided square, which corresponds to the physical realm and material world; yet another link to the cube being the building block of nature (with 'nature' being the material world). We can also logically see that the number four is represented in many forms of our established world. There are the four seasons, the elements (air, fire, earth, and water), signs of the zodiac, cardinal directions, and countless other places.

The Tetractys, or tetrad, is the triangular shape composed of ten points which was a secret, mystical symbol to Pythagoras. It appears in various forms, one of which is arguably the Kabbalah. The ten sephirots of the Kabbalah correspond to the ten points of the Tetractys. If you take 7 of the 10 points to form a cube, you are left with three dots that represent the ethereal invisible nature of the world, while the 7 of the cube represent the material, three dimensional world. We can also make a reasonable relation between Saturn and the cube. I further detail Saturn Worship in *A Grand Unified Conspiracy Theory*:

Black Cube: The black cube is symbolic of Saturn because of occult beliefs in its symbolizing the three dimensional world we live in as a symbol for matter. One of the oddest things surrounding Saturn worship is the observance the NASA Voyager and Cassini missions made when they were taking photos of the poles of Saturn. There is an unexplained hexagon shaped vortex storm on the north pole of Saturn that you can see in the public domain. A hexagon is actually a flattened out cube when viewed at it three dimensionally, so I find it odd that the ancient occult practices somehow knew this and worshipped it before the photographs were taken.

The Beast Aleister Crowley left a heritage of Thelema followers and one of them was the Brotherhood of Saturn. This magical order was similar to the other occult groups, whether it be New Age, Freemasonry or Thelema; they all revolve around the idea of mastery of occult knowledge (e.g. axioms like "*As above, so below*" which emphasize the duality aspects of man and world) in order to advance and evolve one's self in a series of steps and rituals. The Brotherhood of Saturn incorporates 33 steps to achieve the full spectrum of enlightenment, similar to Scottish Rite of Freemasonry who also incorporates 33 degrees. The end of the path for a member of the Brotherhood of Saturn is self-deification, an important concept in Thelema and seen in the realm of music with musicians making themselves god-like (e.g. Kanye West = Yeezus, Jay-Z = Hova, Beyonce = Beysus, etc.).

The Brotherhood established Saturn as the planet of choice because the ancients would focus on polar opposites and at the time they saw Saturn as the outer most planet; furthest from the light of the sun, effectively making it the dark side (hence the reason we see the 'black' cube). The darkness is necessary in order for there to be light, as Stephen E. Flowers, PhD points out in his book *Lords of the Left-Hand Path*:

Saturnian teachings give primacy to darkness. Darkness is said to precede light and to provide a matrix for the manifestation of the light: without darkness there is no light! The "dualism" of the FS does not seek to destroy one pole in favor of the other, but rather it seeks to go beyond the polarities through experience of both extremes.

The book goes on to reveal that the zodiacal sign of Aquarius is ruled by the planetary force of Saturn. The Age of Aquarius is important to the occult because that is the new age of man, or as Crowley defined it the Aeon of Horus. The new age brings about one consciousness and the evolution of man into technology through transhumanism. This concept is threaded back to the ancients' quest for the Golden Age as I point out in my online post on *Saturn Worship: A Beginner's Guide:*

The background of Saturn worship goes back to 600 BC with Greek poet Hesiod's 'Works and Days' where he discusses the various ages of man. One of the ages was referred to as the Golden Age. The Golden Age was referenced in several prominent ancient cultures, similar to how the cultures would adopt each other's gods and rename them. The ancient Romans worshipped the god Saturnus, who was the god of agriculture and time, and his reign was known as the time of Golden Age of peace and harmony. The Greek god that was the same as Saturnus was Cronus, the youngest of the Titans. The Carthaginian god Ba'al (or Moloch) was the same god, and devoured children (similar to Cronus who ate children).

Saturn is often depicted as Baphomet and associated with Satan as a devourer of children. Some theorists claim that the Tree of Knowledge fruit was actually a reference to babies being eaten. There is a belief that Cain actually *ate* Abel and that is where the derivation of the word "Cannibal" comes from.

In the triangles, pyramids and sun section I explore a concept of the Black Sun and The Great Work. "The Great Work" is the journey to be god-like and make something out of nothing. It is initiated with the first step being the alchemical Black Sun. The Black Sun is the first stage in the achievement of enlightenment or immortality, which is accomplished through the philosopher's stone. The philosopher's stone is known for making lead into gold, and the planetary association of Saturn to metal is lead. The planetary association with the Sun is gold, so turning Saturn into the Sun is the alchemical process of the philosopher's stone, based on metal transformation.

Now here is where we start to meld everything together. The Illuminati are the older elites who will prey on the young (an analogy of the Baphomet devouring children). This allows the Illuminati to achieve their quest for the Golden Age by sacrificing the youth to the Devil (aka the material world, aka Saturn) by making them pursue material goods and working a job in never ending servitude based on the masses desire for consumption.

We see this Saturn symbolism all around us including black school gowns worn at graduation with a square (*think cube) mortarboard hat, judicial gowns, Supreme Court Justice gowns, etc.

The holiday of Saturnalia was established by the Romans, as discussed in *Occult & Illuminati holiday traditions*:

The Saturnalia festival featured human sacrifices and ran from December 17th-23rd. There would be gladiator battles and the deaths would be considered more sacrifices to the deity Saturn. There were also concepts of role reversal; with masters feeding their slaves (still practiced today at work Christmas parties when the bosses feed the workers).

The Romans also participated in a festival called Dies Natalis Solis Invicti, or "Birthday of the Unconquered Sun" on December 25th. Sol Invictus was a Roman god of the sun, which could be yet another retelling of Nimrod and Semiramis. The depictions of Sol Invictus appear to mirror that of the Statue of Liberty, who was designed after the Roman goddess Libertas:

We also use the tradition of marriage rings which some claim is an ode to Saturn since it's the only planet with rings.

Another website that covers various aspects of Saturn links it quite easily to Satan and Pan; here is HollywoodSubliminals.com:

Saturn has also been associated with Satan and this, for numerous reasons. First, many authors argue that the word Satan is derived from the word Saturn. Second, Saturn is associated with the color black as well as Satan. Third, Ancients considered Saturn to be the farthest planet from the sun , the latter being associated with the principle of Good. (Note that Pluto never was considered a planet). Saturn is consequently the celestial body that is the less exposed to the sun's divine light and thus associated with the coldness of the principle of Evil. Finally, the "great god Pan", the horned deity, represented Saturn in ancient paganism. This half-man half-goat creature is considered the ancestor of our modern depictions of Satan.

"Pan was a composite creature, the upper part–with the exception of his horns–being human, and the lower part in the form of a goat. (…)The pipes of Pan signify the natural harmony of the spheres, and the god himself is a symbol of Saturn because this planet is enthroned in Capricorn, whose emblem is a goat"
- Manly P. Hall, Secret Teachings of All Ages

So Pan was depicted with horns due to the fact it represented Saturn, the ruler of the house of Capricorn which symbol is a goat.
Pan was the controlling spirit of the lower worlds. He was portrayed roaming through the forests, penis erect, drunk and lascivious, frolicking with nymphs and piping his way

through the wild. We might say he ruled the lower nature of man, its animal side, not unlike Satan.

Despite acknowledging its association with Evil, secret societies find the veneration of Saturn necessary to obtain illumination. It is the necessary counterpart of the principle of Good. Masonic authors clearly associate Saturn with Satan.

One last worthy mention of Saturn symbolism is that of the Freemasonry twin pillars: Boaz and Jachin. These pillars were part of Solomon's Temple and are believed to represent the entrance to a mysterious and sacred place. You can see them on various forms of currency and in American architecture, like the Pennsylvania State Capitol building and the IRS Headquarters Building in Maryland. The lineage of this symbol traces back to the Hermetic mystery schools and it a play on the duality concept. The pillar of light is Jachin, while the pillar of darkness is Boaz.

The book previously incorporated some of the Saturn talk with the Age of Aquarius; suggesting that perhaps the planet has always been a part of the Illuminati agenda, and they want us to worship and devote energy to this master plan of theirs.

Moloch, Owls and the Horns of Satan

One such theme of symbolism used to convey an 'eternal truth' of symbols, is that of horned deities. The oldest mention of a horned deity starts with Nimrod, El, and Moloch. These somewhat-interchangeable deities were thought to be depicted as either a single or double horned-god who was worshipped in the Bronze Ages of Mesopotamian culture. He was one of multiple gods in these ancient pagan cultures that we see the Canaanites, Sumerians, Phoenicians, Assyrians, and Babylonians devoting much energy and bloodshed. They were worshipping this deity to the point of sacrificing their own children (although some argue there is no definitive evidence of this, while others claim a counter-conspiracy cover-up of the disturbing practice). These ancient cultures believed that sacrificing their infants would appease the deity and they would in return have financial blessings, more fertility, good fortunes, or any other type of prayer worthy gift. This form of idolatry is what influenced much of the teachings of the Bible (about having false idols and such).

I talk about various theories involving the pagans of the time with goddess worship like Semiramis in the online post about Occult & Illuminati holiday traditions, while going into Moloch stuff:

The Hanging Gardens of Babylon had a temple of Nimrod (with the single or double horns; represented as aka

Moloch) where sacrifices were given, as referred to in 2nd Kings 23:10:

He also defiled Topheth, which is in the valley of the son of Hinnom, that no man might make his son or his daughter pass through the fire for Molech.

Also in Leviticus 18:21 of the KJV:

And thou shalt not let any of thy seed pass through the fire to Molech, neither shalt thou profane the name of thy God: I am the LORD

Further on in the occult holidays post when talking about St. Patrick's Day:

They believed that Moloch would give them financial blessings if they sacrificed their children, and this is believed to continue to this day, as is evident by the startling number of missing children around the world at any given time. A study from 1999 reported that approximately 800,000 children are missing every year in America. 800,000 is an astoundingly high number, that's about 16,000 per state (if distributed evenly). Getting back to the worship of Moloch, people still wear the horns of Moloch as jewelry, referred to as the Italian Horn.

The unicorn's horn was attributed with healing powers, and was considered one of the most valuable things on earth. The Inquisition would torture those that wouldn't acknowledge the strength and existence of the unicorn and its horn. The unicorn horn spirals (just like the ziggurat of the Tower of Babel), and is yet another reference to Moloch. The horn gives you blessings if you could acquire it as well (again, same logic for the Moloch sacrifices). The leprechaun shillelagh was just another representation of the horn of Moloch with its powers.

Rainbows are also symbolic of the ancient worship of Moloch. At the end of the rainbow there are treasures that leprechaun would do anything to get back. It is depicted as a cauldron filled with gold. Again, it is the financial blessings that Moloch gave you in return for the sacrifice. These cauldrons were used in occult practices, including the sadistic bobbing for apples (see the occult symbolism found in Halloween).

Perhaps this explains why we see the rainbow symbol so often in Stanley Kubrick's *Eyes Wide Shut*, or in *Wizard of Oz*; a tale by Theosophist Frank L. Baum.

Some Greek and Roman records claim that the Phoenicians of Carthage also had children that were sacrificed by fire to the deity of Saturn (Greek) or Cronus (Roman), which was also known as Ba'al Hammon by the Carthaginians. This is where we can tie-in Moloch with Ba'al, even though they were technically different deities. Ba'al was the son of their version of God the Father, El, and they were synonymously referenced. They were also both depicted as bulls, or seen with horns atop their heads.

It should be noted that while the 'sacrifice of children to a deity' concept is refuted by some, the notion still exists that Moloch and/or Ba'al is the deity attributed to death and particularly the blood sacrifice of the youth in exchange for the gifts from an entity of the dark side. In fact, Beelzebub is a common household name for Satan, which derives its origin from Ba'al, or in its Arabic form Ba'al dhubaab (and on the occult holiday of May Day or Beltane Fire Festival, the bailfires are really just Ba'al-fires).

There was also a hollow bronze bull that the ancient Greeks would execute criminals inside of by roasting them to death via applied heat. Perhaps this is a carryover tradition from the days of Moloch worship as well.

Here's NNDB talking about the notorious leader of Sicily, Phalaris, who created the bronze bull as a hail to Ba'al:

After ages have held tip Phalaris to infamy for his excessive cruelty. In his brazen bull, invented, it is said, by Perillus of Athens, the tyrant's victims were shut up and, a fire being kindled beneath, were roasted alive, while their shrieks represented the bellowing of the bull. Perillus himself is said to have been the first victim. There is hardly room to doubt that we have here a tradition of human sacrifice in connection with the worship of the Phoenician Baal (Zeus Atabyrius) such as prevailed at Rhodes; when misfortune threatened Rhodes the brazen bulls in his temple bellowed.

The Rhodians brought this worship to Gela, which they founded conjointly with the Cretans, and from Gela it passed to Agrigentum. Human sacrifices to Baal were common, and, though in Phoenicia proper there is no proof that the victims were burned alive, the Carthaginians had a brazen image of Baal, from whose downturned hands the children slid into a pit of fire; and the story that Minos had a brazen man who pressed people to his glowing breast points to similar rites in Crete, where the child-devouring Minotaur must certainly be connected with Baal and the favorite sacrifice to him of children.

There is another term for the burning sacrifice of human beings that will be easily recognized by the reader, and that is 'holocaust.' Some conspiracy theorists rightly point out the disturbing fact that we still reference the tragic events of

World War II as the 'holocaust' which literally means a 'burnt offering of sacrifice to god.' OneEvil has much more on this concept as well:

The Holocaust- the mass sacrifice of over eighteen million innocent Protestants, Orthodox Christians, ethnic Jews and minority groups by burning several million of them alive in ovens in Poland and Russia less than seventy years ago by Catholic dictators Adolf Hitler S.J. and Fr Joseph Stalin S.J. represents the largest and most expensive act of mass human sacrifice in history.

So vast were the military and logistical resources ordered to be deployed to this "Great Inquisition" from Rome from 1939 to 1945 that it played a major part to the eventual downfall of the Nazi Third Reich. The effort to efficiently sacrifice the largest number of non-Catholics in 24 x 7 purpose-built ovens [24 hours a day, 7 days a week] was a massive logistical effort- not the least of which required the complete genealogy analysis of most of Europe.

The pagan religions of the Middle Ages worshiped both the horned god and the Triple Goddess (Maiden, Mother, and Crone). The horned god is the male aspect of the divine, usually being depicted with the head of an animal, and always with horns atop its head (although it was also referenced with its various forms or 'moods' as the Green Man or Sun God). The male deity is shown with anthropomorphic characteristics because it represents the wild side of human nature, which one could argue is consumed by sex, survival, fear, and violence; all reptilian brain functions that the Illuminati use to their advantage.

To play Devil's advocate, there are claims by anthropologist Margaret Murray that the Christian Church started depicting Satan with horns in order to demonize the pagans with their horned god, and the witches/pagans use this theory to defend themselves from the given label of "Devil worshippers." Continuing on that line of witches and pagans, Wiccan founder Gerald Gardner established the religion through an amalgamation of Occult, Freemasonry, Theosophy, and Aleister Crowley's beliefs from their time together at the Ordo Templi Orientis and Order of the Golden Dawn.

Occultist and magic practitioner Eliphas Levi created the infamous Baphomet image and defined the inverted pentagram with its two points upward (like horns) as the symbol representative of evil. So it seems that through six degrees of separation we can tie evil to horned imagery, to the occult (Levi to Crowley), to witches, to pagans, and then back to Moloch. And of course there is the overarching web of the Illuminati who promote these things subtlety through entertainment and various other forms. Depending on how deep you want to go down this rabbit hole we can claim that the Archon demons from another dimension are really pushing this entire agenda (aka the reptilian shape shifters).

Here's why I say that. In Hebrew, Moloch means 'king' and Ba'al means 'master' or 'owner.' In Greek, Archon means 'to rule'. The rulers of this world (the 'kings'-Moloch, or masters-Ba'al) are the top 1% of the top 1%; the most elite who control all industries of energy, entertainment and media, also known as the Illuminati. The Archons are the shape shifting reptilians who believe they can rule the masses. They are what form the Illuminati. When we see satanic imagery in music videos and films, it's a subliminal message to the masses while at the same time a sign to each of the other members of the Illuminati who understand this esoteric language.

The rituals that were done in Babylon and the ancient world, and continue to this day, are done in a certain sequence in order to appease this dark force that exists in another dimension, unseen to us. The people who are into this have no empathy for others and seek only to please the demons and entities that exist on the dark side of the Kabbalistic Tree of Life. I explain this in the online post about the Kabbalah conspiracy theories & Illuminati symbolism in pop culture post when I talk about 'the other side:'

When broaching the concept of evil, some of the Kabbalah teachings display it through a shadow Sephirot and call it the "Other Side." It is also referred to as the "evil twin," and this "Other Side" is represented by evil spirits known as the Qliphoth. The Hermetic Qabalah actually tries to make contact with the Qliphoth spirits as part of the self-realization process (unlike the Jewish Kabbalah). Some of these evil demons are eerily similar to the Illuminati symbolism we see from the entertainment industry on a regular basis, leading me to believe that the Illuminati are part of this magic ritual trying to contact the dark forces of the Qliphoth For example, the demon Nehemoth (a.k.a. Naamah) means 'whisperer' and is responsible for frightening sounds and exciting the mind with strange desires. This demon was characterized as pleasing and had a proclivity for idolatry and singing songs to pagan deities (does 'American Idol' seem fitting? ...). The symbolism for the Illuminati vow of silence that we see from young men and women in the entertainment industry couldn't convey this point any clearer.

Crowley had a profound impact on the music industry and that is why they partake in these symbols. The musicians are performing these rituals when they use these lyrics and putting on certain performances. We saw Katy Perry perform a very dark ritual with Juicy J on the 2014 Grammy Awards with their performance of her song, *Dark Horse*. The initiate who plays with magic really should know what they are falling for, but that doesn't stop the musicians and Hollywood stars from dabbling anyways. Kenneth Grant wrote about the downfall of playing with magic when one is not ready for it in *The Magical Revival*:

> *In mediaeval times secrecy was restored to more as a safeguard for the occultist than for the world of which he formed a part. The scene is not much different today, except that the tables are turned. The indiscriminate revelation of occult formulae often leads to insanity and death. The unprepared who meddle with occult processes invite trouble.*

So it's no shocker to see that Katy Perry made us watch (and take part) of a ritual with witches, a beast with Moloch horns (horned god symbolism; it's the figure on the far right), and plenty of fire to go around. Crowley said Satan wasn't merely just a Devil with a pitchfork, but rather anyone who is 'God' for the 'other' team. From his book *Magic in Theory and Practice* (retrieved from Hermetic.com):

> *"The Devil" is, historically, the God of any people that one personally dislikes. This has led to so much confusion of thought that THE BEAST 666 has preferred to let names stand as they are, and to proclaim simply that AIWAZ — the solar-phallic-hermetic "Lucifer" is His own Holy Guardian Angel, and "The Devil" SATAN or HADIT of our particular unit of*

the Starry Universe. This serpent, SATAN, is not the enemy of Man, but He who made Gods of our race, knowing Good and Evil; He bade "Know Thyself!" and taught Initiation. He is "the Devil" of the Book of Thoth, and His emblem is BAPHOMET, the Androgyne who is the hieroglyph of arcane perfection. The number of His Atu is XV, which is Yod He, the Monogram of the Eternal, the Father one with the Mother, the Virgin Seed one with all-containing Space. He is therefore Life, and Love.

Evoking these dark entities breaks one down over time to the point that the medium takes on the traits and despises the masses, viewing them as cattle. The victims are destroyed and it affects many others around them. This is why you see public meltdowns from entertainers like Britney Spears shaving her head, Michael Jackson acting the fool and going on spending sprees, Mariah Carey saying goofy stuff on TRL, or one of the many deaths we see (see the 27 club).

The importance of the symbolism is expressed by occultist Manly Palmer Hall in his book *The Secret Teachings of All Ages*:

In the World of Assiah are to be found the demons and tempters. These are likewise reflections of the ten great globes of Atziluth, but because of the distortion of the images resulting from the base substances of the World of Assiah upon which they are reflected, they become evil creatures, called shells by Qabbalists. There are ten hierarchies of these demons to correlate with the ten hierarchies of good spirits composing the Yetziratic World. There are also ten Archdemons, corresponding to the ten Archangels of Briah. The black magicians use these inverted spirits in their efforts to attain

303

their nefarious ends, but in time the demon destroys those who bind themselves to it. The ten orders of demons and the ten Archdemons of the World of Assiah are as follows:

*D1, the evil Crown; the hierarchy is called Thaumiel, the doubles of God, the Two-head; the Archdemons are **Satan and Moloch**.*

The light bearer known as Lucifer is also depicted as a flame, or a torch; particularly that of the Torch of Liberty. The flames and light are a symbol for enlightening and truly allowing man to '*do as thou wilt*.' Crowley oddly echoed the Declaration of Independence which gave men and women many rights to pursue their own form of happiness. The Freemasonic influence of the founding fathers is no doubt imbued in the founding of America, and Lady Liberty (aka Lady Semiramis or the Babylon Whore).

In Texe Marrs' *Codex Magica* he claims that George Bush Sr. once walked into the Oval Office wearing a goat head mask. Combine that oddity with the fact that George Bush Jr. was reading The Pet Goat on 9/11 and one has to wonder?…

Another goat-like depiction of a horned deity is that of Pan. This is the horned god of nature for many pagans. Pan's father is Hermes; the founder of the Hermetic traditions and the Illuminati vow of secrecy. Referencing back to the section about Saturn:

Saturn has also been associated with Satan and this, for numerous reasons. First, many authors argue that the word Satan is derived from the word Saturn. Second, Saturn is associated with the color black as well as Satan. Third, Ancients considered Saturn to be the farthest planet from the sun , the latter being associated with the principle of Good.

(Note that Pluto never was considered a planet). Saturn is consequently the celestial body that is the less exposed to the sun's divine light and thus associated with the coldness of the principle of Evil. Finally, the "great god Pan", the horned deity, represented Saturn in ancient paganism. This half-man half-goat creature is considered the ancestor of our modern depictions of Satan.

"Pan was a composite creature, the upper part—with the exception of his horns—being human, and the lower part in the form of a goat. (...)The pipes of Pan signify the natural harmony of the spheres, and the god himself is a symbol of Saturn because this planet is enthroned in Capricorn, whose emblem is a goat"
- Manly P. Hall, *Secret Teachings of All Ages*

So Pan was depicted with horns due to the fact it represented Saturn, the ruler of the house of Capricorn which symbol is a goat. Pan was the controlling spirit of the lower worlds. He was portrayed roaming through the forests, penis erect, drunk and lascivious, frolicking with nymphs and piping his way through the wild. We might say he ruled the lower nature of man, its animal side, not unlike Satan.

Despite acknowledging its association with evil, secret societies find the veneration of Saturn necessary to obtain illumination. It is the necessary counterpart of the principle of Good. Masonic authors clearly associate Saturn with Satan.

Yet another play on the horns would involve the various astrological ages we know about in recorded history. The order of the astrological ages goes as follows:

Age of Taurus (symbolized by the bull)
Age of Aries (symbolized by the ram and fire)
Age of Pisces (symbolized by fish and monotheism)
Age of Aquarius (symbolized by the water carrier and the New Age movement, freedom and technology)

I know the astute reader will be able to put two and two together and see where we're headed with this. The first age of Taurus was roughly around the pre-Moses time and he destroyed it with the Ten Commandments when God declared *Thou shalt not worship false idols*. This was because the people were worshipping Moloch and the bronze bull gods at that time.

The next age was Aries and the ram (more horns). This was around the time of Akhenaten who was the Egyptian pharaoh who attempted to supplant the polytheistic worship of multiple deities with a monotheistic one. Moses continued to condemn the practice of worshipping the false idols, and the concept of a single God started to take foothold.

Next up, the Age of Pisces is the age of the Christian, brought forth by Jesus Christ, hence the reason we see the fish as a symbol of Christianity.

Lastly we have the Age of Aquarius which some argue already started, while others claim they are pushing us towards. The massive amount of change that has taken place over the last 100 years makes one think we are in a period of serious transition, especially with the transhumanism movement which takes technology and "reforms" God's creation of man to make an artificial evolution into a new form of biological robot.

So you can see that the horns of the ancient ages of astrology are the Illuminati's way of saying that they are continuing to defy Christianity and that they are laying low

306

until the Age of Aquarius can take over and they can make all of us transhumanistic robots and slaves to their purpose. The film Zeitgeist did a good job of going through this theory if you're interested in learning more.

One more thing I feel I should point out is the improper conflation of the bull deities (e.g. Ba'al, Moloch, etc.) with the owl deities. The owl is actually symbolism for the goddess, which is depicted with the various goddesses like the Greek Athena, and then the Roman Minerva. The owl was depicted as the symbol for wisdom because it had an ability to see in the dark. It was a metaphor because it would illuminate the darkness of the masses and educate the ignorant. It was able to transcend illusions and deception and see the ultimate truths of the world.

We see the owl all over the place in the realm of conspiracy, including its most infamous use at Bohemian Grove during the Cremation of Care ceremony where 'mock' sacrifices of children are given up to the owl-god. Richard Cassaro has a great post about owl symbolism, and one of the sections is entirely about the Cremation of Care. From RichardCassaro.com:

The ceremony involves the poling of a small boat across a lake containing an effigy of Care ("Dull Care"). Dark, hooded individuals receive the effigy from the ferryman which is placed on an altar and, at the end of the ceremony, is set on fire.

Domhoff notes: "this is the body of Care, symbolizing the concerns and woes that afflict all men during their daily lives."

The occult meaning of this ceremony seems clear. These men carry the cares of the world and use a symbolic ritual to cast it off. The remaining time at the Club represents a careless period, or vacation of sorts, during which time no business is conducted.

By "cremating" care, they expunge the negative energy of such emotions as worry, fear, and anxiety; it is the goal and magical effect of the ritual, which could more properly be called the "Cremation of worry" or "Cremation of negative energy."

The pertinent evidence to the present article, of course, is the fact that the ceremony takes place next to a 45 foot (14m) high concrete owl statue, symbolizing knowledge and wisdom. The voice of the owl during the ceremony is former newsman Walter Cronkite, himself a member of the Bohemian Club, and music and fireworks accompany the ritual for dramatic effect.

And of course, we tie right back into magic when referencing the ridding of stresses from this ritual:

Magical thinking applies here: they believe they have done it, and so they have.

The owl is connected to magic because Native Americans and Africans both used it as symbolism for magic, prophecy, divination, and protection from evil spirits. Some believe that the owl carries messages back and forth between the nether world and ours. From RichardCassaro.com:

Shamans called upon Owl medicine for insight. Plains Indians wore owl feathers to protect against evil spirits. The Cree and Apache believed the Boreal Owl was a summoning to the spirit world. To this day, Native Americans associate the owl with spiritual vision; the owl is viewed with respect and associated with the souls of deceased ancestors. African cultures viewed the owl similarly to the Native Americans, heralding them as messengers of secrets as well as the bird of sorcerers, witches, and warlocks. In Madagascar owls are said to dance on the graves of the dead, and to the Aboriginal Australians they are companions to medicine people.

Some theorists claim the owl is the female evocation of god, while the bull is the male aspect; hence the confusion. I've also heard David Icke describe this concept with the ancient goddess symbolism of the moon crescent on the head which is another example of horns. The Greek moon goddess Selene and the Egyptian goddess Isis are seen depicted with the crescent moon on top of their heads.

The Mano Cornuto hand gesture (aka El Diablo, Hook 'Em Horns, Il Cornuto, Devil Horns, etc.) is the most commonly flashed Illuminati symbol. This symbol has been transformed entirely to a 'harmless' sign of rock 'n' roll expression. Its present day meaning is much more inconspicuous than one would think, but ultimately it's just another expression of black magic and evil. The horns are synonymous with the Moloch deity and that is why the rock 'n' roll industry popularized it. Think about what the purpose really is; drugs, sex, music, etc. and all of these things are low vibration concepts that do nothing but harm to one's self (*if used improperly; there's inherently nothing wrong with all three of those things, but they are improperly used most of the time).

In Milton's *Paradise Lost* tale there is a fallen angel named Moloch. Since I haven't read it, here's DarknessVisible:

The name means 'king' in Hebrew. Moloch also goes by the name of Baal and is best known for his inordinate

309

fondness for child sacrifice. In Book II he is basically Rambo without the weapons: 'the strongest and the fiercest spirit | That fought in heaven; now fiercer by despair' (II.44). He characterizes a brawn-not-brains mentality as he advises open war because he cannot stand being defeated and surviving. The samurai ethic of hara-kiri is perhaps brought to mind. However, instead of disembowelling himself, Moloch clamours for another battle which he knows – but won't admit – cannot be won. This would make for good theatre, but Milton (perhaps regrettably!) chooses to stick to the biblical narrative and so Moloch is overruled.

Dan Brown's *Lost Symbol* book features an antagonist named Mal'akh that is said to be covered in tattoos and he has rituals all over the book as well. The film *Metropolis* has an industrial demonic machine named Moloch that accepts humans as sacrifices to the fire (also note the figures inside of the mouth with the horns). Stargate SG-1's Moloc demands female children be sacrificed by fire. From the Stargate Wikia:

Moloc (also called Molech, Molekh, Molok, Molek, Melech, Milcom, Molcom, and most commonly, Moloch) was a Goa'uldSystem Lord. While on Earth, he was worshiped by the Canaanites and Phoenicians. During his reign, he became known for his demand of child sacrifice, a trait which he took with him after leaving Earth.

Stargate SG-1's Baal is an alien, here's the Wikia:

First seen during the Second Goa'uld Dynasty, Ba'al was originally one of Ra's prominent underlords in service to him on Earth where he was thought to be the son of El—who was, in actuality, Ra—by the Canaanites. It was in this role that he oversaw many cultures' development of an agricultural system, the Canaanites and Phoenicians among them. Ba'al's influence spread throughout these cultures so much that he was known over the entire Mediterranean basin and, eventually, most of the planet.

He was rarely seen to be a kind overseer, however, and indeed whenever his people failed to meet his strict food production quotas he very often issued orders for the mass sacrifice of Human lives.

The *Watchmen* comic has Moloch the Mystic and Arthur C. Clarke's novel *Childhood's End* features a dark tale of horned aliens called the Overlords (another name for the reptilian shape shifters known as the Archons).

The point behind all of this is unknown and left open for debate and speculation. The one undeniable truth is that it exists; whether or not you want to believe it's for nefarious purposes or not is up to you. Our God given free will allows us to choose which path of energetic donation we want to explore. If you want to enjoy artwork that features these types of symbolism, I believe that is fine (especially considering that I continue to do so as well). The only request one can reasonably make is that you remain educated and wary for manipulative practice and magic symbols all around you.

Special Thanks:

First and foremost God for giving me the abilities to carry this out, and my family who gets thanks for not choking me out while I'm consumed at my computer or watching conspiracy theory videos. I couldn't do it without the support and encouragement you provide.

Special Thanks to Susan, Sandman, Freeman and Jamie Hanshaw, and inspirations & knowledge from David Icke, Mr. Gates, Bloodstain Lane, JD Boaz, Marty Leeds, Greg Carlwood, Professor Griff, and Prodigy.

Super big shout outs to the Watchers out there who are helping me launch this project:

Aja	
Amanda B.	Abduraham
Brynne W.	Adam H.
Carolina	Ali313
Cecilia S.	Amy G.
Fleurdamour	Bronson
Idasa T.	Chriss L.A.
John McG.	Christo C.
Jon C.	Christopher W.
Laura	Connor
Pete	Daketo
Ryan B.	Emmanuel C.
Sandman	ExposeIlluminati
Seenb4in84	K
Thomas	Kizza B.
Tyler	Liam J.

Sources:

I wrote this book over the course of two years (2012-2014). I've compiled as many of the links as I could, but they are not all in order (due to the last minute decision to include links).

Flowers, Stephen E. *Lords of the Left-hand Path: Forbidden Practices & Spiritual Heresies*. Rochester, VT: Inner Traditions, 2012. Print.

Marrs, Texe, *Codex Magica: Secret Signs, Mysterious Symbols, and Hidden Codes of the Illuminati*. Austin, TX: RiverCrest Publishing, 2005. Print.

Hanshaw, Jamie, and Freeman Fly, *Weird Stuff (Operation: Culture Creation Book 1 and 2)*. 2013-2014. Print.

Byrne, Rhonda, *The Secret*. 2010. Hillsboro, Oregon: Atria Books and Beyond Words Publishing. Print.

Weishaupt, Isaac, *A Grand Unified Conspiracy Theory: The Illuminati, Ancient Aliens, and Pop Culture*. 2013. Print.

http://www.jsonline.com/blogs/news/211190351.html
http://www.scarletwoman.org/docs/docs_egc.html
http://www.sacred-texts.com/oto/engccxx.htm
http://illuminatiwatcher.com/aleister-crowley-the-illuminati-magick-trance-on-the-entertainment-industry/
http://www.rap-up.com/2012/02/13/nicki-minaj-talks-grammy-performance-madonna-m-i-a-starships/
http://illuminatiwatcher.com/illuminati-symbolism-in-miley-cyrus-we-cant-stop-music-video/
http://articles.latimes.com/1998/jan/22/business/fi-10797

https://www.goodreads.com/quotes

http://www.jashow.org/2012/02/06/mormons-new-secret-names-marriage/

http://www.youtube.com/watch?v=LdmclVMGWxs

https://www.youtube.com/watch?v=jhhRUX9n6zE

http://www.nytimes.com/2007/09/02/magazine/02rubin.t.html?pagewanted=7&_r=0

http://www.unc.edu/~ltolles/illuminati/Believe.html

https://www.lds.org/topics/becoming-like-God?lang=eng#2

http://www.cfr.org/about/membership/roster.html?letter=W

http://www.texemarrs.com/022007/occult_theocracy.htm

http://blogs.houstonpress.com/rocks/2011/05/kesha_wants_you_to_send_her_yo.php

http://www.sfexaminer.com/sanfrancisco/madonna-to-cleanup-team-leave-no-dna-behind/Content?oid=2200643

http://memory.loc.gov/cgi-bin/query/r?ammem/mgw:@field%28DOCID+@lit%28gw360395%29%29

https://www.sigmapiphi.org/home/history_of_the_boule.php?page=1

http://books.google.com/books?id=zBgDPupR_lMC&pg=PA184#v=onepage&q&f=false

http://admeter.usatoday.com/story/sports/ad-meter/super-bowl/2014/01/20/ad-meter-story-super-bowl-ad-costs/4476441/

http://consumerfed.org/news/594-the-financial-status-and-decision-making-of-the-american-middle-class

http://www.asc.upenn.edu/gerbner/Asset.aspx?assetID=2744

http://nationalhumanitiescenter.org/tserve/freedom/1609-1865/essays/aafamilies.htm

http://www.dol.gov/oasam/programs/history/moynchapter3.htm

http://www.hrw.org/legacy/reports/2000/usa/Rcedrg00-05.htm

http://www.huffingtonpost.com/john-w-whitehead/prison-privatization_b_1414467.html

http://www.globalresearch.ca/the-prison-industry-in-the-united-states-big-business-or-a-new-form-of-slavery/8289

http://www.newyorker.com/arts/critics/atlarge/2012/01/30/120130crat_atlarge_gopnik?currentPage=all

http://www.huffingtonpost.com/2014/03/10/war-on-drugs-prisons-infographic_n_4914884.html

http://www.huffingtonpost.com/2013/04/08/drug-war-mass-incarceration_n_3034310.html

http://www.justicepolicy.org/uploads/justicepolicy/documents/gaming_the_system.pdf

http://ir.correctionscorp.com/phoenix.zhtml?c=117983&p=irol-faq

http://www.hiphopisread.com/2012/04/secret-meeting-that-changed-rap-music.html

http://www.geogroup.com/history

http://www.mtv.com/news/1699264/kesha-die-young-sandy-hook-shootings/

http://listverse.com/2011/12/12/10-famous-people-who-avoided-death-on-911/

http://www.thepeoplehistory.com/november12th.html

http://www.dailymail.co.uk/femail/article-2063262/Lady-Gagas-monstrous-fragrance-smell-like-expensive-hooker.html

http://rollingout.com/music/2-chainz-blames-video-directors-for-illuminati-imagery/#_

diaryofahollywoodstreetking.com/**jaden-smith**-reppin-booze-**black-magic**/

http://www.pnas.org/content/111/24/8788.abstract?tab=author-info

www.lifeandstylemag.com/.../move-over-sasha-fierce-meet-**beyonce**-s-new- **alter-ego**-yonce-33807

http://news.bbc.co.uk/2/hi/entertainment/7688799.stm

https://twitter.com/rihanna/status/192485591106064386

http://abcnews.go.com/Entertainment/Health/story?id=2885048&page=1

http://www.people.com/people/article/0,,20012207_20012195,00.html

http://www.gq.com/entertainment/music/201111/survivors-music-portfolio-eminem-rap

http://www.mtv.com/news/1574995/jay-z-behind-the-rhymes-hov-reveals-why-he-hasnt-written-down-lyrics-in-a-decade/

http://pitchfork.com/reviews/albums/13740-rated-r/

http://www.merriam-webster.com/dictionary/rain

http://dictionary.reference.com/browse/rain

http://mic.com/articles/95260/the-music-industry-is-literally-brainwashing-you-to-like-bad-pop-songs-here-s-how

http://mediasmarts.ca/marketing-consumerism/how-marketers-target-kids

http://www.ftc.gov/news-events/press-releases/2000/09/ftc-releases-report-marketing-violent-entertainment-children

http://perezhilton.com/2013-12-27-miley-cyrus-ariana-grande-discusses-corrupting-pop-star-association-celebrity-friends#.U-eIg2OTLgJ

http://illuminatiwatcher.com/ariana-grande-illuminati-yes/

http://en.wikipedia.org/wiki/Symbol_of_Chaos

http://illuminatiwatcher.com/kaballah-conspiracy-theories-illuminati-symbolism-in-pop-culture/

http://www.drugabuse.gov/sites/default/files/rrprescription.pdf

http://newsfeed.time.com/2012/12/08/gangnam-rile-psys-past-anti-american-performances-stir-controversy/

http://aftermathnews.wordpress.com/2008/11/07/prodigy-says-jay-z-sides-with-the-evil-illuminati/

http://www.billboard.com/articles/news/472374/snoop-dogg-blasted-for-promoting-caffeine-laced-alcoholic-drink

http://en.wikipedia.org/wiki/Metropolis_(1927_film)#cite_note-20

http://www.goodreads.com/list/show/23942.Books_Read_by_Tupac_Shakur_

http://www.npr.org/templates/story/story.php?storyId=5614846

http://en.wikipedia.org/wiki/Astrological_age#The_Age_of_Taurus_.28The_Taurean_Age.29

https://www.youtube.com/watch?v=6YHi6bYgp8I

http://gawker.com/leaked-secret-tape-of-kanye-west-ranting-about-taylor-827192453

http://www.tmz.com/2009/06/25/michael-jackson-dies-death-dead-cardiac-arrest/

http://www.cnn.com/2009/SHOWBIZ/Music/06/25/michael.jackson/index.html

http://en.wikipedia.org/wiki/Michael_Jackson

http://en.wikipedia.org/wiki/Death_of_Michael_Jackson

http://abcnews.go.com/GMA/michael-jackson-attorney-fbi-files-vindication/story?id=9407615&page=2

http://news.bbc.co.uk/onthisday/hi/dates/stories/august/24/newsid_2512000/2512077.stm

http://transcripts.cnn.com/TRANSCRIPTS/0906/29/sitroom.01.html

http://www.thesmokinggun.com/documents/celebrity/michael-jacksons-15-million-payoff

http://www.dailymail.co.uk/news/article-1196009/Im-better-dead-Im-How-Michael-Jackson-predicted-death-months-ago.html

http://books.google.com/books?id=lWxxodXkQ4UC&pg=PA62&lpg=PA62&dq=shockaholic+carrie+fisher+evan+chandler&source=bl&ots=Px1XxOhOR8&sig=uThcspclUQ43_B_JaepxGYLzoBY&hl=en&sa=X&ei=xdLWU7yQMNeyyASH1oHQ

Bw&ved=0CDEQ6AEwAg#v=onepage&q=shockaholic%20ca
rrie%20fisher%20evan%20chandler&f=false
http://www.ancientegyptonline.co.uk/eye.html
http://mysticalnumbers.com/number-10-in-kabbalah
http://www.philadelphiaweekly.com/news-and-opinion/cover-
story/over_the_waterfall-38359394.html
http://www.bible-history.com/isbe/C/CORNER-STONE/
http://www.masonicworld.com/education/files/jun03/evolution
_of_the_cornerstone_cer.htm
http://www.history.com/this-day-in-history/capitol-
cornerstone-is-laid
http://en.wikipedia.org/wiki/Human_sacrifice
http://en.wikipedia.org/wiki/Blood_libel
http://web.stanford.edu/dept/archaeology/journal/newdraft/garn
and/paper.pdf
http://www.dailymail.co.uk/sciencetech/article-
2544728/Ancient-Greek-stories-ritual-child-sacrifice-Carthage-
TRUE-study-claims.html
esoteric.msu.edu (Unleashing the Beast article)
http://www.theroot.com/articles/history/2009/10/michelle_oba
ma_has_a_white_greatgreatgreatgranddaddy.html?page=0,1
http://www.brainyquote.com/quotes/quotes/q/quincyjone60156
7.html
http://uproxx.com/smokingsection/2013/08/rashida-jones-
tupac-letter/
http://www.huffingtonpost.com/2012/12/21/katt-williams-
jamie-foxx-gay-django-unchained-role_n_2347945.html
http://diaryofahollywoodstreetking.com/chris-mack-daddy-
kelly-dead-at-34/
http://www.dailymail.co.uk/news/article-2651584/How-king-
pop-1-5billion-dead-body-Five-years-Michael-Jacksons-
posthumous-fortune-broken-records-Now-brilliant-report-asks-
IS-making-mint-death.html

http://www.michaeljacksonhoaxforum.com/forum/index.php/page,the_weird_list.html

http://transcripts.cnn.com/TRANSCRIPTS/0906/29/sitroom.01.html

http://newsbusters.org/blogs/noel-sheppard/2012/02/26/20-richest-oscar-winners-all-time

http://www.rollingstone.com/music/news/quincy-jones-sues-michael-jackson-estate-20131026

http://www.theguardian.com/music/2011/jun/23/michael-jackson-la-toya

http://nypost.com/2014/08/10/michael-jacksons-ex-maids-reveal-madness-at-neverland/

http://www.express.co.uk/news/showbiz/479900/Michael-Jackson-bodyguards-book-briefcase-woman-credit-card

http://www.vh1.com/news/articles/1455976/20020708/jackson_michael.jhtml

http://www.deseretnews.com/article/705313897/Jackson-family-faces-criticism-since-Michaels-death.html?pg=all

jwjackson.com/?p=1461

Mobile.nytimes.com/2012/09/23/magazine/the-pop-diplomacy-of-quincy-jones.html?

http://prince.org/msg/8/348905

http://www.huffingtonpost.com/g-flint-taylor/the-fbi-cointelpro-progra_b_4375527.html

http://en.wikipedia.org/wiki/Fred_Hampton#FBI_investigation

http://en.wikipedia.org/wiki/Mark_Clark_(Black_Panther)

http://en.wikipedia.org/wiki/COINTELPRO

http://www.hiphopdx.com/index/news/id.29392/title.chuck-d-shares-tupac-letter-/Prisons

http://www.thedailybeast.com/articles/2011/04/09/10-revelations-from-notorious-bigs-fbi-files-on-murder.html#

http://www.crimelibrary.com/notorious_murders/celebrity/shakur_BIG/5b.html

http://www2.citypaper.com/film/story.asp?id=20324

http://madamenoire.com/445773/hurtful-extremely-upsetting-jennifer-hudson-crazy-claims-sacrificed-family-members-illuminati/#sthash.fpWy3O0f.dpuf

http://web.archive.org/web/20090429075620/http://www.rollingstone.com/news/story/8898338/the_unsolved_mystery_of_the_notorious_big

http://theboombox.com/tupac-shakur-blank-on-blank-pbs-digital-features/

http://www.oprah.com/omagazine/Oprah-Interviews-Mary-J-Blige

http://www.huffingtonpost.com/2011/08/30/outlawz-confirm-they-smoked-tupacs-ashes_n_942106.html

http://www.songlyrics.com/richie-rich-f-2pac/niggaz-done-changed-lyrics/

http://www.nytimes.com/2004/05/29/nyregion/record-company-can-sue-over-popular-singer-s-death.html

http://www.foxnews.com/entertainment/2012/02/13/whitney-houstons-daughter-bobbi-pulled-from-tub-day-before-moms-death-report/

http://www.theafrolounge.com/2013/02/04/rapper-amil-left-the-music-industry-because-she-refused-to-sell-her-soul/

http://www.metrolyrics.com/quarrels-lyrics-amil.html

http://www.rollingstone.com/music/news/the-epic-life-of-carlos-santana-20000316

http://abcnews.go.com/Entertainment/MichaelJackson/story?id=8314753

http://pitchfork.com/news/45043-read-ol-dirty-bastards-fbi-file/

http://www.independent.co.uk/news/people/profiles/whats-new-pussycat-nicole-sherzinger-on-being-a-global-pop-star-and-conquering-an-eating-disorder-8523189.html

http://www.rollingstone.com/music/features/suge-knight-endless-fall-20150706#ixzz3h36Y1JUt

http://www.rollingstone.com/music/news/lil-wayne-tour-bus-shooter-receives-20-year-sentence-20151120

http://www.people.com/article/bobbi-kristina-brown-medical-examiners-hold-autopsy-report

http://www.11alive.com/story/news/2016/01/18/fake-nurse-who-cared-bobbi-kristina-charged-again/78970444/

http://radaronline.com/celebrity-news/debra-reis-brooks-reveals-new-details-morning-friend-bobbi-kristina-brown-found-tub/

Further Down the Rabbit Hole...

A GRAND UNIFIED CONSPIRACY THEORY:

THE ILLUMINATI, ANCIENT ALIENS AND POP CULTURE

This is a comprehensive beginner's guide to ALL things conspiracy!

'A Grand Unified Conspiracy Theory: The Illuminati, Ancient Aliens, and Pop Culture' is a culmination project of several years of

research and taking notes on taboo and fringe subjects from various theorists, philosophies, and academic walks of life. I focus a lot of the material on the philosophy of David Icke, so if you wanted an independent third party assessment on why he thinks reptilian shape shifters control our planet (and why he could be correct); this is the book for you!

I explore links between all of the Illuminati conspiracy theories, the music, film, and entertainment industry's infiltration, and brainwashing symbolism found in all of these venues (e.g. the All Seeing Eye, pyramids, etc.). Ancient cultures, Nazis and occult worship still play a key role in today's control system, and I provide insight into these topics, including a never before released review of a controversial and banned documentary of Princess Diana's murder. This film has never been released and I was able to watch a copy of it and review its findings.

More original theories are presented such as Rihanna's occult origins, red dragons and their symbolism, and the Illuminati eugenics program being deployed through a transhuman robotic agenda. I also explain how David Icke's theories of the Moon Matrix and Saturn Worship operate to manipulate us into a false reality.

I wrap the book up with a conclusion of what actually works out of all this mess. It includes an assessment of David Icke's reptilian shape shifters explained through a legitimate cognitive style model theory in academia called 'Adaption-Innovation' theory.

KUBRICK'S CODE

In this book, author and independent researcher Isaac Weishaupt presents hundreds of images and analysis from Stanley Kubrick's most popular films- *2001: A Space Odyssey, A Clockwork Orange, The Shining*, and *Eyes Wide Shut*.

Learn all about the conspiracy theory of the secret message Kubrick tried to convey about the occult and the Illuminati before his untimely passing. This book lays out

examples of scenes and covertly placed messages and themes within Kubrick's films that supports the idea he was privy to the Illuminati secret agenda.

The full-color images taken directly from the films are explained with analysis that suggests Kubrick knew much more than many people believe. This book contains some adult themes, but some images (specifically the *Eyes Wide Shut* scenes) have been edited to ensure no full nudity.

THE DESERT ENIGMA: AN ANALYSIS OF OCCULT SYMBOLISM IN PAULO COELHO'S "THE ALCHEMIST"

In *THE DESERT ENIGMA: AN ANALYSIS OF OCCULT SYMBOLISM IN PAULO COELHO'S "THE ALCHEMIST"*; author, blogger, and independent investigator Isaac "The IlluminatiWatcher" Weishaupt reveals the hidden occult messages found in Paulo Coelho's novel: "The Alchemist."

This analysis takes an honest look at the history of author Paulo Coelho and his degrees of separation from ceremonial magick, Aleister Crowley, Charles Manson, Kenneth Grant, Alejandro Jodorowsky, witchcraft, satanism, and more.

A review of themes and messages in "The Alchemist" are juxtaposed with actual occult teachings in an attempt to unravel the core belief system at play.

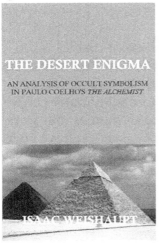

Learn how the New Age movement could be leading many astray and into the clutches of an Illuminati belief system that embraces the occult "evolution of consciousness" which seeks to open up a portal to other-dimensional entities, and ultimately; the Antichrist...

328

Printed in Great Britain
by Amazon

49701254R00189